THE AMERICAN INDIAN AND ALASKA NATIVE

STUDENT'S GUIDE TO COLLEGE SUCCESS

CHiXapkaid (D. Michael Pavel)

and

Ella Inglebret

GREENWOOD PRESS

Westport, Connecticut • London

Library of Congress Cataloging-in-Publication Data

Pavel, D. Michael.
  The American Indian and Alaska Native student's guide to college success /
D. Michael Pavel and Ella Inglebret.
      p. cm.
  Includes bibliographical references and index.
  ISBN 978-0-313-32958-6 (alk. paper)
  1. College student orientation—United States. 2. College choice—United
States. 3. Indian universities and colleges—United States. 4. Indian college
students—Life skills guides. I. Inglebret, Ella. II. Title.
    LB2343.32.P38 2007
    378.1'9829976073—dc22   2007002973

British Library Cataloguing in Publication Data is available.

Library of Congress Catalog Card Number: 2007002973
ISBN-13: 978-0-313-32958-6
ISBN-10: 0-313-32958-3

First published in 2007

Greenwood Press, 88 Post Road West, Westport, CT 06881
An imprint of Greenwood Publishing Group, Inc.
www.greenwood.com

Printed in the United States of America

The paper used in this book complies with the
Permanent Paper Standard issued by the National
Information Standards Organization (Z39.48-1984).

10 9 8 7 6 5 4 3 2 1

This guide is dedicated to all the
American Indian and Alaska Native students
who have touched our lives
with stories of success over the years.

CONTENTS

FIGURES AND TABLES

PREFACE

The Old Woman and the Young Woman

(Attafii qieibun!)

The old woman bent and gave the young woman her hand.

"I am too tired," said the young woman. "I cannot get up. I do not want to try."

And when she finished speaking that young woman lay back in the snow to die. She closed her eyes and brought up her legs. She decided life had ended.

But that old woman, she sighed, and she rubbed her stooped back, and she stomped her cold feet. She looked at the stars, and at her white breath in the cold, cold air. She looked at the young woman in the snow. She thought perhaps she should join her.

"I also am tired, and I do not want to try either," she said quietly. Only the small stars and the thin air heard her. Only the cold in her feet and the ache in her back answered her words. She saw no wisdom in the dead grass. She heard no song in the dark sky.

But the brightness of her spirit told her what to do.

And that old woman bent her body, and she lifted that young woman onto her back.

And that is why we are here today.

—A. Noelle Phillips

WHAT THIS BOOK IS ABOUT

At first glance, American Indian and Alaska Native higher education participation and achievement rates seem to lag behind national norms. Closer examination of trends and developments, however, reveals a sense of accomplishment and success in the number of American Indian and Alaska Native students going to college and graduating from a range of academic programs. Overall college success among American Indian and Alaska Native people is evidenced by the increase in enrollment and graduation rates, development of Native-focused student services and academic programs, and students finding gainful employment after graduation (many of whom return to their own communities).

As shown in Appendix A, the literature on American Indians and Alaska Natives in higher education is replete with success stories of individual students. Reports and studies have proven the increasing positive impact of institutional programs designed to meet the needs of American Indian and Alaska Native peoples and the growing positive influence of tribal governments. This book advances insights believed to be associated with the college success of American Indians and Alaska Natives and will hopefully provide you with information on how to be successful in fulfilling your own postsecondary aspirations, intentions, and commitments.

A complex array of events and circumstances can either enliven the prospect of success or conspire against American Indians and Alaska Natives getting into college and making the most of the experience. One important aspect of promoting college success is for all the important stakeholders to acknowledge that they feel a part of the process. If postsecondary representatives read this book, they might understand the depth of commitment needed to ensure that American Indians and Alaska Natives have a successful experience in college.

Attention must be paid to making the individual, institutional, and governmental factors that lead to college success as achievable as possible. Clearly a range of stakeholders need to be present to ensure widespread postsecondary achievement among American Indians and Alaska Natives. However, this book is written for the individual student who aspires to start and finish a college education culminating in a degree while going on to achieve meaningful life goals afterward.

The two themes that frame *The American Indian and Alaska Native Student's Guide to College Success* are:

- there is college success among American Indians and Alaska Natives, and
- individual American Indian and Alaska Native students can continue this overall success.

This book reflects a spirit of enthusiasm and positive outlook for American Indian and Alaska Native peoples and communities. It is a step in the direction of focusing on the successes, not the failures. We are motivated to address healthy social developments rather than reacting to a problem. It is important to tell the stories of making a difference as powerful reminders of what is possible in our lives.

WHO SHOULD READ THIS BOOK

One of the major questions we asked ourselves when writing this book was who should read it? The simple answer to this question is that this book is written for any American Indian or Alaska Native person who desires a postsecondary education. On one level, this means that it is written for the American Indian or Alaska Native individual who graduates from high school or achieves a GED irregardless of age, gender, economic background, chosen degree field, or potential area of study. However, this book is also intended to be helpful to a broader range of American Indian and Alaska Native people.

In addition to high school students, this book is for the Lummi tribal member who, at forty-five years of age, decides to pursue her lifelong dream of becoming a teacher. It is for the Seneca tribal elder who wants to take advantage of getting a college degree to demonstrate that she can do it! It is for the tribal member on the Fort Belknap Reservation in Montana, who after years of being a rancher has made a commitment to pursue a degree in natural resources to help his tribe.

This book is for the traditional cultural leaders and Native language speakers who are lifelong residents of the Navajo reservation and see the importance of learning how to develop Native cultural and language programs that keep alive the traditional culture and Native language in their communities. It can be for the traditional medicine man from Skokomish or traditional medicine woman from Yakama who could probably teach any college faculty about the healing power of plants. This book is for any and every American Indian and Alaska Native person who wants to successfully get a college degree.

WHY YOU SHOULD READ THIS BOOK

The literature is saturated with books on college success. Coupled with the overwhelming burden of choosing among the mass literature is the question, "Is the information targeted to American Indians and Alaska Natives?" In fact, it is largely a result of gathering information on American Indians and Alaska Natives in higher education that we developed the framework for *The American Indian and Alaska Native Student's Guide to College Success*. You should read this book because it is based on the many real stories of American Indian and Alaska Native people going to and succeeding in college.

Stories are important because how we refer to human knowledge and how we preserve it has changed significantly since the development of written languages. Shared knowledge of cultural concepts is a tool for survival and prosperity. For example, the Southern Puget Salish people developed a belief in a common origin and history, a moral and ethical system, a story symbology, and a spiritual belief system. These beliefs form the foundation for character development and a formal educational system. They believe, for example, that the plants and animals were placed on the Earth first, before human beings. The plants and animals were the first created and were charged by the Creator to experience all the trials and tribulations necessary to survive in the world at that time. The experiences of the plants and animals told through stories would become the teachings on which the humans would base their cultural system of moral, ethical, and spiritual values; it would become their system of counseling and educating one another. These stories taught the people how to learn from the environment as well as from their own life experiences.

Now we live in a time when we can draw on the stories of American Indian and Alaska Native people for inspiration, advice, and motivation. When you have successfully completed college, your story of success will be added to the growing number of others who aspired to and achieved a college degree, many of whom have given back to their communities.

It is your inherent right to pursue aspirations that will improve your life. This was one of the most important considerations of American Indian and Alaska Native leaders who signed treaties or negotiated agreements between the federal government and sovereign Native communities. The exchange of land and natural resources for certain goods and services contained in these treaties and agreements created a trust relationship between the U.S. government and American Indian and Alaska Native people. It is indeed a trusted and sacred responsibility to ensure that all citizens of this country have the opportunity to fulfill their education dreams.

BRIEF OVERVIEW AND PRIMER

Take a moment and think about what it would be like to know what to expect in life. Imagine how good it feels to be engaged in something meaningful that can make a profound and positive difference in the lives of American Indian and Alaska Native people. Consider that you are not alone in your awareness that increased levels of education offer deeper insights into myriad complex subjects ranging from science and the humanities to the spirit.

In Chapter 1, you will find successful college students talking about success that will stimulate a variety of meanings in your mind: providing for others, giving back, starting and finishing tasks, setting and accomplishing goals, learning about your traditional culture, representing your people with pride, living life with integrity, getting a good job, raising your children right, and graduating from college. These and other thoughts are examples of why we wrote this book. The remainder of this preface provides a brief overview of the topics addressed in more detail.

Where to Begin the Journey

In Chapter 2, we introduce the idea that American Indian and Alaska Native worldviews are important when advocating postsecondary access and achievement and are critical to understanding where one should begin the journey. Otherwise, this might as well be a book written for non-Indian America. But it is not. It is written specifically with the American Indian and Alaska Native people in mind. That is why we indicate that it is important to begin the journey being embraced by the ancestral experience of higher learning. This conceptual and intellectual space holds the seeds of the ancient philosophic foundation that has guided American Indian and Alaska Native people for countless generations.

The core values characterized by harmony, nature, and the circle offer universal and widely applicable teachings. We encounter ideas associated with ancestral time that deepen our understanding of purpose and attentiveness to fulfilling that purpose. The value of identity becomes so pronounced it is second nature to think Native identity must—indeed needs to—intertwine with and be inseparable from postsecondary pursuits. The ancestral experience of higher learning is about education in all of its manifestations. This is what allows American Indians and Alaska Natives to be simultaneously consumed by activities that contribute to increased well-being and quiet accepting of what is.

We ask, "Why go to college?" From the outset we make it clear that first and foremost is because you *can*. American Indians and Alaska Natives have not always had the opportunity to freely seek out postsecondary opportunities. Historically, over at least the last 350 or so years, American Indians and Alaska Natives have been grossly underrepresented in America's higher education institutions. Only in the late 1960s did American Indians and Alaska Natives begin enrolling in colleges and universities in measurable numbers and tribal communities resurrected the practice of creating tribal colleges and universities. Currently, America's higher education institutions are learning to be more receptive, sensitive, and respectful of American Indians and Alaska Natives.

This evolution of American higher education is a good thing. It is welcomed because there are many benefits of getting a higher degree. The most intimate benefit of pursuing a postsecondary degree is the fact that education, in and of itself, is a meaningful experience. We honor the very act of being human any time we broaden our intellectual horizons while gaining a deeper understanding of some area of interest.

Many traditional elders convey that to be human is to accept the responsibility to carry forth a love of learning. This love of learning encompasses remembering traditional teachings and preparing to live in tomorrow. It is a sacred responsibility to gain knowledge throughout one's life on how to care for others, maintain a sense of harmony, enjoy life, nurture new life, carry on the positive cycle of existence, and deal with hardship.

True, such levels of intimacy of learning and sharing can and do occur outside the realm of accredited higher education systems. However, more and more society is embracing movements that hail the need for educated people to meet and exceed stated standards with regard to skills associated with writing, reading, math, and science. We live in an increasingly credential, technological, and knowledge-oriented society that sees a college degree as a prerequisite to gaining entry into many career fields. Job announcements abound with "bachelor's degree required, master's degree preferred" or "master's degree required, doctoral degree preferred." Of course, it would be more or less impossible to practice in certain professional fields (e.g., law, medicine, business, psychology, science, etc.) without the prerequisite degree credential and/or certification.

Along with the college degree is the proven increased wages that college graduates earn compared with students who have not completed high school or have a limited postsecondary education. The differences can be staggering, particularly when measured over the course of twenty to thirty years. From the outset, the annual salaries of college graduates can be two to three times higher than those of high school graduates. Beyond the security of increased wage earnings, college graduates enjoy better health benefits and coverage. College graduates are more involved in selecting our political leaders. They are more physically active and less likely to be overweight. They are less likely to have multiple risk factors for heart disease. To which we say, "Go forth college graduate—live long and prosper."

A college education is made accessible to many because there are a lot of institutions of higher education to choose from. Although going to college is an important decision, just choosing one may be a more challenging and exciting point in the whole experience. The decision to attend a particular college has to be made with careful thought and consideration. With over 4,500 accredited institutions of higher education in the United States, you have to decide the best fit (i.e., public, private, technical schools, small, large, rural, urban). You start this process by looking at the school that offers the program of study that best fits your needs. Important considerations are cost and location; if possible, visiting the campus is always helpful. Transfer students will want to talk with institutional representatives to ensure that credits will transfer. Also, don't forget that college is about enjoying yourself, so look for available recreational opportunities.

American Indians and Alaska Natives should consider other factors in their college choice decision. For example, find out how many other American Indians and Alaska Natives attend, their graduation rate, Native student organizations, Native faculty, Native-related activities, and what kinds of Native student support services are available. Unless you are considering a tribal college or university, most U.S. colleges and universities will have pluses and minuses when specifically taking into account factors that make you feel comfortable. Be open to the fact it is unlikely there is a campus that meets all your expectations as an American Indian or Alaska Native student, and take personal responsibility to make it work for you. Even so, don't go overboard on analyzing what college you choose to attend, but be smart about what to expect and how to handle ambiguity.

An essential part of being successful in college is clarifying aspirations, intentions, and vision. You have to believe in yourself and believe that it is natural for you to have postsecondary aspirations. Every college and university in America is there for you to choose from once you make the decision to pursue a higher education. The opportunity of going to college is a way to realize your educational goals. It is yet one more chance for you to follow a vision that inspires you to fulfill a commitment to make a positive difference for American Indian and Alaska Native people.

Seriously considering our futures is something good to experience. Whether induced by ceremony or by personal choice, doing so can have a profound impact on the direction you take in life. For American Indian and Alaska Native people, it is rarely meaningful to undertake thoughts of the future from an individual perspective. More likely, such serious considerations are done with family and community in mind. The development of new skills and abilities to engage in reflection and conversation clarify what you truly care about in life. Do so by being sincere in your communication with yourself and other people.

Develop new awareness and sensibilities that provide fulfillment and result in intellectual growth. Newfound levels of understanding and insight enable you to deal with the complexity and interrelatedness of the world. You won't be alone—the college world affords you with many opportunities to experience dialogue about things that matter to you and other American Indian and Alaska Native people. Imagine new attitudes and beliefs that await you each day in college—and know that these attitudes and beliefs were there before.

Financial Aid

In Chapter 3, we explain that going to college has associated costs, of course. Your success may be enhanced by understanding college pricing and financial aid. College pricing enables you to compare the cost of different institutions. This will have an influence on the overall budget that you should develop to cover tuition and fees, books and supplies, room and board, transportation, and other expenses. Many American Indian and Alaska Native students may have additional expenses related to daycare (particularly among female heads of households), attending cultural events, and so on.

Going to college is often a family decision due to the cultural dynamics of kinships. It is important to know what we need to do to support each other when we go to college. Even though it might seem expensive at first glance, a college education is still one of the best investments that a person can make. Besides scholarships, American Indian and Alaska Native families and students should be knowledgeable of an array of financial aid opportunities and financial aid terms to demystify the complex world of college financial aid (see Appendix B for financial aid terminology).

Most American Indian and Alaska Native students receive federal financial student aid, and still, a major barrier to college success often cited by Natives is a lack of money. To ensure the maximum financial aid award, find out if you are eligible for the variety of financial aid programs (grants that you don't have to pay back, money that you earn through work study, and loans which must be paid back). Follow some simple steps to manage the financial aid process and know what kind of helpful information you can and should be able to get from any college or university.

It will be difficult to determine how much financial aid you can receive until you fill out and submit the proper applications and required paperwork. Following a checklist helps you keep track of doing things in a timely manner. If you are like most American Indian and Alaska Native students, working while going to college is going to be a reality. Working can have a positive influence on persistence and degree completion. Although working while pursuing a college degree may be challenging, it does have rewards.

If you do work and attend college, feel fortunate—not everyone has the opportunity to pursue their postsecondary dreams at all. Therefore, you would be wise to learn about debt management and terms of loans, budgeting, increasing income, reducing expenses, using debit and credit cards, and exit counseling.

Spiritual, Mental, and Physical Well-Being

Chapter 4 focuses on the fact that going to college can be a lonely experience, so be strong of spirit and have the support of at least one other person. Try not to party too much, and don't abuse alcohol and drugs; substance abuse is not an Indian problem but adversely affects college students from all backgrounds. Instead, preoccupy yourself with cultivating resilience. Resilience for American Indian and Alaska Native people is an ability to address adversity and overcome challenges experienced by countless generations.

Today, American Indian and Alaska Native college students can further cultivate resilience by positively developing their attitudes and emotions, social competence, and physical health. Achieve a high degree of resilience for the sake of yourself, your family and community, and future generations of Americans Indian and Alaska Natives. Create a world of prosperity and fully experience the joy of life. Don't suffer. Laugh more. Enjoy each others' company. College is as good a place as any to experience this joy.

Getting Prepared to Ensure Success in College

Chapter 5 covers what matters most on the way to being successful in college. It will help you out now and most certainly be helpful to future generations as you consider the role of parent and adult care takers in having high expectations and voicing encouragement. Cultivate your abilities and believe you have the talent to be successful in college. Embark on the search process of naming particular institutions you want to attend. Prepare for and be ready to take certain standardized tests used by college admission personnel in making admission decisions. Always strive to improve your writing, read and comprehend more, and gain higher levels of understanding.

Engage in positive experiences that will define your collegiate experience in a powerful way. Think about what you will learn outside the classroom and appreciate the depth of knowledge gained through formal coursework. Imagine the people who took an interest in your life and the time you took to interact with others. Going to college provides another possibility to become a better person with a greater appreciation of life. You can become a person whose skills, abilities, and knowledge convey the intellectual vision and creativity, individually or collectively, to address issues affecting American Indian and Alaska Native peoples. The final stages of your collegiate experience can lead into career maturity and occupational awareness.

There are many intervention strategies to help you along the way. Expose yourself to activities that nurture college aspirations and commitments, and seek assistance whenever possible. Don't wait until the last moment. Seeking help early is the easiest and best thing that people looking to be successful in college can do, and it is generally free. Locate and participate in orientation and academic programs whenever possible. Colleges and universities should embrace the responsibility to provide a range of student support services that will meet the needs of American Indian and Alaska Native students. Nevertheless, you need to take personal responsibility to be successful.

The concept of academic and social preparation is closely aligned to the idea of integration. Beside tribal colleges and universities, there are a relative handful of higher education institutions that fully accommodate the needs of American Indians and Alaska Natives. So be academically prepared and take a rigorous course load in high school that includes several classes of English, mathematics (particularly the highest levels), science (with labs), languages, social studies, and technology-related courses (i.e., computer science).

Some schools serving American Indians and Alaska Natives may not be offering an array of rigorous or college-prep courses. So pressure the school board and administration to offer these courses and also find out what is available at community colleges or through distance education. Challenge yourself by reading more, writing more, taking tests, being a creative problem solver, critiquing literature, looking at reports produced by your tribe or about American Indians and Alaska Natives, sharing your views, expanding your vocabulary, learning traditional songs, studying your tribal history, learning the scientific and traditional names of plants, looking at the mathematics inherent in art, and so on. These are just a few of the ideas you can embrace to expand and develop your intellectual capabilities. When you get to college, try to stay continuously enrolled, preferably at the same institution, while making time to get the best grades possible and progressively improving over time.

Social preparation can be deceptively difficult. Develop a schedule and establish priorities, enjoy your college experience, be confident, and cultivate friends who will become your family. We are sure there is more that you will discover. Preparing socially for college is one of those life skills that comes in handy long after graduation.

Being successful in college will not be easy, and there are barriers that require you to develop persistence. Draw on the spiritual strength of your ancestors. Prosper spiritually while feeling a sense of purpose and accomplishment. Place importance on commitment to community and be deeply motivated to do well in college with the goal of helping American Indian and Alaska Native peoples. Develop the ability to do well in all kinds of settings, educational or otherwise. The intrinsic gift of spirituality can keep you on the right path. Praying to the Creator and our ancestors reminds us of the humble journey we all walk when in service of our peoples' welfare. Become a role model and mentor, setting an example that achieving in a good way is an ancient and time-honored tradition that we must all embrace. Make the conscious decision to succeed in college because of the strengths of your cultural background.

Develop Problem-Solving and Critical-Thinking Skills

Chapter 6 provides an overview of how you can enhance your academic success by mastering two important intellectual skills: (a) problem solving and (b) critical thinking. Problem solving is a process that involves defining the problem, getting information to arrive at a solution, and assessing the solution while keeping in mind there are a limited number of solutions. The purpose of problem solving is to find and implement a solution, usually to a well-defined and well-structured problem. Specific problem-solving skills are understanding the problem, obtaining background knowledge, generating possible solutions, identifying and evaluating constraints, choosing a solution, group problem solving, evaluation, and dispositions. Critical thinking deals with reasoning in an open-ended manner and trying to identify an unlimited number of solutions. Individual skills that define critical thinking include interpretation, analysis, evaluation, inference, presenting arguments, reflection, and dispositions. Problem solving and critical thinking can be used across various academic disciplines and interchangeably; you may find that problem solving is often associated with math, engineering, and science-related fields and critical thinking generally aligns with behavioral science disciplines.

Internet Resources

The problem is not finding a helpful Web site you can visit for practical advice about preparing for, doing well during, and transitioning after college. There so many sites that the problem is choosing which ones to visit. In scanning through and critiquing literally hundreds of Web sites, we organized and present in Chapter 7 a nice cross-section around three areas: (a) general Web sites dedicated to improving postsecondary access and achievement, (b) sites dedicated to improving Native postsecondary access and achievement, and (c) state-supported Web sites dedicated to assisting parents and students. Visiting these particular Web sites will allow you to better decide and search for additional internet resources on your own.

Exemplary Four-Year Institutions and Tribal Colleges and Universities

There are thousands of accredited postsecondary institutions from which to choose. A number of them take the lead in connecting with American Indian and Alaska Native philosophy and culture. Chapter 8 profiles institutions that can be considered exemplary or models of achievement in moving toward the ideal of high levels of American Indian and Alaska Native college student success and respect for tribal sovereignty and Native identity. Primary characteristics of exemplary colleges and universities are a holistic approach to offering assistance during the transition into college, providing opportunities to connect with Native culture through coursework and tribal partnership programs, promoting Native scholarship and research, and promoting leadership skills for American Indian and Alaska Native students.

Tribal colleges and universities (TCUs) stand out among all other post-secondary institutions in their ability to nurture traditional cultural values and beliefs that help develop a social and economic vision for the future of American Indian and Alaska Native peoples. Although a recent development in higher education, TCUs have had a profound impact on enrollment, graduation, and success among Native college students. Obviously TCUs meet the educational needs of Native students in a way that no other type of educational institution has before. The stories of student success and pride are numerous and positively overwhelming.

The Circle of Success

Chapter 9 presents a model depicting the Circle of Success. We feel that cultural identity is the core of American Indian and Alaska Native student success. Closely linked to cultural identity are the interrelated components of individual, family, community, and tribe. There are three phases of the journey through college. It begins with preparation for the transition into college. This is followed by the actual experience associated with enrollment in college. The final phase is connecting back to American Indian and Alaska Native communities, both locally and more broadly, through a process of returning to serve Native peoples. Following the pattern of life itself, you become part of the circle that represents the continuity and interconnectedness of all aspects of the educational journey.

More Profiles of Successful College Graduates

In Chapter 10, we bring the journey of this guide full circle with the stories of three additional college graduates. They describe in a powerful manner their experiences in navigating through higher education. Clearly, the reader will see the doors that have been opened to these successful college graduates as a result of their college degrees.

TRANSITION THOUGHT

We approach this book together, as a Native and a non-Native educator concerned with promoting the success of American Indian and Alaska Native students in higher education. Your journey along the educational pathways of a college or university will bring you in contact with a diverse array of faculty. While the number of Native faculty in higher education is steadily increasing, you are likely to enter into many learning experiences with non-Native faculty. Our voices join together in this book to help you understand that both non-Native and Native faculty can play an important role in building bridges between the culture of a university and the culture of your home community.

CHiXapkaid's (Dr. Michael Pavel's) Voice: I am an enrolled member of the Skokomish Nation, and given the charge at the age of 15 by my elders to get a Ph.D. It was then and throughout my life that I have been guided by the vision to make a powerful and positive contribution to improving American

Indian and Alaska Native postsecondary access and achievement. The most important foundation informing my vision is derived from traditional teachings and ancestral wisdom, while exploring ways to incorporate contemporary knowledge to live the possibility that we (as Native people) can achieve our dreams. The most important message I hope you gain from this guide is to say to yourself, "I can succeed in college and life. I did it and I helped others do the same."

Ella Inglebret's Voice: As a non-Native faculty member, I have had the opportunity to teach and learn from numerous Native students over the past 17 years. Students bring their individual cultural backgrounds to their educational pursuits. I see it as my responsibility to work with students in exploring their cultural values, beliefs, and concerns as part of the educational process. At the same time, I bring my own cultural background to our exchanges. Many of our basic values overlap, while others are vastly different. What is important is that we are respectful of what it is that we each bring to this shared educational journey. The synergy of our different perspectives helps bring to light potential means for linking traditional cultural knowledge and skills with the learning that occurs in a formal institutional setting. We all benefit from this exchange.

You may come across something in this book that helps you on your postsecondary journey, whether you are a high school freshman, currently enrolled in college, out of school but thinking about going to college, helping other American Indians and Alaska Natives go to college, or parents who want their children to feel comfortable about wanting to and actually pursuing a degree. Maybe this book is even for those who don't want American Indians and Alaska Natives to succeed in college; they should see the depth of passion and our orientation to sharing insights about what it might take to be successful in college from a Native worldview. Read the rest of this book in such a way as to give yourself a chance to succeed. You *are* good enough. You can be successful in college.

Once, I Saw Our Path

We are strong because
We have lived through winter massacres,
starved marches, and
influenzas
decimating.
We are strong because we caught
fish, killed bear and buffalo, and
ate the goodness
of our lands.
We are strong because we wade through
their words, and ours,
because we survive
alcoholism,
diabetes,
poverty,
abuse.

Why are we strong?

Because we have to be, because
we were to get here.
We are strong because
we made it this far,
and we have grown
longer legs
to take the next big steps.

Success?
Is living off past strength to become
strength of the future.
Is fighting back with
healthy families,
good dreams,
strong selves.

Success?
Is grandchildren hugging grandmothers,
the rich smell of smoked salmon,
proud generations, toothless smiles.
It is a free flowing of our rivers,
and of the rivers of our peoples.
It is our fist raised to the sky,
while our feet grow deep,
so deep,
into this
earth.

—A. Noelle Phillips

CHAPTER 1

Profiles of Successful College Graduates

With each passing year, more American Indians and Alaska Natives achieve success in colleges and universities. The journey to success takes on a variety of forms with unique opportunities and challenges for each individual. We felt that the best guide to college success would come from the stories of actual American Indian and Alaska Native graduates. We include stories of men and women who have ventured into higher education and have come away with skills and knowledge that they now use in making contributions to Native peoples and society more broadly. These stories teach us about what is important for students today—and those in the future. The stories of college success shared here are organized around a series of interview-style questions.

- Tell me about your experience as a student in higher education.
- How did you choose the higher education institution you attend(ed)?
- What factors contributed to your success in higher education?
- What challenges did you face as a student in higher education?
- How did you adapt to meet these challenges?
- What advice would you give to American Indian and Alaska Native individuals interested in obtaining a higher education degree?
- What would your life be like without having gone to college or getting a degree?
- Please describe what you feel are the benefits of going to college and earning a degree.

These questions assisted successful college graduates in organizing their thinking about the process they went through as students. Their stories are important in helping us understand what it takes to be successful in higher education, and we encourage you to use these questions to guide your own reflection. As you read these stories, think about what might positively influence your own success story. Think about the challenges you might face and the strategies that you will use. You will someday be in a position to contribute to the next generation of students by sharing your own story of success. Think about the advice that you will give to these incoming students and how you will describe the benefits of a college education.

We share three stories of student success here. The stories vary widely, and you will have your own unique story as well. The way the stories are told also differs quite significantly. This reflects our belief that it is important to retell the stories in the words and style selected by the graduates themselves. What is important is that you think about the possibilities for yourself—you, too, can become the narrator for a similar story of your own success.

MARY PAVEL of the Skokomish Nation was born and raised on the Skokomish Reservation in the state of Washington. She had only been on an airplane three times before she headed across the country to attend Dartmouth College at age eighteen. Mary attended Dartmouth from 1984 to 1988, at which time she received her bachelor of arts degree in sociology. She then was accepted into the Law School at the University of Washington in 1989 and graduated with a juris doctor in 1992. An active member of her tribal community, Mary is a leader within the traditional society in the House of slanay on the Skokomish Reservation and frequently finds time to return home and practice her traditions while maintaining her family and professional responsibilities. She is currently a partner with the highly regarded national law firm Sonosky, Chambers, Sachse, Endreson and Perry. She works in all phases of the firm's practice, with special emphasis in legislative matters pending before Congress. She is the founding president of the Native American Bar Association of Washington, DC, and serves on the Dartmouth College Alumni Council. Her bar and court admissions include the Washington State Bar (1992), U.S. Court of Appeals for the 8th Circuit (1997), District of Columbia (1998), Superior Court (1998), and U.S. District Court for the District of Columbia (2003).

Tell me about your experience as a student in higher education.

I feel very fortunate that both my undergraduate and graduate experiences were positive. In both instances I was able to find a community of friends, who while not like me in terms of where we grew up and the culture that we grew up in, shared the same basic sense of core values of what is important in life and were able to teach me things and share with me experiences that I do not think I would have been able to have without going to college and law school.

How did you choose the higher education institutions you attended?

I selected Dartmouth because my vocational nursing instructor had suggested that I consider Dartmouth because of its strong commitment to educating Indian students. She was familiar with Dartmouth because her husband had attended it and because of another student from Shelton who had attended Dartmouth a few years earlier.

I selected the University of Washington because I wanted to go home to go to law school and the University of Washington is one of the top ten public law schools in the country. In addition, one of the preeminent scholars in Indian law, Ralph Johnson, was a professor there at that time.

What factors contributed to your success in higher education?

The biggest factor in any success [I] have achieved in higher education is my parents. They provided me with a solid foundation for meeting my academic requirements throughout my life and expected nothing less when I went to college. They then provided me with the necessary support to be successful in terms of financial and moral support.

What challenges did you face as a student in higher education?

The greatest challenge I faced in higher education, at least for my undergraduate years, was finding my voice and becoming the person I aspired to be. In any community there are cliques and because I had grown up in a small community with a very large family, the only clique that I knew was my family, and so, I had to determine how to have a social life that had nothing to do with family.

Academically, I suppose my greatest challenge [was] getting the necessary grade in Italian so that I could attend my language study program abroad in Siena, Italy. There was something associated with the study of language that gave me a great deal of anxiety during test taking. I could speak the language as well as any beginning student, and I tested orally just fine, but almost failed miserably on the written exams.

How did you adapt to meet these challenges?

In terms of finding a social core to sustain me, I opened myself up to a cross-section of people and experiences that allowed me to build my own personal circle of friends, who while they didn't have a lot in common with one another had me in common. These people remain my best friends today. In addition the Native American Program at Dartmouth was wonderful. This is true because it opened me up to a whole world of Indian people that I knew nothing about. And, regardless of what else was going on, there was always the program office, where you could go and laugh and relax and rejuvenate yourself.

In terms of the academic challenge, I learned to be humble enough to talk to my professor and ask for help. This was difficult for me because I had always excelled academically—the idea that I could be failing anything was very humiliating. My professor was terrific. He talked about test taking and anxiety, and he worked with me to create an environment where I could take his exams so that I would not feel under pressure. I succeeded and was able to attend the program in Siena, Italy. That experience taught me the valuable lesson of being humble enough to ask for help.

What advice would you give to American Indian and Alaska Native individuals interested in obtaining a higher education degree?

You should go and try, whether it is at a community college or a four-year school. Higher education will only empower you and teach you about worlds and people that you knew nothing about before. It is hard, there can be no doubt, but nothing in this world worth having is not hard. The only way to fail at it is not to put your effort into the academic work. In going away to undergraduate [school], it is easy to get caught up in the numerous outside activities that have nothing to do with going to school and getting passing grades. Once you are at school, the number one priority needs to be whether you are doing all that you need to do to get a passing grade in the classes that you are taking. All the external stuff is simply irrelevant to that primary objective.

What would your life be like without having gone to college or getting a college degree?

I certainly wouldn't be a lawyer. I also wouldn't have seen Europe at twenty. I would not have had the experience of getting on a plane at eighteen and traveling to Boston by myself. These things have shaped who I am today, and while they seemed excruciatingly difficult at the time, I survived them and became a better and stronger person. Financially, I would probably not be in the same place. I have the luxury of not living paycheck to paycheck. I have a home, a car that runs, and resources available for any emergency that I or my family may encounter. I have health care and a retirement plan. Finally, I would not have had the chance to serve the many tribes throughout the country that I serve and make the lives of the Indian people on these reservations better.

   In short, I don't think that my core values would be any different, I just would not have had the range of experiences and opportunities that I have had, which I think have made my life great.

Please describe what you feel are the benefits of going to college and earning a degree.

I think the benefits—other than the monetary ones, which are substantial—are the opportunities to learn and understand new things and new thinking. This makes you a better person for your community and for Indian country in general.

JUSTIN JACOBS, of the Yakama Nation, received his bachelor of science in mathematics, a secondary teaching certificate, and an engineering degree at Washington State University. He grew up working on the family orchard while playing lots of sports. His family values education, and his mother kept him involved in school activities like clubs and summer enrichment programs. He was able to take college prep courses in high school and had the chance to know one grandparent well. He managed to cope with the death of his brother. Justin taught high school math for four years on the Yakama Reservation at Wapato High School before returning to college for his engineering degree. He taught calculus to Native students at the University of New Mexico for the TRIBES Program in summer 1998 and to minority students in a summer program at the Jet Propulsion Laboratory (JPL) while working with the Transmitter Group designing Deep Space Network test equipment. A former *USA Today* Academic All American, Justin shares his story in the following responses.

Tell me about your experience as a student in higher education.

University of Colorado (Summer 1993): Received a scholarship for the TRIBES (Tribal Resource Institute in Business, Engineering and Science) program. It's a program for Native American students who just graduated from high school. The program served as a bridge to the university setting. We took [courses in] tribal government and advanced expository English. The classes were very demanding, but there was a big support system in place to help us learn how to take the academic pressure placed upon us.

   Washington State University (1993): I felt out of place at the beginning, socially and academically. Socially, I was a brown kid in a sea of white kids. Fortunately, I was athletic, and that helped me fit in. It took some time, but I realized my actions and words formed others' perceptions about Yakamas and Native Americans in general. Being the competitive person that I am, I embraced this challenge and used it as motivation. As [my] confidence level and success levels increased, I began to succeed even more, ask questions, and seek mastery from my courses instead of survival.

   Heritage College (1999): Learned a bunch of Sahaptin the first two semesters, but the rate at which the instructor was teaching new material fell off to better meet the needs of the majority of the class. The cost of attendance was not justified, so I stopped a couple weeks into the third semester.

   Central Washington University (Summer 2000): Three summer program for teachers to earn their master's degree. Only liked one of the five classes I took the first summer. Really disliked one instructor. I only went to increase my earning potential since teachers only get raises for years served and credits earned. Resented the fact that my teacher certification depended on whether I took fifteen credits every five years. I wasn't making that much money, and I was forced to take expensive classes and pay for them myself. Legislative decisions and limited options for advancement in the teaching profession made me decide to find another career. Didn't return to Central after the first summer.

   Washington State University (2002): Successful in both research and classes while with the microengine group. Liked my advisors and group leaders, but I realized I didn't want to raise a family away from the Yakama

Reservation and that having a career in microdevices in the Yakama area was not likely in the near future. I changed to civil engineering, and I am happy with the decision.

How did you choose the higher education institutions you attended?

University of Colorado: I decided to attend the program because my brother and a good friend had attended it in previous years and recommended the program and spoke well of the people that ran the program.

Washington State University (WSU): In state, close to home, good scholarship package, weather better than University of Washington.

Heritage College: I wanted to know more Sahaptin. They offered Sahaptin. My brother and his wife were in the class. I thought I might teach Sahaptin at Wapato High School some day. College credits increased my pay as a teacher.

Central Washington University: To earn a graduate degree in teaching mathematics to increase my earning ability as a teacher. Close to home. Wife was in the program.

WSU: Wanted to have an option to do something other than teach my whole life. To earn a graduate degree in mechanical engineering with a focus on microdevices. WSU had a great research team developing a micro-engine that I wanted to work with. Good financial support from WSU and the microdevices research group. Wife's family is close by.

What factors contributed to your success in higher education?

Parent support in academics and extracurricular activities. Work ethic learned growing up on a farm. Lessons in competitiveness and teamwork from athletics. Commitment to succeed. Willingness to participate in support programs. Participation in summer enrichment programs while in high school and college—broadened my scope. Scholarships and family support—didn't have to have a job my first couple years in college.

What challenges did you face as a student in higher education?

   a. Choosing a major. It was difficult to commit to one field of study thinking you would have to work in that field the rest of your life.
   b. Believing in myself enough to take the more difficult math and science classes and not take the path of least resistance.
   c. Balancing physical activity, socializing, and academics. I found that too much studying would lead to unhappiness and poor performance would follow. Too much basketball, weight lifting, and partying and academics suffered.

How did you adapt to meet these challenges?

   a. I kept my options open by taking the harder classes to allow me to make a decision later without limitations. I ended up choosing a major that I felt allowed the most options.
   b. Became a more disciplined student by taking advantage of tutorial sessions, office hours, and study groups. This extra work outside of the

classroom made me a better student and gave me the confidence needed to push forward.

c. I set a schedule. Physical activity was daily. Socialize Thursday evening and Saturday. Studied at various locations to break up the monotony.

What advice would you give to American Indian and Alaska Native individuals interested in obtaining a higher education degree?

a. Learn to recognize when your life is in and out of balance as early as you can. This applies to all, not just those pursuing higher ed. Must constantly evaluate the way you feel and understand what influences both successful and unsuccessful moments in your life. If you learn how to keep yourself balanced and strong, you will greatly increase the probability of reaching your goals.

b. Participate in summer programs and internships to broaden your scope, learn to apply what you are learning in school, meet new people, and learn about different areas of the country or world. Positive experiences may lead to a career, and negative experiences will help you make a better choice in careers. I have been involved in many summer programs and internships. No matter whether I enjoyed the experience or not, I learned a lot. Learning to work with people from different places helps broaden your perspective and increases your ability to successfully understand and adapt to future difficult situations.

What would your life be like without having gone to college or getting a college degree?

a. Would not have had the opportunity to teach high school math on my reservation. Learned a lot about myself, my community, and our future leaders while teaching.

b. My earning power would be diminished.

c. Would have lost the experience that I gained teaching very bright Native American students in summer programs such as TRIBES and at JPL. These were very rewarding summer programs to be involved in.

Please describe what you feel are the benefits of going to college and getting your college degree.

Increase your options for career opportunities and advancement. Increase earning power. Increase the possibility of my kids going to college and having similar experiences that I enjoyed. Give young Yakama students another role model that may help them choose to pursue higher education as well.

MARY KIM TITLA is San Carlos Apache and was born and raised on the San Carlos Apache Reservation. Her father was a sophomore in high school when she was born. Mary Kim lived with her grandparents in her early childhood, and they had no plumbing or electricity. Her parents eventually landed good jobs, and they moved into a home her father built. It had plumbing and electricity but only two bedrooms. She shared one room with four siblings until going off to a boarding high school. Mary Kim was Arizona's first and only Native American television news reporter, and then she resigned from her highly successful Channel 12 (KPNX) position to devote herself to the online magazine she created for Native American youths, *Native Youth Magazine* (www.nativeyouthmagazine.com). It is filled with profiles, articles, commentaries, poems, and artwork produced by young Native Americans. Titla said she believes her calling now is about molding young Native storytellers and will showcase their talents and lifestyles through the magazine. "I think the magazine fills a void, there's nothing of this magnitude in the U.S.," she said. "My sons didn't have a place on the Internet to go to. They go to mainstream sites. *Native Youth Magazine* is a place for all young Native people whether they are interested in fashion, writing or art."

Please describe your experience as a student in higher education.

I enjoyed my college experience. I enrolled in a junior college, and it was a good fit for me because I came from a very small boarding school. The teacher–student ratio was similar to a large high school, and my teachers knew my name. Community colleges are great for students coming from rural areas, including Indian reservations. I think it makes for an easier transition. I eventually transferred to the University of Oklahoma, which was a culture shock. The class sizes were huge and impersonal, but I had developed good study habits, which helped. I became involved in extracurricular activities at both schools and was a social butterfly. I endured all the hardships many Native American students endure—homesickness, no extra money, no transportation, and no nearby support system. I nearly had to drop out of school at one point due to bad grades, but I made a commitment to turn my grades around. As long as I can remember my parents stressed the importance of a college education. I was the oldest of five children, and it was up to me to be an example. I must've inspired my siblings. They now all have college degrees. What's great is my parents also enrolled in college and graduated with one of my brothers.

How did you choose the higher education institutions you attended?

I chose Eastern Arizona College because it was close to home, about an hour away. I really didn't give much thought to going any place else. I wanted to be close to home because many of my friends were still in high school as well as a younger sister. Being close to home made it easier to see them on the weekends. My journalism instructor at Eastern was a graduate of the University of Oklahoma. He said they had a good school of journalism. I also knew Oklahoma had the second highest population of American Indians, which was attractive and an organization I became involved with was based there [United National Indian Tribal Youth, Inc., or UNITY]. The executive director, J. R. Cook, became my mentor.

What factors contributed to your success in higher education?

I developed good study habits in high school. I also had a supportive family who encouraged me every step of the way. I was self-motivated, which is very important.

What challenges did you face as a student in higher education?

Homesickness, no extra money, no transportation, and no nearby support system [at OU].

How did you adapt to meet these challenges?

I made friends quickly, I got a job, and I gave myself pep talks.

What advice would you give to American Indian and Alaska Native individuals interested in obtaining a higher education degree?

Don't give up. If I can do it, you can do it, too.

What would your life be like without having gone to college or getting a college degree?

That's a good question. I've given speeches where I said, "I wouldn't be where I'm at today if I hadn't stayed in school," but I've never really thought about what my life would be like without a college degree. Knowing me, I would strive to be in a leadership position because of sheer determination and hard work.

Please describe what you feel are the benefits of going to college and getting your college degree.

I made many friends in college who are now in leadership positions around the country. Having a college degree made it easier for me to land a job as a news reporter in one of the largest cities in America (Phoenix). I also earned a very good salary.

CHAPTER 2

Where to Begin the Journey

CHiXapkaid

A Student's Voice

When I was at home, I always knew where I was (by the river with the billowing grass), who my family was (wrinkled "old friends" and relatives both), and what was expected of me: pulling in the gill nets, taking care of the horses, watching brothers and sisters and cousins. . . . When I left for school I had to "solidify" who I was when all of those things were removed from me. It was hard, and scary, and no one I met truly knew who I was, because no one identified with my life experience. But throughout the process, I learned to share my life more bravely with others. I held tight to *where* I was from, *who* my family was, and *what* was expected (hoped) of me, even as those expectations grew and changed. . . . In a sense I took the seed of my identity and swallowed it, only to have it grow inside. Now more than ever it pervades my eyes, my ears, my mouth. I link everywhere I am and everything I do back home.

THE ANCESTRAL EXPERIENCE OF HIGHER LEARNING

This chapter begins with a brief discussion about the ancestral experience of higher learning for American Indian and Alaska Native peoples. It was natural to engage in this discussion from a Native worldview (specifically, that of CHiXapkaid), informed from years of traditional training among the Coast Salish spiritual leaders and interaction with other prominent traditional elders throughout the Native world. This American Indian and Alaska Native guide to college success is more than simply offering the student and other stakeholders advice and guidance about starting and completing a college education. It is about setting out a life plan that fits within one's life experiences and is inspired by our ancestors. Along the way of unforeseen and unexpected events, your intentions and aspirations can also inspire other Native students to persevere and be resilient to hardships and challenges. This section is about orienting Native students to the postsecondary experience in a way that helps them prepare spiritually, psychologically, and intellectually by factoring in social and cultural influences that are implicit and explicit in our ancestry.

Our Philosophical Foundation

In many ways, going to college is about searching for meaning and purpose about our lives as well as engaging in a deep philosophical orientation to life itself. This sounds deep, I know. However, it helps to think about college from this perspective because it is at the heart of a holistic point of view that characterizes many (if not all) Native values. Although values are not always visible, easily articulated, or upheld in every situation, we subconsciously and consciously are influenced by values to decide among choices, define who we are, to whom we belong, and to define the orientation of other people. Briefly, many American Indian and Alaska Native value systems focus on common tribal values, such as individual autonomy, putting the interest of community ahead of personal accomplishments, the ability to endure deprivation, bravery, the proclivity for practical jokes, and a belief system in the existence and essence of supernatural powers.

There are many tribal elders who widely believe that philosophical values play an important factor in our introspective view, individually and collectively speaking. Values and philosophy go hand in hand. Philosophy is a search for a general understanding of values and reality by chiefly speculative means; it is an overall vision of life and its purposes. Philosophy plays an integral part in how and why we, as American Indian and Alaska Native people, view ourselves as a part of the whole. Within this philosophic view of self and others, most of us see ourselves from a holistic perspective. Holistic people conceive the universe, living nature, and themselves in terms of interacting wholes that are more than the mere sum of elementary particles. As such, it was told to me by Paul Bernal, a respected Taos elder who has since passed on, that going to college is not simply about getting an education at the mental level, it is a physical and spiritual journey this is most effectively accomplished by group effort. In conducting traditional ceremonies and rituals, we are often called to work in one mind and in one spirit. So say to yourself, "If higher learning is important, we need to support each in one mind and in one spirit." Say it at least once a day while praying to the Creator to watch over you and your people.

Harmony, Nature, and the Circle

The sun is a circle. The moon is a circle. The sky is a circle. The birds make their nest in the form of a circle. I see the horizon as a great circle. The seasons are in a circle. The process of birth, childhood, adolescence, adulthood, and old age, when we regress to our earliest memories, is a circle. A circle symbolizes the theme of closure, completion, and empowerment. All important decisions were made within a circle. All important information was imparted in a circle. We use expressions such as "social circle," "circle round," "come full circle," and "talking circle." To get to the conclusion of a problem we must return to the beginning, and that is a circle. In circle philosophy everything is related (like the ripple effect). Our personal actions influence others, beginning with our immediate families, then our friends, our community, and finally our tribe. What we do to the Earth will be done to us. In the philosophy of the circle, it is important to consider how your actions will affect yourself, your people, and generations yet to come.

In one sense everything you do will come back to either haunt you or give you personal satisfaction. So doing positive things for yourself is to do positive things for others. For instance, going to college and graduating. There is a moment, in time and space, that you will realize that your actions represent your people, that how people perceive you is how they perceive Native people. No pressure—it is just part of the reality of quietly and confidently accepting the responsibility of being a positive role model to encourage other American Indians and Alaska Natives to value the skill of lifelong learning. True, the act of being a lifelong learner is not relegated to just the college experience. Nevertheless we, you and I, need to present a very real world to future generations to have more opportunities in life (not fewer), to experience an expanded awareness (without drugs), and to contribute to the positive cycle of prosperity (instead of failure). Believe me when I say that if more of us go to college and make a positive difference in our communities, we will inspire even more American Indians and Alaska Natives in the next generation to pursue college. We are all connected.

Ancestral Time

Native peoples' sense of present time is often recognized as differing from that of American and Western European culture. We view time as in a rhythmic, circular pattern. Aboriginally, we marked the passage of time in seasons rather than weeks, months, or years. The passage of a day was not marked by seconds, minutes, or hours but by the position of the sun, moon, our internal senses, or even the tide. Our ancestors placed themselves within history not by number dates but by when major events took place. Time shared in common was marked by major events that the whole social unit could correspond to, such as the Treaty Time, the Year of the Spotted Sickness, or the Year the Trees Exploded in the Cold, and so on. Personal time was marked by such events as My Puberty Ceremony, My Vision Quest, When I Got My Ancestral Name, When I Married, and so on.

Often we can feel our own internal clock dictating when it is time to do something, but many times we are not sensitive to these urges because of our own ego-driven feelings. We see it all the time with Native people who are in their mid-twenties and finally look at their life and say it is time to get serious about their education. Get serious about your education early because it makes life much easier to live over time, particularly if you want to pursue a college degree. The ancestral concept of time is not always about rationalizing why you are late and using the unsophisticated excuse that you are operating on "Indian time."

The ancestral concept of time is to be tuned into the seasons, to be prepared when it is time to harvest and getting yourself and your gathering tools ready. It is about knowing when you have gathered enough to survive during lean times. We don't know what tomorrow brings; we can only prepare ourselves and our children to confront and overcome anything they will experience and encounter. Record the day you go to college, celebrate the first classes you pass, and remember that nobody can take away what you earned when you complete your college education. These and other events will be the times that define the story of when you successfully completed college.

The Value of Identity

A good identity is one of the most valuable forms of strength a person can possess. A sense of identity for our ancestors was considered to be like a garment: it could be soiled and devalued. Individuals who are part of a tribal community were reminded that their actions from that day on would affect the honor of not only themselves but their families and the tribal community as well. You need to carry the identity of your tribal heritage with pride and respect. In virtually all Native cultures, the concept of tribal identity enables us to distinguish one thing or entity from another. The word *identity* has connotations of reputation, fame, character, title, celebrity, notable, and importance.

To not have pride in your heritage is to be destitute and lack resilience. If we lose the ability to respect our Native culture, then we lose the value of the identity that we carry. The need to be recognized is part of the character of being human, humans that belong to a community. When we lose a sense of achieving in the good name of our people, we lose our sense of belonging. We search for an identity and sense of family or belonging in different ways, such as gangs, social groups, religious cults, drinking buddies, or partners in crime. We try to make a name for ourselves to belong. Imagine that American Indians and Alaska Natives are widely recognized as being successful in college without losing our identity—that seems like a good thing, doesn't it? It certainly does. Retaining your Native identity while going to college has been and will continually be advocated by grandmothers and grandfathers, approved by mothers and fathers, and endorsed by aunties and uncles.

Education

The plants and the animals were our first teachers. The plants were created first. They were given a common goal to achieve: to hold the Earth together for others who would come along in the future. They were instructed to develop the strongest method of teaching possible, called *teaching by example*. The animals were the next to be created, and they were told to live through all the trials and tribulations of life. They were told that the stories of their struggles of survival or demise would serve as teachings for the humans who were yet to come. Through the teachings of these stories would come the moral and ethical values of the first humans who were created. We need to stick together and support one another in our pursuit of getting an education, just like the plants are holding the Earth together. We need to look back at the trials and tribulations of those who have gone on to college ahead of us and learn from their experiences, just like the humans looked to the animals' experiences. We need to be part of the story, a story of being successful in college in significant numbers.

Acceptance of What Is

In many ways the concept of acceptance (which is peculiarly indicative of Indigenous peoples) has helped American Indians and Alaska Natives survive under the adverse circumstances that they have encountered in the past 500 years. Researchers note a general tendency of non-Indian culture to take charge or manipulate nature to fit its needs as opposed to the Native value of accepting natural and sometimes unnatural events as they are.

This peculiar value of accepting things as they are is often described as being-in-becoming, as opposed to the non-Indian value of doing something about the situation. Researchers indicate that this acceptance of events is representative of the Native belief that these happenings occur as part of the nature of life or destiny, and one must learn to live with life and accept what comes, both good and bad. Some therapists view this value of acceptance by Native peoples as an explanation for why we do not impose ourselves or our views and problems on others unless asked.

I am often asked by people, "Why do such a low percentage of American Indian and Alaska Native people go to and succeed in college?" Sometimes I just answer, "Because they don't." These people are puzzled at first, and I then explain, "In time we will be asking ourselves why there is such a high percentage of American Indian and Alaska Native people that go to and succeed in college. It is a long life. Be patient."

A Student's Voice

How do we tie our ancestral experience to higher learning? One way to tie our ancestral experience to higher education is create and maintain a sense of community once in college. Newly enrolled Native students need a place or community to connect with—a community where they have shared experiences. Whether it's a place to share cultures, languages, songs, art, or a sense of humor, these values are crucial to adaptability and persistence while in college. Among Indian people, the family structures within tribal communities are interdependent, wherein the burdens of an individual are often felt (or shared) by the community at large. For example, I've observed that it is rare to find a homeless person on a reservation because there is always someone who will take him or her in and provide shelter. This close-knit community creates such a strong support system that it engenders interdependence, which in some cases makes leaving this support system very difficult for community members when one encounters adversity. Therefore, it is very important for Native students to find a "family" or community while in college to maintain this sense of community common to our ancestor's way of life.

WHY GO TO COLLEGE?

A Student's Voice

College is hard. College is stressful, and I don't like stress. Sometimes when I'm stressed I just want to go home. . . . There is a very thin thread holding me here at school. But you know, that thread is pretty interesting. . . . My parents want me to learn stuff, and to be able to get a good job when I go home. I personally want to be able to do something that really helps our community, and I feel like what I'm learning here will make a difference to a lot of kids back home. It's true that college is hard, but boy does it open up doors. It shows you doors you didn't even know existed, and then shows you to turn the handle and walk through. And once you know how to do that, you can show others.

There are many ways to prepare for and fulfill the admirable goal of getting a college education, and most of the ways can be viewed as process-oriented strategies. To me, it is the "why" question (i.e., why go to college?) that creates the postsecondary intentions and aspirations that serve as the foundations for being motivated to engage in a successful experience. So let's ask the question, "Why go to college?"

First and Foremost, Because You Can

It is an inherent right of all human beings to seek ways of self-improvement, pursue greater levels of understanding, and follow dreams yet born. From the very beginning of European contact over 500 years ago, however, this was not always true for the many American Indians and Alaska Natives who are our ancestors. It has only been recently, in fact in the past forty years, that Native people have been welcomed into the domain of America's colleges and universities in any great numbers. It seem ironic in that when they signed many of the treaties, our ancestral leaders exchanged aboriginal claim to vast tracts of land and natural resources based on the promise that their children and future generations would have equal access to quality educational services. So whether young or old, all Native people should feel comfortable with the thought of choosing to go to college for the simple reason that it is their right. It was not so true several generations ago. This is why you should consider going to college and becoming a change agent who contributes to the spirit of our ancestors. Choose to go to college because you *can*.

American Indian and Alaska Native success in college can be a contributing factor in the continued progress of Native people throughout the nation. Getting to college may be no easy task for many of us, and if we do go to college, it may not be easy to finish. Going to college should not be a difficult choice; choosing between whether to buy medicine or food is a difficult choice. Choosing to pursue a college education can be done in our best interests and honors our ancestors while preserving our culture. It is not really a choice at all but the reality of being American Indian and Alaska Native in our society today. Testimony in a recent report by the National Indian Education Association is quite revealing.[1]

> As students enter high school in these rural areas [of Alaska], some parents send their students to Mount Edge, which is the state-wide boarding school, or send them to relatives in Fairbanks or Anchorage or they move there themselves. In the small high school, where maybe you only have a dozen students, there are not a lot of opportunities to take languages and other things that may help them to get into colleges. So we have, I guess, a brain drain in the rural communities to the urban areas. The students that are left in the rural community's high schools are those that require special education. And so when it comes to AYP, they don't fare as well. (p. 12)

> Tribal sovereignty and our children's cultural identity become undermined unless tribes are directly involved in all efforts to develop policy, set standards, guide curriculum, develop a palate of assessments and lead in the development of culturally appropriate pedagogy. (p. 20)

> I think it's time to raise our voices and ask that we be heard and we can do it. For me, I could go on and on because I can see so much out there and I really firmly believe; and, the people in this room, you're all models of that, is that education is the key to wiping out poverty on our reservations. Just a little bit of knowledge goes a long way. (p. 21)

The future of American Indian and Alaska Native people is entrusted to those who understand the significance of overcoming the barriers of getting into and succeeding in college. This impressive group of people represents all sectors of our society—the high school graduate looking to be the first person in their family to complete college, working adults aspiring to a better position, single women seeking more security for their children, and elders who have always known the inherent value of an education. We represent all sectors of our communities and refuse to quit, despite the obstacles and barriers. It may take some of us longer to get into college, and some of us may take longer to graduate. Although it is important that we choose to pursue a college degree, gain access to college, and graduate, it still matters that we try our best.

A Student's Voice

There are a number of reasons why one should go to college, but one of the most important reasons is that a college education provides opportunities and options. In the society we live in today, education equals social mobility. Without a college education, career mobility and advancement are severely limited. When people lack opportunities and options, they lose a sense of drive and purpose. They languish in hopelessness and mediocrity. All they see are obstacles. I see this too often on my reservation, and it breaks my heart. Far too many tribal members on my reservation complain that the tribe hires too many non-Indians, and I always say to myself, it's because they have the credentials that the job requires! Why not go to college and earn a degree? But I also understand that for Indian people, this is easier said than done because historically, higher education, or education in general, has left a bad taste in the mouths of Indian people after years of colonizing practices. Despite these wounds, I believe that one no longer has to compromise Indian identity and ways of life to pursue a college education. It wasn't until my junior year that realize how blessed I have been to even go to college and, more important, to have a strong support system that encourages me along the way. I realized that I am the beneficiary of the sacrifices that my ancestors went through to give me the opportunity to earn a college education. My mother's tireless work ethic and my father's determination made an indelible impression on me. I believe a better educated citizenry is bound to be more resourceful and innovative and is able to determine its own destiny, whereas an uneducated citizenry is bound to be captive to poverty and helplessness. This is why more Native people need to go to college, because we can use our education to break the cycle of poverty and hopelessness on our respective reservations. This, to me, is the value of education and why I am a strong advocate for the highest quality of education for our children and the generations to come.

There is a story I have heard and like to share that is about several non-Native and Native scholars talking about persistence in higher education (e.g., students maintaining enrollment until graduation). One of the Native scholars explained that he knew an elder who took seven years to get his associate of arts degree from a two-year college. On hearing the story, a non-Native scholar said, "How sad it was that it took him so long and how nice it would have been if he completed it in two years."

The Native scholar who brought up the story replied, "You sound like he could have done it differently. We are talking about persistence. Staying on course despite the costs, time and effort it takes, and events that transpire in your life as a college student. The particular elder that I am referring to started college, then within the first year lost a wife to cancer, in the second year lost a son to an automobile accident, was living on commodities throughout his college experience, had to depend on rides to college to attend classes, was involved in his traditional ceremonies, and supported three other children. Get the picture? That is persistence in higher education for quite a few American Indian people. It is not always getting into college right after high school, staying enrolled full-time for four years, and then graduating. That is good. We all know that. What we need are the stories of courage and pride that our people tap into to overcome whatever we face in life."

There was silence in the group. Then the non-Native scholar nodded his head affirmatively while saying to the group, "Then let us document the stories of courage and pride that inspire all of us to envision persistence in terms of the elder who has changed my view of what it means to be an American Indian in higher education." All nodded in agreement.

Villegas and Prieto's 2006 study, *Alaska Native Student Vitality: Community Perspectives on Supporting Student Success*,[2] offers a dynamic definition of success. Drawing upon the strength of knowing what it is to be a good human being, the definition of Alaska Native student success from the student's perspective is about gaining the ability to

> set and achieve goals because she knows her own worth and value, understands her responsibilities, to her community, and is prepared to pursue whatever life path she chooses. This image of success is distinct because it fundamentally challenges the idea that there are two separate worlds that Alaska Native students must bridge. In the media, educational research, policy, and daily discussions about schooling these two worlds could be the "Western world" and the "Native world"; or they might be the "school world" and the "community world"; or they could be the "world of individual academic achievement" and the "world of collective success." Whatever form they take, they are framed as having competing and conflicting values that students must learn to navigate and somehow hold together in order to be successful. The definition that respondents offered, however, sees individual and community success as woven together, unable to be separated from one another. (p. 35)

To be successful, students must realize they are valued by their communities and have an opportunity to help improve life for themselves, their communities, and indeed all of society. There is no separation of individual and community success. A community cannot excel and prosper when people suffer and individuals cannot succeed while their communities suffer.

A recent focus group of tribal college administrators agreed that student success is not about who graduates in the shortest period of time.[3] Too often American Indian and Alaska Native students enroll in college without basic skills in reading, science, and math. "When their skills improve enough to enroll in core curriculum courses, the college and the student have experienced success. Students who come to get a certificate in carpentry or take a Native language class have achieved their own personal goals" (p. 9). The experience of many educators and higher education leaders is that our students move in and out of the college due to financial and family circumstances; nevertheless, many of these American Indian and Alaska Native students do keep enrolling and then graduate from college. "By focusing upon the number who graduate in the shortest period of time, it devalues the persistence of those who stay for many years."

A Student's Voice

By getting a college education, you expand your boundaries of where you can work, who you can work with, and how you impact the younger native children within the community you are in by being a positive role model and possibly mentor.

There Are Many Benefits to Getting a Higher Education

Pursuing a postsecondary education is a meaningful experience. It is a time to broaden your intellectual horizons while gaining a deeper understanding of some area of interest. We all should embrace and accept the responsibility to be lifelong learners who remember ancestral teachings and prepare for the future. To gain knowledge throughout one's life is a sacred responsibility. We can also experience higher learning outside accredited higher education systems. However, we live in a standards-obsessed society that has ordained the college degree as a prerequisite to gaining entry into many career fields (i.e., job announcements with "bachelor's degree required, master's degree preferred"), and it is unlikely that anyone can practice in professional fields (i.e., law, medicine, business, psychology, science, etc.) without the degree credential and/or certification.

The College Board's Trends in Higher Education Series includes a report that offers an overview of the benefits of higher education for individuals and society.[4] From a financial perspective, four-year college graduates earn about 62 percent more per year than high school graduates (i.e., nearly $50,000 compared to around $30,000). "Those with master's degrees earned almost twice as much, and those with professional degrees over three times as much per year as high school graduates" (p. 2). There are other benefits that attract a growing participation in higher education.

- An increasing number of people realize that education pays off. In 2004 at least 53 percent of the population age twenty-five and older had completed post–high school education (compared to only 10 percent in 1940); nearly 30 percent hold a four-year college degree.
- College graduates are more likely to have health benefits and coverage. Among only high school graduates, half of the private-sector employees had health coverage compared to two-thirds of the college graduates.
- College graduates are more involved in selecting our political leaders. Among high school graduates, only about half voted in the presidential elections compared to two-thirds of college graduates.

- College graduates are more physically active. In 2003, a whopping 80 percent of individuals never graduating from high school reported *never* engaging in vigorous exercise. On the other hand, 91 percent of individuals with a bachelor's degree or higher reporting engaging in vigorous physical activity at least once per week (56 percent) or three or more times per week (35 percent).
- College graduates are less likely to be overweight. In 2001, 27 percent of individuals never graduating from high school were obese compared with 16 percent of individuals with a bachelor's degree or higher.
- College graduates are less likely to have multiple risk factors for heart disease. In 2003, 53 percent of individuals never graduating from high school had two or more high-risk factors, compared to 26 percent of individuals with a bachelor's degree or higher.

Table 2.1 provides a detailed listing of benefits resulting from Native peoples' success in higher education. Benefits to reservations are particularly attributed to tribal colleges and universities. It is clear that every Native person who successfully completes his or her college degree does so to have experiences that go beyond their own personal world. Families, the public at large, and Native communities enjoy a range of economic and social benefits that have a lasting impact on the future for all American Indians and Alaska Natives.

Table 2.1. Personal, Public, and Reservation Benefits Resulting from Higher Education

	Individual/Family	Public	Reservation
Economic	• Higher salaries and benefits • Employment • Higher savings levels • Improved working conditions • Personal/professional mobility	• Increased tax revenues • Greater productivity • Increased consumption • Increased workforce flexibility • Decreased reliance on government financial support	• Workforce and skills development • Greater opportunities for leadership and small businesses • Economic growth and development • Employment for graduates on reservations • Agriculture and land development
Social	• Improved health/life expectancy • Improved quality of life for offspring • Better consumer decision making • Increased personal status • More hobbies and leisure activities	• Reduced crime rates • Increased charitable giving and community service • Increased quality of civic life • Social cohesion/appreciation of diversity • Improved ability to adapt and use technology	• Mitigation of social problems • Centers for preservation of culture, language, and traditions • Provision of further educational opportunities • Technology transfer • Community program

Source: Institution for Higher Education Policy, American Indian Higher Education Consortium, and American Indian College Fund (February 2007), *The Path of Many Journeys: The Benefits of Higher Education for Native People and Communities* (Washington, DC: Institution for Higher Education Policy). Available at www.usafunds.org/forms/school_lender/path_of_many_journeys.pdf.

There Are a Lot of Institutions of Higher Education to Choose From

College choice is an exciting journey that should be embarked on with careful thought and consideration. There are many higher education institutions in every state: public, private, technical schools, small, large, rural, urban, and so on. At last count there were over 4,500 accredited institutions of higher education in America. Once you have decided to go, there is considerable literature on the topic of college choice, and the advice is fairly uniform. A perspective that is both straightforward and thoughtful comes from Jeffrey Dransfeldt.[5] I like his approach because he first reminds us of the experience where we anxiously await the mail each day, looking for an envelope from a college admissions office that, when opened, starts out with "Congratulations!" This is a positive perspective that is grounded by some solid advice for students in general, and that is a good place to start.

- Research the countless universities and available programs fitting your needs.
- Consider cost, location, and size of the institution.
- Look at colleges at varying distance from home (close, in state, out of state).
- Visit or find out about the campus through publications and the Internet and make contact with a campus representative to talk about degree requirements, campus involvement activities, and housing and financial aid opportunities.
- In the case of transfers, talk directly to an academic advisor to be clear about how many credits will be transferred.
- Survey recreational opportunities because college is also about enjoying yourself and meeting new people.

For American Indians and Alaska Natives, I add that it is important to choose a college that makes you feel comfortable. You might want to consider asking these questions:

- How many Native students attend?
- What is the Native student graduation rate?
- Is there a Native student organization, and how many students are involved?
- How many traditional celebrations, events, or gatherings are held on campus?
- How many Native faculty are on campus and in what academic areas?
- What kinds of student support services are available for American Indians and Alaska Natives?
- Are there financial aid opportunities for American Indians and Alaska Natives?
- Is there dedicated Native student housing?
- Have there been controversial events involving Native people at the campus?

Obviously, positive information about these and other questions speak well for any college campus. Imagine asking these questions and getting the response that (a) there are lots of Native students from all over the country enrolled in the college; (b) almost all Native students graduate with honors and those that did not graduate left for a high-paying job; (c) every Native person on campus is involved in the Native student organization; (d) there is a Native event every day; (e) there is a large Native faculty in every field, and they are available any time; (f) you will find all kinds of money available for Native students to buy computers, cars, and even for spending money; (g) there is a big, private American Indian and Alaska Native house with all the latest gadgets, along with free parking; and (h) there is lots of love for Native people in the college and community. However, wake up. That would be nice, but highly unlikely. Maybe someday.

The reality is that most campuses will have pluses and minuses when specifically taking into account factors that make you feel comfortable. My advice is to be open to the fact probably no campus can meet all your expectations. Take personal responsibility to make it work for you. That said, don't go overboard on analyzing what college you choose to attend, but be smart about what to expect and how to handle ambiguity. This approach can serve you well in all areas of your life, including relationships.

A Student's Voice

I remember the advice my grandmother gave me about woman and relationships. I was having difficulty with a girlfriend in high school and my grandmother noticed I was upset. She asked what was wrong and I solemnly said, "Nothin'." She prodded a bit, and I finally relented that I could not understand my girlfriend. "Well," while handing me a pencil and piece of paper, she said, "Why don't you list all the things in a woman that you like and want in a girlfriend?" I paused for a bit and then began to list one thing, then another, and then another until I had a list of about forty-five things that I desired in a woman. Proudly, I handed it to my grandmother, feeling like I really knew what I wanted. She frowned, looked at me and said, "No wonder you're having trouble with your girlfriend and I am sad to say you will never be happy with anyone. Look at this list; nobody can live up to these expectations. You better change your way of looking about relationships and what you desire in a woman. And burn this list as a good start."

My perspective is a bit simplistic. Jay Mathews offers a more insightful outlook in his article, "Six Ways to Be Happy with Your College Choice."[6] He draws on a book written by Barry Schwartz, *The Paradox of Choice: Why More Is Less*,[7] which covers the experiences of students choosing and then attending college. I relate to Jay's six points of advice drawn from Barry's book and feel that all American Indian and Alaska Native students should consider these points. I add my own insights with the italicized comments after each item.

1. **Listen to your viscera.** Mathews explains that feelings matter more than facts, and an unexamined emotional response is often a better guide to our

long-term needs than careful analysis of our thoughts. Schwartz cites a study in which college students were asked to evaluate posters for their dorm rooms. Some were asked to write down their feelings about the posters. Some were not. Both groups were told they could take home the posters they preferred. Those who analyzed their thinking and wrote down their feelings before making their choices were less happy with their posters weeks later than those who went with their instincts. *This is listening to the spirit, a place where the most important destiny we fulfill as Native people is the destiny that our ancestors encouraged us to follow. Many of our ancestors promoted getting an education to care for our people. You can feel their voices guiding you in the right direction.*

2. **Count your blessings.** Schwartz says gratitude has been scientifically proven so powerful in enhancing happiness that people should write in a bedside notebook each day five things that happened for which they were grateful. *For American Indians and Alaska Natives, this is the essence of being humble. We don't need everything, but we need to pray each day for everything that the Creator has blessed us with. Those of us who have been fortunate enough to be in a position to attend college, to escape drugs and alcohol, and offset the gripping effects of poverty should be thankful because we were given a chance to make a difference for every other American Indian and Alaska Native who may not have been as fortunate.*

3. **Satisfice.** Mathews notes that Schwartz uses this particular made-up word as a verb, as in, "You need to satisfice more." Although *satisfice* does not appear in any dictionary, the term resonates throughout the book. "To satisfice," Schwartz says, "is to settle for something that is good enough and not worry about the possibility that there might be something better." *The ancestral teachings of many Native cultures warn against being greedy or taking more than what we need. It keeps us from thinking we deserve more and taking more than we need. In terms of American Indians and Alaska Natives going to college, we often do so lacking the financial resources that could make things easier. However, I remember being so broke that I had to borrow pencils (pencils basically cost a nickel) to get by. Instead of worrying about being broke and wanting something more (a laptop would have been nice), it was fulfilling to use that pencil to do my homework.*

4. **Regret less.** Mathews reveals that his favorite mental exercise when wondering if he was right to have made a certain choice is to concede that he might have been hit by a bus if he had taken the alternate road. Schwartz endorses this vehicular approach to mental health. *For Native people, this may mean thinking less about what we miss out on if we went to college and more about what we gain from investing in the future of our people.*

5. **Anticipate adaptation.** Schwartz describes the process of adaptation this way: "We get used to things, and then we start to take them for granted." He is interested in the way adaptation sucks some of the thrill out of good things. Recognizing that this tendency is important will make you less likely to misinterpret it as a sign that you made the wrong choice. *Of the many reasons Native people are thankful for all the Creator's gifts (i.e., the sun, the water, the land, the plants, the animals, the wind) is that they greet us each day to be with us in our struggles and our joys. As we adapt to modern life, we should never forget to honor our ancestors and all that surrounds us in the environment; it keeps us thankful, and that is a good thing. The act of going to college is a daily ritual of personal improvement, which is a lifelong process. Don't get tired of it after a week of school, after one semester, three years, or ever. Be thankful you have been given a chance to make a positive difference each and every day of your life, and never lose a sense of thankfulness about this opportunity.*

6. **Avoid conversations about choice with maximizers.** Mathews relays that maximizers are people who obsess over every decision, who don't know how to satisfice. In these situations, try to change the subject to matters over which you have little control but are still fun to talk about. *My uncle, a renowned spiritual leader in the Pacific Northwest, would often tell me to approach life more organically and enjoy, indeed welcome how things can happen naturally. This relates to a lot of decisions regarding your college education, from what classes to take to what you'll do on weekends. You have to talk about things, and it is a good process to examine all sides, but you'll know when such decisions become unwieldy. When that happens, just pose the question, "What if we did nothing?" Wait a few moments, look around, then smile, and say, "Okay, let's make a decision, move on, and live with whatever we decide."*

A Student's Voice

I chose my first college (which I came to hate) purely on the basis of money and location. It was on the East Coast, which sounded cool to me, and offered me a very tempting financial aid package, which I took. My mom visited it with me, and tried to talk me out of going there, but I was stubborn and wanted to assert my independence, so I went anyway. Within a year I had transferred to my second-choice school, which my mom had really liked and which had offered me a good (but not quite as spectacular) financial package. The moral of the story is listen to others when making your decision, and don't make the decision of where to go to school entirely based on money. Money can make all the difference, but go where you feel you have the highest chances of success. You can always take out loans to make the financial stuff work out, and there are many scholarships available to Native students. I didn't succeed at my first college for many reasons, but I succeeded quite well at my second one and in grad school later on. Changing schools was the best decision I made. If things aren't working out, don't be afraid to change schools. Or majors, either. I went through five majors in my undergrad before I found my niche.

CLARIFYING ASPIRATIONS, INTENTIONS, AND VISION

A Student's Voice

If you don't know where you are going, how are you going to get there? Having a vision or a dream is a must. It fuels your fire and desire to accomplish it. Once it is established, you are able to move forward in the direction you need to go and seek out the assistance or guidance you will need in reaching it.

Academic preparation is important to succeed in college. At the same time, you'll probably find out very quickly that being familiar with the campus social environment helps you negotiate the complexity of college life. All of these and other new skills and capabilities are created by the attention you give to aspirations, intentions, and vision. Aspirations offer an important reason why you should begin thinking that every college and university is for us, as Native people regaining our prosperity to further our notion of place in this world. We need to say that we as a people belong in this world, that we are important as distinct members of society, and that our cultural intelligence can contribute to the betterment of humanity. The exceptional opportunity of going to college should give us power to realize the dream of survival that our ancestors promoted during the darkest times of our histories, when violence, famine, and extinction were all too real and where peace, contentment, and prosperity are only a tomorrow away.

There is a powerful body of literature on learning organizations that espouses skills and abilities that allow us and our communities to adapt readily to change and new challenges. In 1990, Peter Senge authored a book titled *The Fifth Discipline: The Art and Practice of the Learning Organization*. This is a profound book, and I encourage you to read it along with the collection of books that followed (i.e., *The Fifth Discipline Fieldbook, The Dance of Change,* and *Schools That Learn*).[8] Senge and his colleagues have put together wisdom from across the lands, and their central tenet of systems thinking honors the worldview of Native people.

What I want to briefly share with you here deals with one of the five core disciplines called *personal mastery* (the others are systems thinking, mental models, building shared vision, and team learning). Personal mastery is particularly relevant to this guide because it covers the importance of "articulating a personal vision, seeing current reality clearly, and choosing: making a commitment to creating the results you want."[9] The visioning process inherent in developing personal mastery is the same thing that occurs for Native people when we achieve a mental state that connects our past to the present world in such a way it guides us into the future. There is little hope for us to withstand the rigors of pursuing a postsecondary degree or even to live life fully without a personal vision of succeeding and being happy, however we define success or happiness.

For some Native people, the very act of seriously considering future goals in life can satisfy the deep search for meaning that will result in a personal vision. For others it requires a ceremonial involvement that allows the spirit to reveal the meaning and purpose that comes with a profound direction to take in life. However we arrive at the place in our minds that is our personal vision, we know when it happens. It is a special place mostly surrounded by deep desires to contribute meaningfully to our families and communities; rarely are personal visions among Native people about self or selfish purposes. So unique and special is this process that I refrain from providing specific direction on clarifying your personal vision. I do encourage you to contact your parents, adult mentors, or elders to ask them how you might develop a personal vision about going to college. You can also read publications by Senge and colleagues I mentioned here.

HELPFUL RESOURCES

There are at least three "must be aware of" publications among the many resources that are helpful guides for American Indians and Alaska Natives with postsecondary aspirations.

The American Indian Graduate Center (AIGC) publishes the amazing pamphlet, "Journey to College," which provides tips for Native youth, elders, and parents; describes the difference between the SAT and ACT, federal student aid at a glance, eligibility requirements for tribal higher education grants, and myths about financial aid; provides a glossary of college terms, importance of the essay, and top-ten tips for submitting a winning scholarship application. One side of the foldout has a wonderful poster that lays out the journey to college. Contact AIGC at www.aigcs.org.

The other two publications are magazines for American Indians and Alaska Natives who want timely information about higher education opportunities. *Winds of Change* is published by the American Indian Science and Engineering Society and focuses on career and educational advancement for Native people. Each year in September, the Annual College Guide is published in time for the fall recruitment season; it is one of most informative and attractive publications and includes data on colleges, universities, and financial aid for American Indian students; resources and references specific to American Indians; articles on applying to college, preparing for university life, and cultural support on campus; and words of wisdom from successful students. Visit www.aises.org.

Indian Country Today, the newspaper, puts out an annual feature magazine, *Education*, that is designed to be your guide to higher learning in Indian country. It has a comprehensive listing of tribal colleges and American Indian Studies programs, as well as scholarships and internships targeting Native students. Another attractive and informative resource, it is the perfect tool for high school students and their parents who want to decide on what to do and where to go after graduation. Visit *Indian Country Today* at www.indiancountrytoday.org.

Both of the magazines are loaded with advertisements from colleges and universities as well as organizations promoting programs specifically for American Indians and Alaska Natives.

I want to add that the essence of developing new skills and abilities to make college the most rewarding experience possible will involve clarifying your aspirations, engaging in reflection and conversation, and conceptualization. Aspirations express what you truly care about in life so that you live accordingly because it is something you want to do. Engaging in reflection and conversation means to be sincere in your communication with yourself and other people; it is the ability to express your feelings while being real. There is no need to lie to anybody (especially yourself) about something as important as your life and going to college. Conceptualization is about seeing the whole experience of going to college and keeping in mind the day when you graduate—actually visualize the day when you are done. Tripping over one bad day, horrible class, or low grade is not conceptualizing.

As a human being committed to learning and adapting to life, you will develop new awareness and sensibilities that will provide fulfillment.

The resulting intellectual growth will be conducive to understanding the complexity and interrelatedness of the world and profound insights about life that were very clear to our ancestors. These insights will be brought forth in experiences fostered by dialogue, a communication skill perfected by many Indigenous cultures because it uniquely lets us become aware of the presence or absence of the spirit. Newfound attitudes and beliefs await you each day so that you incorporate each into your life as if it always belonged there. I know this sounds strange. It can also be wonderful. Let me add that you don't have to go to college to arrive at this state of mind. On the other hand, you can achieve this state of mind in college. Ultimately, you make the decision.

A Student's Voice

Well, I knew I wanted to go to college, and I thought I wanted to be a vet. Turns out, I didn't! So what then? I met several times with my school advisor, and talked to a favorite professor and my mom a lot. I didn't know what to do, but I knew that organic chemistry and putting dogs down wasn't for me. I continued taking classes in areas I enjoyed, but didn't want to major in, so I have a minor in history and one in biology as well. I love to write, and finally I chose to major in what I loved. . . . So I ended up graduating with a degree in creative writing. Fine and good, and I don't regret it, but in my small Alaskan town there aren't many good jobs for creative writers. So, after living from miserable paycheck to miserable paycheck, I went back to grad school, thinking, "I need to do something worthwhile, that I will like, that will support me so I can be independent, and that dovetails with some of my interests." For me that turned out to be speech pathology. I get to directly affect the lives of my clients for the better, in my home community or wherever I go, and I am in demand. It is very gratifying. And I can always write poetry, my first love, on the side!

CHAPTER 3

Financial Aid

A Student's Voice

One of the worst things about going to school is working out the financial aid. I said to myself, "I'm poor to begin with. How in the world am I gonna afford school?" Well, the thing to remember is that there are a lot of funding possibilities out there. . . . I think it's especially important to talk to an advisor and an Office of Diversity person on campus. They seem to know what money is available and how to get it, and can be really helpful figuring out all the paperwork. There are loans, too. But don't take them out unless you're committed! *If* you're committed, then between scholarships and loans there's a way to make it happen for pretty much anybody.

COLLEGE PRICING AND FINANCIAL AID

College Pricing

The reality is that going to college will encumber a financial cost of some kind. Simply said, you will have to spend money to get an education. You will have to pay more or less depending on where you decide to attend college. You need to be ready for this and plan accordingly. The College

Table 3.1. One-Year Increase in Total Charges at Four-Year Public and Private Institutions

Sector	Total Charges			
	2005–6	2004–5	$ Change	% Change
Four-Year Public	$12,127	$11,376	$751	6.6%
Four-Year Private	$29,026	$27,465	$1,561	5.7%

Source: College Board (2005b), p. 5.

Board's Trends on Higher Education Series offers two recent reports that explain information on college charges and available financial assistance.[1] Let's look at *Trends in College Pricing* first. This particular report provides the kind of evidence that has been consistent throughout time: college pricing tends to increase each year. For example, average published charges for undergraduates at four-year public and private institutions reflected about a 6 percent increase from 2004–5 to 2005–6 (see Table 3.1).

According to *Trends in College Pricing*, the type of postsecondary institution has a dramatic influence on the overall budget you should anticipate. For example, Table 3.2 shows that on average costs associated with two-year public commuter institutions are much lower ($11,692) than attending a four-year private residential college ($31,916). Factoring in out-of-state tuition would probably make the difference even more dramatic.

These estimated budgets factor in such costs as (a) tuition and fees, (b) books and supplies, (c) room and board, (d) transportation, and (e) other expenses. However, many American Indian and Alaska Native students may have additional expenses related to day care (particularly among female heads of households), attending cultural events, and so on. These additional costs are difficult to calculate. It has been our experience that American Indian and Alaska Native students, particularly from tightly knit extended families, experience unavoidable trips to and from home at least once or twice a year to fulfill family and community responsibilities.

For many American Indian and Alaska Native students going to college is often a family decision due to the cultural dynamics of kinships and the fact that many Native family incomes are in the lower quartiles. This is important not because American Indian and Alaska Native students and families need to factor in what it will cost the family but, more important, to help us all anticipate and be proactive about what we need to do to

Table 3.2. Total Average Student Budgets by Type of Postsecondary Institution

Type of Institution	Total Estimated Average Student Budget
Two-Year Public Commuter	$11,692
Four-Year Public In-State Resident	$15,566
Four-Year Public Out-of-State Resident	$23,239
Four-Year Private Resident	$31,916

Source: College Board (2005b), p. 6.

support each other when we go to college. For example, "The average public net cost of attendance for dependent students from the lowest income quartile represents 37 percent of average family income."[2] Simply put, the proportion of family income needed to cover the cost of college attendance is generally greater for lower income families when compared to higher income families. Financial aid can and does help alleviate this discrepancy for many American Indian and Alaska Native families.

A Student's Voice

Start the fall of your senior year in high school. Apply to many different colleges that you like. This will give you choices if accepted into more than one. Plus you can weigh it based on financial aid offered by each institution. Be sure to visit the campuses if you can. This will give you a feeling for the campus life and meeting of instructors or Native American personnel, so if you do choose one, you will have familiar people to see. Start searching for scholarships as early as possible—see your guidance counselor at your high school. Talk with your parents about their backgrounds because you might qualify as a child of a veteran, or first-generation college student, or foster child. Have all your information ready before you do your search. Make sure you have someone proofread your essay for scholarships to ensure cohesiveness of your ideas of why you qualify for the scholarship.

Financial Aid

It is important to note that *Trends in Student Aid* explains that "students and their families pay only a fraction of the costs of higher education; the balance comes from a variety of sources."[3] This may not always appear to be the case as American Indian and Alaska Native parents and students prepare to write personal checks to cover certain expenses of college attendance. But a college education is still one of the best investments that a person can make in terms of actual expenditures compared with the actual costs of providing the postsecondary educational opportunities given that states, the federal government, and private foundations provide large subsidies.

Besides scholarships, American Indian and Alaska Native families and students should be knowledgeable of an array of financial aid opportunities, such as those listed below:

- Federally supported programs
  - Grants: federal Pell grants, federal SEOG, federal LEAP, federal veterans, federal military/other grants
  - Federal work study

— Loans: federal Perkins, federal subsidized Stafford, federal unsubsidized Stafford, federal PLUS, other federal loans (i.e., higher education grants for Indian Students, American Indian scholarships, Indian Health Service scholarships)

- Education tax benefits
- State grant programs
- Tribal grant programs
- Institutional grant programs
- Private and employer grants
- Nonfederal loans

Please refer to Appendix B to review and master the glossary of terms that relate to these programs and financial aid for college study in general. American Indian and Alaska Native families and students will want to get familiar with this vocabulary to become aware of and demystify the complex world of college financial aid. Indeed, the world of college financial aid is pretty complex, both in researching opportunities and filling out the myriad forms. However, it is time well spent, and it is unlikely that you will receive more of a return on any investment of effort over your lifetime. Besides, you do essentially the same thing year after year (i.e., fill out forms, provide income information, etc.), so it should get easier once you start. Spend two to three hours to fill out federal grant applications, and you might receive anywhere from $2,000 to $3,000 per academic year, and that basically works out to a $1,000 per hour spent on the forms! We have not come close to such a return in our professional careers even after receiving our doctorates and becoming faculty members at a major research university.

IMPORTANT ADVICE ABOUT FINANCIAL AID

Sources of Federal Student Aid and Steps to Take

One of the essential resources on financial aid is *Funding Education Beyond High School: The Guide to Federal Student Aid*.[4] Like most students, the vast majority of student financial assistance received by American Indians and Alaska Natives is awarded by the federal government. However, the advice offered in *The Guide to Federal Student Aid* is applicable to most efforts to secure financial assistance to fund your college education. The report states,

> Our nation is built on opportunity for all. Our guide might just give you the boost you need to make community college, university, or trade school a reality for you. As you make progress on your personal path to achievement, all American benefits. So take advantage of the resources we provide: we're here to help you as you go forward into new successes. (p. v)

We like the sound and sincerity of this statement. You should, too. One of the major barriers to college success cited by American Indians and Alaska Natives is the lack of money. This lack should not necessarily be a prohibitive factor to college attendance with over $70 billion in student financial aid awarded by the Department of Education each year. So let's take the Federal Student Aid Team up on their offer and take advantage of the resources they provide. A good place to begin is a summary of critical information available in the *Guide to Federal Student Aid* and at the Web site www.federalstudentaid.ed.gov. They recommend that you know what federal student aid is: financial assistance available from the Department of Education if you're enrolled in an eligible program as a regular student at a school participating in federal student aid programs. As shown in Table 3.3, there are a variety of financial aid programs that range from grants that you don't have to pay back, money that you earn through work study, and loans that must be paid back. The Federal Student Aid Team then recommends that you follow a manageable seven-step process (see Table 3.4) to answer the question of how you can apply for federal student aid.

Getting Helpful Information from the School

The Federal Student Aid Team also feels that it is important to find out about financial aid at the college of your choice. Everyone—and that includes you—has the right to receive the following information from schools administering federal financial aid:

- The location, hours, and counseling procedures for the school's financial aid office.
- The financial aid assistance available, including federal, state, local, private, and institutional programs.
- The procedures and deadlines for submitting applications for each available financial aid program.
- The school's criteria for selecting financial aid recipients.
- The school's process for determining your financial need.
- The school's process for determining the type and amount of assistance in your financial aid package.
- The method and timing of aid payments.
- The school's basis for determining whether you're making satisfactory academic progress, and what happens if you're not. (Whether you continue to receive federal financial aid depends in part on whether you make satisfactory academic progress.)
- If you're offered a federal work study job, the nature of the job, the hours you must work, your duties, the pay, and the method and timing of payment to you.[5]

Are You Eligible and How Much Can You Receive?

One of the first things to find out about federal student financial aid is whether you are eligible. To receive federal aid, you must meet certain criteria. You must establish financial need. There are educational requirements

Table 3.3. Federal Student Aid Summary Chart

Federal Student Aid Program	Type of Aid	Program Details	Annual Award Limits
Federal Pell grant	Grant: does not have to be repaid	Available almost exclusively to undergraduates; all eligible students will receive the federal Pell grant amount they qualify for	$400 to $4,050 for 2006–7
Federal Supplemental Educational Opportunity grant (FSEOG)	Grant: does not have to be repaid	For undergraduates with exceptional financial need; priority is given to federal Pell grant recipients; funds depend on availability at school. This is why it's so important to apply early to be considered for these funds. Not everyone who qualifies for an FSEOG gets one	$100 to $4,000
Federal work study	Money is earned while attending school; does not have to be repaid	For undergraduate and graduate students; jobs can be on campus or off campus; students are paid at least federal minimum wage	No annual minimum or maximum award amounts
Federal Perkins loan	Loan: must be repaid	Interest charged on this loan is 5% for both undergraduate and graduate students; payment is owed to the school that made the loan	$4,000 maximum for undergraduate students; $6,000 maximum for graduate and professional students; no minimum award amount
Subsidized direct or FFEL Stafford loan	Loan: must be repaid	Subsidized: U.S. Department of Education pays interest while borrower is in school and during grace and deferment periods; you must be at least a half-time student	$2,625 to $8,500, depending on grade level
Unsubsidized direct or FFEL Stafford loan	Loan: must be repaid	Unsubsidized: Borrower is responsible for interest during life of the loan; you must be at least a half-time student; financial need is not a requirement	$2,625 to $18,500, depending on grade level (includes any subsidized amounts received for the same period)
Direct or FFEL PLUS Loan	Loan: must be repaid	Available to parents of dependent undergraduate students who are enrolled at least half-time	Maximum amount is cost of attendance minus any other financial aid the student receives; no minimum award amount

Source: U.S. Department of Education (2006), p. xii.

Table 3.4. Seven Steps to Take and Processes to Follow on How to Apply for Student Aid

Steps to Take	Process to Follow
Step 1	Get a personal identification number (PIN). A PIN lets you apply, "sign" your online forms, make corrections to your application information, and more—all online. Go to www.pin.ed.gov.
Step 2	Collect the documents needed to apply, including income tax returns, W-2 forms, and other records of income. A full list of what you need is available at www.fafsa.ed.gov. Tax return not completed at the time you apply? Estimate the tax information, apply, and correct the information later.
Step 3	Complete the Free Application for Federal Student Aid (FAFSA) between January 1 (i.e., 2007) and July 2 of the following year (i.e., 2008). Make sure to know the correct dates as there are no exceptions. Apply as soon as possible after January 1 to meet school and state aid deadlines. Apply online by going to www.fafsa.ed.gov.
Step 4	Review your Student Aid Report (SAR)—the result of your FAFSA application. If necessary, make changes or corrections and resubmit your SAR for reprocessing. Your complete, correct SAR will contain your Expected Family Contribution (EFC)—the number used to determine your federal student aid eligibility.
Step 5	If you are selected for verification, your school's financial aid office will ask you to submit tax returns and other documents as appropriate. Be sure to meet the school's deadline, or you will not be able to get federal student aid.
Step 6	Whether you're selected for verification or not, make sure the financial aid office at the school has all the information needed to determine your eligibility.
Step 7	All students: Contact the financial aid office if you have any questions about the aid being offered. First-time applicants: Review award letters from schools to compare amounts and types of aid being offered. Decide which school to attend based on a combination of (a) how well the school suits your needs and (b) its affordability after all aid is taken into account.

Source: U.S. Department of Education (2006), p. xii.

that demonstrate you are qualified to enroll in postsecondary education and other legal requirements.

- Have a high school diploma or a GED.
- Pass an approved ability-to-benefit (ATB) test. If you don't have a diploma or a GED, you can take an approved ATB test to determine whether you can benefit from the education offered at that school.
- Meet other state and federal standards.
- Complete a high school education in a home school setting approved under state law.
- You must be enrolled or accepted for enrollment as a regular student working toward a degree or certificate in an eligible program.

- You must meet satisfactory academic progress standards set by the postsecondary school you are or will be attending.

- You must be a U.S. citizen or eligible noncitizen.

- You must have a valid Social Security number (SSN) (unless you're from the Republic of the Marshall Islands, the Federated States of Micronesia, or the Republic of Palau). If you need an SSN, you can find out more about applying for one online at www.ssa.gov or by calling (800) 772-1213 (TTY users can call (800) 325-0778).

- You must certify that you will use federal student aid only for educational purposes. You must also certify that you are not in default on a federal student loan and do not owe money on a federal student grant (which could happen if you withdraw from school, for example). You certify these items when you apply for federal student aid and sign a promissory note to obtain these funds.

- You must comply with Selective Service registration. If you're a male, aged eighteen through twenty-five and you have not registered, you can do so at the same time you complete your FAFSA by giving the Selective Service System permission to register you by means of the FAFSA. You can also register online at www.sss.gov or call (847) 688-6888 (TTY users can call (847) 688-2567).

- You must answer question 31 on the FAFSA, "Have you ever been convicted of possessing or selling illegal drugs?" If you leave it blank, you automatically become ineligible for federal student aid. You may be eligible to receive federal student aid even if you have been convicted under federal or state law of selling or possessing illegal drugs. For information or to find out about your status, call (800) 4-FED-AID (433-3243) or go to www.fafsa.ed.gov, click on "Worksheets" in the left column, then select "Drug Worksheet."[6]

Nobody knows how much financial aid you can receive until you fill out and submit the proper applications and required paperwork. However, an important process in receiving federal student financial aid from most of the programs (except for unsubsidized Stafford loans and PLUS loans) is to determine financial need and expected family contribution (EFC). Check out information about the EFC formula at the U.S. Department of Education Web site (www.studentaid.ed.gov/pubs) or contact the Federal Student Aid Information Center at (800) 4-FED-AID (433-3243).[7] The folks at the Information Center are pretty helpful but often swamped with calls all day long. Be persistent, gracious, and respectful in contacting them because they are trying to help you get the most aid that you are eligible to receive.

Additional Publications and Checklists

There are a bunch of helpful federal student aid publications, and every one is filled with information just for you! The following publications can be found at Web site studentaid.ed.gov or by searching the Internet using the title of the publication:

- *College Preparation Checklist*
- *The Student Aid Audio Guide*

- *Looking for Student Aid*
- *Completing the FAFSA*
- *Repaying Your Student Loans*
- *Stafford Loan Forgiveness Program for Teachers*

The *College Preparation Checklist* is very helpful, and a workable checklist is offered in Table 3.5. Getting financial aid is only one factor to ensure that going to college is an experience you are prepared for academically and personally. The checklist is basically geared to traditional age college students (i.e., those coming out of high school). If you are an older or returning student, look at some items in the checklist metaphorically, and notice that others apply to anyone.

Table 3.5. Federal Student Aid College Preparation Checklist

Pre–High School

- Start saving for college if you haven't already. Look into college savings plans that your state may offer.
- Take classes that challenge you.
- Do your best in school. If you are having difficulty, don't give up—get help from a teacher, tutor, or mentor.
- Investigate which high schools or special programs will most benefit your future interests.
- Become involved in school- or community-based extracurricular activities that enable you to explore your interests, meet new people and learn new things.

High School: Every Year

- Continue to save for college.
- Take challenging classes in core academic subjects: most colleges require four years of English, at least three years of social studies (history, civics, geography, economics, etc.), three years of mathematics, and three years of science, and many require two years of a foreign language. Round out your course load with classes in computer science and the arts.
- Stay involved in school- or community-based extracurricular activities that interest you or enable you to explore career interests. Consider working or volunteering. Remember: it's quality (not quantity) that counts.
- Save copies of your report cards, awards, honors, and best work for your academic portfolio. Athletes, artists, scholars, and others should start collecting items for their portfolios (such as game tapes, newspaper clippings, stats, awards, artwork, photographs, school papers, etc.).

Ninth Grade

- Take challenging core classes. (Core subjects are listed above, under "Every Year.")
- Start planning for college and thinking about your career interests. At www.federal studentaid.ed.gov you can register with MyFSA and research your career and college options.

Tenth Grade

- Continue to take challenging core classes. (Core subjects are listed above, under "Every Year.")
- Meet with your school counselor or mentor to discuss colleges and their requirements.
- Talk to adults about what they like and dislike in their jobs and about what kind of education is needed for each kind of job.
- Consider taking a practice Preliminary SAT (PSAT), or the PLAN exam, also known as the pre-ACT. Register for all tests in advance, and be sure to give yourself time to prepare appropriately. If you have difficulty paying a registration fee, see your school counselor about getting a fee waiver.
- Ask your teachers and counselors whether Advanced Placement classes are offered in your school. You may want to consider taking them in your junior year.
- Plan to use your summer wisely: work, volunteer, and/or take a summer course (away or at a local college).

Eleventh Grade: All Year

- Continue to save money for college.
- Continue to challenge yourself academically. (Core subjects are listed above, under "Every Year.")
- Stay involved in school- or community-based extracurricular activities that interest you or enable you to explore career interests. Consider working or volunteering. Remember: it's quality (not quantity) that counts.
- Update your portfolio. (A portfolio might include awards, game tapes, newspaper clippings, artwork, etc.)
- Talk to people you know who went to college to learn about what to expect.
- Research colleges that interest you. Visit them and talk to students. Make lists to help you compare different colleges. Think about things like location, size, special programs, and costs.
- Go to college fairs and presentations by college representatives.
- Investigate financial aid, including scholarships. Understand the different types of aid and sources for aid. Check your school's scholarship postings, colleges' financial aid Web pages, and your library for directories of special scholarships.
- For more information about scholarships and federal student aid opportunities, visit www.federalstudentAid.ed.gov.

Eleventh Grade: Fall

- Take the PSAT/National Merit Scholarship Qualifying Test. Even if you took it for practice last year, you must take the test in eleventh grade to qualify for scholarships and programs associated with the National Merit Program.
- Write to your U.S. senator or representative if you would like to attend a U.S. military academy.
- See your school counselor if you are interested in participating in a Reserve Officer Training Corps (ROTC) program.

(*continued*)

Table 3.5. Continued

Eleventh Grade: Spring

- Register for and take exams for college admission. Register for all tests in advance and be sure to give yourself time to prepare appropriately. If you have difficulty paying a registration fee, see your school counselor about getting a fee waiver. Many colleges accept the SAT I and/or SAT II: Subject Test, whereas others accept the ACT. Check with colleges you are interested in to see what tests they require.
- Make sure you file with the NCAA (National Collegiate Athletic Association) Clearinghouse if you want to play for a Division I or II team. When registering for and taking the SAT or ACT, enter "9999" as one of the college choices to have test scores sent to the Clearinghouse.

Summer Before Twelfth Grade

- Narrow down the list of colleges you are interested in attending. If you can, visit schools that interest you.
- Contact colleges to request information and applications for admission. Ask about financial aid, admission requirements, and deadlines.
- Decide whether you are going to apply under a particular college's early decision or early action program. Be sure to learn about the program deadlines and requirements.
- Begin preparing for the application process: draft application essays; collect writing samples; assemble portfolios or audition tapes.
- If you are an athlete and plan to play in college, contact the coaches at the schools to which you are applying and ask about intercollegiate and intramural sports programs and athletic scholarships.

Twelfth Grade: All Year

- Keep taking classes that challenge you. (Core subjects are listed above, under "Every Year.")
- Update your portfolio. (A portfolio might include awards, game tapes, newspaper clippings, artwork, etc.)
- Work hard all year; second-semester grades can affect scholarship eligibility.
- Stay involved and seek leadership roles in your activities.

Twelfth Grade: Fall

- Meet with your school counselor: are you on track to graduate and fulfill college admission requirements?
- If you haven't done so already, register for and take exams such as the SAT I, SAT II: Subject Test, or ACT for college admission. Check with the colleges you are interested in to see what tests they require. Register for all tests in advance and be sure to give yourself time to prepare appropriately. If you have difficulty paying a registration fee, see your school counselor about getting a fee waiver.
- Apply to the colleges you have chosen. Prepare your application carefully. Follow the instructions, and *pay close attention to deadlines!*
- Well before your application deadlines, ask your counselor and teachers to submit required documents (e.g., transcript, letters of recommendation) to the colleges to which you're applying.

- To prepare to apply for federal student aid, be sure to get a PIN at www.pin.ed.gov so that you can complete your application and access your information online. One of your parents must also get a PIN.

Twelfth Grade: Winter

- Encourage your parent(s) to complete income tax forms early. If your parent(s) have not completed the tax forms, you can provide estimated information on your federal student aid application, but remember to make any necessary changes later.

- As soon after January 1 as possible, complete and submit your FAFSA, along with any other financial aid applications your school(s) of choice may require. You can complete the FAFSA online at www.fafsa.ed.gov or on paper, but completing the application online is faster and easier. You should submit your FAFSA by the earliest financial aid deadline of the schools to which you are applying, usually by early February.

- If you have questions about the federal student aid programs or need assistance with the application process, call (800) 4-FED-AID (433-3243) or TTY for the hearing-impaired, (800) 730-8913.

- After you submit the FAFSA, you should receive your Student Aid Report within one to four weeks. Quickly make any necessary corrections and submit them to the FAFSA processor.

- If the schools you are applying to require it, complete the CSS Profile. Many private colleges and universities use this information to help them award nonfederal student aid funds.

- Complete scholarship applications. Apply for as many as you can—you may be eligible for more than you think.

- Parents should check their eligibility for the Hope Credit, Lifetime Learning Credit, or other tax benefits.

Twelfth Grade: Spring

- Visit colleges that have invited you to enroll.
- Review your college acceptances and compare financial aid packages.
- When you decide which school you want to attend, notify that school of your commitment and submit any required financial deposit. Many schools require this notification and deposit by May 1.

Source: Adapted from College Preparation Checklist. Available at www.studentaid.ed.gov/PORTALSWebApp/students/english/checklist.jsp.

WORKING AND GOING TO COLLEGE

A recent American Council on Education (ACE) *Issue Brief* examined the issue of students working while they made their way through college and how this has an impact on the college experience.[8] This is an important topic because most American Indians and Alaska Natives may have to work while pursuing an undergraduate degree. They will not be alone, as the ACT study found that nearly 80 percent of all students work while going to college. If done in the right way, it seems that working can have a positive influence on persistence and degree completion—that is, if you only need fifteen or fewer hours a week and score a good work study job that aligns perfectly with your academic interests. Let's imagine that your supervisor gives you lots of time off (with pay), to study for tests and complete course assignments. This could happen and it could be you, so keep praying.

The cool sense of reality that is probably going to be the case might be a morning breeze you feel while waking up halfway to that Dunk'n Fried Bread stand you open up at 5 a.m. to catch the morning rush and working for minimum wage. You work there until 9 a.m. to catch a 9:30 a.m. class, take three more classes throughout the day, study for an hour or so just before dinner, then hop and skip to your next employment opportunity stacking shelves at Megafoods supermarket from 7 to 11 p.m. You study a bit more, hang out, and then crash to start the whole cycle again. Just like salmon. Sound fun?

On a different note, working while pursuing a college degree may be challenging, but it does have its rewards. You have to play it smart and know your limitations. The smart side? Get a job that interests you and somehow can give you working experience in an academic field of your choice. That Dunk'n Fried Bread stand you run would be related to entrepreneurship and business-related professions. Stacking shelves at Megafoods? That's a clear example of marketing research if ever there was one. You say you're in sociology? Well look for that job working the concession stand at the local theater so that you can examine human interaction as customers come and go.

Whatever you do while working and going to college, feel fortunate. Most of us had to work, most of us do work, and most of us will continue to work while pursuing our dream of higher education. It is still a right of Native people to have access to and an opportunity to graduate from college. However, we need to take on a high degree of personal responsibility to make that dream a reality. If we need to work, then we work. The ultimate achievement is to finish college. There are a number of helpful suggestions if you choose or need to work while going to college.

- Don't work too much. Only you can really determine what too much is. A good indicator of too much is when you start pouring coffee in the sugar cup (which is full of sugar).
- Don't work the wrong job. Only you can tell what the wrong job is. A good indicator of the wrong job is when the supervisor says, again, "Yuz ain't meant for college . . . loser anyway."
- Don't work a job where the cost of getting the job outweighs the potential earnings you make. Just about anybody can tell you if a job will cost you too much money. A good indicator? You have to buy the suit, the car, and so on to get the job and you are only going to be working long enough to pay half the debt you incurred to get the job. Make sense?
- Don't think you can juggle work and college without telling your supervisor or others at work. It is not good to keep it to yourself that you are sneaking off and getting a college education. A good indicator that you are not being open and honest with your boss is when she asks you what's up about some textbooks you have and you reply, "I'm part of a book club."

There are more helpful suggestions, of course. You'll figure these out as you go along. Just don't let anything prevent you from accomplishing your goal to finish college—especially work.

DEBT MANAGEMENT MATERIAL

Another great source of helpful brochures and guides is the federal agency Nellie Mae,[9] which has the positive opening line on their Web site (www.nelliemae.com):

> Nellie Mae helps you be brilliant by providing intelligent student loan programs to help families pay for college. We work in partnership with the brightest school administrators to make student loans accessible and offer timely guidance about borrowing wisely. With an array of federal and private student loans, Nellie Mae has the right loan combination for you.

In particular, the debt management materials are very helpful with advice to first-time student loan borrowers regarding terms of federal loans, budgeting, increasing income, reducing expenses, using debit and credit cards, and exit counseling. Sound great? It *is* great because the information allows you to get an insider understanding of student financial aid and other related financial issues you will come across while completing your college education.

Nellie Mae's brochure *Entrance Counseling Guide for First-time Borrowers* is particularly helpful for thinking about and following through on developing a budget. Like all their brochures, this one has a straightforward and engaging style of writing. For example,

> The term "budget" may remind you of the same kind of drudgery as cleaning your room or doing your laundry. But think about what would happen if you didn't have a plan for handling your money. . . . At some point in time, you simply wouldn't have any left (just like you would eventually run out of clean clothes if you never did your laundry)! (p. 6)

Financial aid is often disbursed in lump installments, and you have to make it last for an extended period of time (i.e., semester or quarter). A budget helps keep you on track with regard to your financial resources in comparison to your spending. A basic budget helps you keep a record of your monthly income (financial aid, part-time employment, etc.) while subtracting your monthly expenses.[10] Try not to blow any extra money, if there is any, because you may need it later on—especially when your expenses are greater than your income.

When expenses are greater than income, it is usual to think about the need to increase income. However, a wiser choice might be to reduce expenses. Think about the little items that nickel and dime you to death. For example, it is easy to overlook your spending habits when there goes $3.50 for something, $5 for something else, $2.25 on yet another thing you just had to have, each and every day. Add this up each day for a week the total will be $75.25, and every month it comes to $301. Over the course of one semester (three months), those little "harmless" not-very-much-at-one-time spending habits comes to hefty $903. Whoa, you ask yourself, where did all my money go? Hamburgers, pizza, bottled water, gas, dry cleaning, cell phone, long-distance charges, shopping spree, I'll buy this round, cigarettes, triple-shot latté with hazelnut flavoring, midnight withdrawals from the ATM, and new-release DVDs.

Nellie Mae offers sound advice in that you should take your lump-sum financial aid disbursement and put it "into a savings account and only transfer a budgeted amount each week or month into your checking account" (p. 7). At the same time, take advantage of discounts and coupons, avoid driving your own car whenever possible, learn to cook economically, avoid using credit cards, and pay them off each month if you can. There's more, but no need to bore you with the details here. Debt management can be a lifelong skill that will help you help yourself and others. For more advice, visit Nellie Mae's Web site, or you may order a hard copy of any of the following brochures by e-mailing your name and address to loancounselors@ nelliemae.com.

- *Entrance Counseling Guide for First-time Borrowers.* This booklet for the first-time student loan borrower outlines the terms of federal student loans, the importance of budgeting, and ways to increase income and reduce expenses while in school. Also included are borrower's rights and responsibilities, tips on avoiding credit card debt, helpful Web sites and phone numbers, and a glossary of student loan terms.

- *A Student's Guide to Borrowing and Using Credit.* This guide addresses the financial concerns of high school students as they transition to college. Topics cover borrowing and repayment, budgeting, and using debit and credit cards.

- *Exit Counseling for Student Borrowers.* This publication emphasizes the importance of understanding loan terms and keeping track of loans after leaving school. It also includes repayment options and estimated monthly loan payments, and it outlines the differences between deferment, forbearance, cancellation, and loan forgiveness. Also included are credit card and budgeting tips, borrower's rights and responsibilities, student loan–related contacts, and a glossary.

- *Steps to Success: A Comprehensive Guide to Preparing and Paying for College.* This brochure for high school juniors and seniors and their families features an overview of the financial aid process and types of aid available, as well as helpful resources, such as an award letter comparison worksheet and glossary of financial aid terms.

- *Tuition 101: A Comprehensive Guide to Funding Your Undergraduate Education.* This guide for undergraduates outlines federal and private student loan options, steps to apply for financial aid and scholarships, and tips for budgeting and reducing expenses while in school. A college planning checklist is also included.

- *A Student's Guide to Federal Stafford Loans and the MPN.* This question-and-answer guide for students outlines the terms, benefits, and repayment options of federal Stafford loans and explains the purpose of the Master Promissory Note (MPN).

- *A Graduate Student's Guide to Federal PLUS Loans and MPN.* This question-and-answer guide outlines the terms, benefits, and repayment options of new federal PLUS loans for graduate students and explains the purpose of the MPN.

- *A Parent's Guide to Federal PLUS Loan and MPN.* This publication for parents explains the terms, benefits, and repayment options of the Parent PLUS loan and outlines the application process using the MPN.

- *Learning by Degrees: A Financial Aid Guide for Community College Students.* This brochure for community college and other two-year program transfer students addresses steps to apply for financial aid and scholarships, borrowing limits, earning potential, and tips for budgeting and reducing expenses during school. Terms and repayment options for federal and private student loans are also included, along with a transfer checklist.
- *Master Plan—Funding Graduate School.* A complete guide to graduate school preparation, this brochure addresses borrowing limits and future earnings, budgeting tips, and federal and private student loan options. Steps to apply for financial aid, suggestions for reducing expenses during school, and a graduate school checklist are also included.

SCHOLARSHIPS

Knowing where to find scholarship opportunities can be difficult, so you may find visiting the College Board's Scholarship Search! Web site an essential first step. Search the Internet or go to apps.collegeboard.com/cbsearch_ss/welcome.jsp. The College Board "created this online tool to help you locate scholarships, internships, grants, and loans that match your education level, talents, and background. Complete the brief questionnaire and Scholarship Search will find potential opportunities from our database of more than 2,300 sources of college funding, totaling nearly $3 BILLION in available aid!" They recommend "that the more personal information you enter, the better the odds that Scholarship Search will be able to match you to financial aid sources. So don't be shy and be sure to complete all the sections of the questionnaire." The American Indian Graduate Center (AIGC) in partnership with Peterson's offers a scholarship search service at www.petersons.com/ss/code/prompt.asp?sponsor=1678.

AIGC also partners with the United Negro College Fund (UNCF) to administer the American Indian and Alaska Native portion of the Gates Millennium Scholarship, which is a scholarship program funded by a $1 billion grant from the Bill & Melinda Gates Foundation. The grant is a twenty-year commitment designed to fund the college education of 20,000 high achieving, underrepresented minority students. This program is also designed to help develop a group of leaders that represent the ethnic diversity of America in the 21st century. The application period runs from October to January 1 (deadline) each academic year. The goals of the program are:

- To reduce the financial barriers for American Indian and Alaska Native students with high academic and leadership promise who are at a significant economic disadvantage.
- To increase the representation of these target groups in the disciplines of mathematics, science, engineering, education and library science, where these groups are severely underrepresented.
- To develop a diversified cadre of future leaders for America by facilitating successful completion of bachelor's, master's and doctoral degrees.
- To provide seamless support from undergraduate through doctoral programs for students entering target disciplines.

For additional information you may call (877) 690-GMSP, or AIGC Scholars at (866) 884-7007 toll free.

Once you have found potential scholarships, the next step is to submit the best possible scholarship application. There is a great deal of information on how to apply for scholarships. Susie McGee offers suggestions online at www.howtodothings.com/education/a3557-how-to-apply-for-scholarships. html. She recommends that you attend to six important areas:

1. **Getting Organized.** The first step in the scholarship application process is to get organized! Gather together important information from your high school years, such as organization memberships, extracurricular activities, transcripts, standardized test scores, upper level academic courses, volunteer projects, financial aid forms, achievements, and awards. You will repeatedly refer to this information as you begin applying for scholarships. Create a separate file folder for each scholarship. Place these files in the order that the scholarships are due, so that you won't miss any deadlines.

2. **Applying Early.** This is so important! You need time to gather all of your information together, compile a folder of references, and receive the proper application materials. Many scholarship applications must be received no later than the fall of your senior year in high school.

3. **Determining Eligibility.** If you have any doubts about your eligibility status for a particular scholarship, contact the financial aid department of that institution before you begin the application process. [Tribal enrollment status is often required for American Indian and Alaska Native–related scholarships.]

4. **Completing Applications.** Proofread! Proofread! Proofread! Remember that you are in competition with hundreds, even thousands, of other students for this scholarship. Common spelling and grammatical errors can mean the difference between success and defeat! Sign and date everything. Be sure you've included the correct number of references, and make sure the information regarding those references is correct. You should plan on mailing your scholarship application ahead of time. A missed deadline means you won't be receiving that scholarship!

5. **Preparing for Essays and Interviews.** Many scholarship applications require an essay. Some scholarship applications also require that a personal interview should be set up. Your essay or interview is the best way for you to express and portray yourself. This is your opportunity to stand out among all of the other applicants. With this in mind, don't go overboard! Stick to the word limit for the essay. Don't add additional materials unless they are requested. Above all, stick to the topic that has been given. Check and double check your writing. Have another person proofread it as well. Be sure your essay is organized, neatly written, and expresses your thoughts clearly. If you must set up a personal interview, dress neatly in business clothing. Don't wear a lot of jewelry. Speak clearly and confidently.

6. **Finding Success.** The scholarship application process can be an arduous journey. However, if you focus on sending complete applications that are error free and include all of the necessary information and a well-written essay (if required), you have already stepped closer to the front of the line!

There are two important areas that you should commit to and prepare yourself for to get scholarships. The first is to establish a track record of achievement (i.e., good grades, community involvement, extracurricular activities, recognitions and awards, leadership roles, etc.). The second is to focus on producing a well-written personal statement, which is often part of the scholarship application.

Marianne Ragins (www.scholarshipworkshop.com/tips.html) lists the following habits of scholarship winners:

- Successful students always remember the five P's—Prior preparation prevents poor performance. Prepare for the scholarship search early. Do not wait until your senior year.
- Successful students do not rely on their parents to do all the work.
- Successful students vigorously avoid mistakes on their essays and applications. They always spell-check, proofread, and allow one other person to proofread their applications and essay for errors.
- Successful students do not ignore scholarships that may be local or those for small amounts. Scholarship amounts, even as small as $50, can add up.
- Successful students do not rely on only one source such as the Internet for their scholarship search. They use many resources. Many scholarships on the Internet or in the free scholarship searches that you find on the World Wide Web are nationally known and are harder to win due to greater competition. Local and regional scholarships are not found as easily through an Internet search, although they may be easier to win because the applicant pool is smaller. You have to use a combination of resources to find as many scholarships to apply for as possible.
- Successful students market themselves well. In their applications, they highlight positive aspects about their lives, especially community involvement.
- Successful students do not apply to one or two scholarships and wait for the best. They apply for all scholarships they are eligible to win. They keep applying until the total they have won exceeds what they need to pay for the college they want to attend or until they graduate with a degree.
- Successful students are organized. They keep track of deadlines and materials required to complete an application.
- Successful students are well rounded. They participate in extracurricular and community activities. They write about these activities in scholarship and college essays in a descriptive manner. They try to benefit others as well as themselves with the extracurricular and community activities in which they are involved.
- Successful students understand that SAT scores and grades alone do not win most scholarships. Scholarship programs look at many factors such as community activities, leadership, presentation of your application package, special or unusual talents or skills, etc.
- Successful students do not look for the easy way out. It is harder for them to believe in a scholarship scam that promises to do all the work for them. They understand that those things for which we work hardest often bring the greatest rewards. Hard work in the scholarship process as a high school student could result in an easy college life without work later, or a loan-free life after college.
- Avoid common mistakes made on college and scholarship applications:
  1. Not following directions.
  2. Missing the deadline.

3. Not typing your application or sending in a sloppy application.
4. Forgetting to spell check and to proofread after you spell check.
5. Not including information such as a transcript or recommendation.
6. Not answering the essay question or another question asked.

AIGC's tips for winning scholarship applications include:

- Apply only if you are eligible.
- Complete the application in full.
- Follow directions.
- Neatness counts.
- Write an essay that makes a strong impression.
- Watch all deadlines.
- Make sure your application gets where it needs to go.
- Keep a back-up file in case anything goes wrong.
- Give it a final once-over and have someone else read it before submitting.
- Ask for help if you need it.
- Make sure letters of recommendation are sent to the right place and on time.

"101 TIPS FROM THE PROS"

Everyone knows and understands that securing financial aid is a complicated and daunting process. Knowing someone who deals with the topic every day can make it a lot less frightening. Peterson's recently surveyed education professionals to find out what they think are the most important things families need to know about financial aid (available online at www.petersons.com). In our opinion, the results of this survey produced one of the best lists of tips to help parents and students work with financial aid officers available. These tips are organized by topics: Preparation and Fact-Finding for Parents (numbers 1–12), Preparation and Fact-Finding for Students (13–37), The Application Process (38–62), Decision Time and Evaluating Financial Aid Awards (63–74), Appealing a Financial Aid Award (75–84), Cash Flow and Savings (85–98), and Things to Consider (99–101). The following excerpt is reprinted with permission from Peterson's Guides, *Get a Jump!: The Financial Aid Answer Book* (Lawrenceville, NJ: Peterson's—a Nelnet company, 2004, 81–100).

Preparation and Fact-Finding for Parents

1. Talk with your child about your ability and willingness to pay for college. Keep the lines of communication open about finances. Parents and students who don't discuss finances as part of the college selection process often have a difficult time when a student's first-choice college turns out to be the one the parents can't afford. Be clear and realistic about your financial limitations as well as your expectations of the role your child will take in the process and in financing.

2. Find out how much college really costs. A figure that continually appears in the media is $30,000 a year. But just as the cost of an automobile depends

on the make and model, college costs can vary widely. If your son or daughter attends a local community college and lives at home, your out-of-pocket costs for the entire academic year may only be a few thousand dollars. A state-supported public university will have a total cost of education anywhere from $10,000 to $17,000 a year. An Ivy League college education can easily cost $35,000 annually. (These costs are for the nine-month academic year and include tuition and fees, books and supplies, transportation expenses, room and board, etc.)

3. Everyone should apply for financial aid. There are so many different factors that determine aid eligibility that no one can give you a simple answer as to whether or not you are eligible for aid. Family income and assets are not the only aspects that determine eligibility for need-based aid; family size and number of children in college are almost as important.

4. Parents should make sure students are involved in and understand the financial aid process. At most schools, the student is the first point of contact for administrative issues. In addition, many times the financial aid process is the first step that students take in learning to manage their own financial matters.

5. Parents should complete a sample Free Application for Federal Student Aid (FAFSA) when the student becomes a junior in high school. This will give you an idea of what your Expected Family Contribution (EFC) will be. The results can assist you in selecting affordable colleges. This can be done at most high school career centers or by using any of the Need Analysis Calculators on the Internet. [See www.petersons.com.]

6. If you haven't started any kind of savings for college, start putting some money aside now. The money you put in the bank today can be used as a resource for college. More importantly, you have created an ongoing resource in your family budget that can be used for a loan payment or monthly payment plan when your child is in college.

7. Invest in a Qualified State Tuition Plan (QSTP), more commonly referred to as an I-529 Plan. (Derived from Internal Revenue Service Code I-529.) There are two types of plans under I-529. The Prepaid College Tuition Plan allows for investors to invest funds in a state plan that freezes the cost of tuition at the present rate and guarantees against tuition inflation in the future. The second is the College Investment Plan, which allows investors (sponsors) to invest in a I-529 plan at any point they wish to contribute. There is no guarantee on meeting tuition costs, but there are many benefits when participating in a state-sponsored college investment plan, including state income tax deductions, federal tax-free earnings, tax-deferred savings, and exemption of listing this asset as a student asset on the Free Application for Federal Student Aid. Many states give tax benefits at the state level as well as federal tax-free benefits when funds are used for college students. This asset is exempt from being listed on the Free Application for Federal Student Aid.

8. Ask your employer(s), union, and any community clubs to which you belong if they offer financial aid to students.

9. Investigate scholarship search services. If your child is an exceptional student and you feel she might qualify for academic scholarship recognition, there are many free scholarship search services available, such as Peterson's (www.petersons.com). You never need to pay for such assistance.

10. Investigate PLUS loans. If you have sufficient resources to finance your child's college costs but are concerned that you may not have enough cash on hand for all those expenses, the federal government has created a non-need-based loan program, Parent Loan for Undergraduate Students (PLUS). All families can take advantage of this program regardless of current income. While it is important to remember that this program is a loan, it is nevertheless available to all parents regardless of income and currently is at a historically low interest rate (4.86%). Through the PLUS loan program, you can borrow up to the full cost of education less any financial aid awarded.

11. Reduce your child's savings. If you have shifted significant resources into your children's names to lessen your federal income tax burden, this could reduce your children's financial aid eligibility. In the calculations for financial aid eligibility, the student's savings are taxed at a much higher rate than those savings reported for parents.

12. Be careful about listening to neighbors and friends who tell you what to do or what will happen. Unless you see their tax return or bank statement, you really don't know much about their finances. You only see how they spent their money.

Preparation and Fact-Finding for Students

13. Listen when your parents talk with you about financing. This is big bucks!

14. View your education as an investment. It will pay for itself many times over in the course of your lifetime. Both men and women benefit from postsecondary education. You can earn up to $1.2 million more over your lifetime by obtaining a bachelor's degree. However, the return is not the same if you do not complete your degree so don't quit!

15. Think about what you can do now to prepare. If you have a job, start putting away some money from each paycheck for college.

16. Do not allow the cost of college to spoil your education plans. Financial aid and other money may be available from a variety of sources.

17. Start your search up close and personal. The most likely source of scholarships for most students is geographically close to home, and the best single identifying source of these local opportunities resides in the high school guidance office.

18. Public libraries have resource books to help you research scholarships.

19. Early is essential. Start looking at the beginning of your junior year in high school. Begin the financial aid investigation process at the same time you begin the college selection process.

20. Be sure to confirm with your high school counselor that you have completed appropriate applications in the junior year to qualify for aid after your senior year. For example, to qualify for the National Merit Scholarship program you must have completed the PSAT exams in the junior year of high school. Many states have scholarship programs for distinguished high school scholars, but the letters of recommendation must be received by the state scholarship administration while the student is a junior in high school.

21. Become informed by talking with your counselor about the advantages of taking tests or classes while in high school for college credit. This will help you save money later.

22. The College-Level Examination Program (CLEP) allows students to demonstrate their proficiency at the college level. By doing so, it allows the college to exempt the student from college courses (save money), lets students advance to higher level courses to complete the college requirements earlier (save more money), and exempts students from taking prerequisites or introductory courses (save even more money).

23. The Advanced Placement (AP) program allows students to experience college-level work while still in high school. Many colleges give credit or advanced placement to students who receive qualifying grades on AP exams.

24. Marketing yourself is probably the most important aspect of receiving a merit award. Too many students depend on grades alone to get merit scholarships for school. As many schools are looking beyond test scores for admission, the same is true for merit awards. A student who has excelled in school and contributed to other areas of interest is more likely to receive these types of scholarships. Schools are looking for students who have challenged themselves academically while still maintaining a separate life of volunteering, publishing, or conducting research.

25. Promote yourself. Many local scholarship donors ask that high schools do their selections. This is the focal point of your self-promotional and search activities.

26. Don't wait for financial aid to award your job. Apply for part-time work at a local campus while you're still in high school, even if you don't plan to attend there. College departments prefer to hire experienced employees just as other employers do. Need-based, financial aid awarded jobs are often a small proportion of campus jobs.

27. Make a folder for each school as you narrow down your choices. In that folder keep information about cost, type of aid offered, deadlines, and any special scholarships the school offers. You can get the base information from brochures or from the schools Web site.

28. Examine the free scholarship automated services that are available on most university Web sites.

29. Ask to talk with someone in financial aid when you visit campuses. Admission officers know the basics of financial aid, but you want to get more detail than that. If you can't visit in person, call and ask for a phone appointment. If possible, get a name from the school's Web site and ask to talk with that particular person. Financial aid titles vary, but a counselor or assistant/associate director or officer will most likely be a person who actually evaluates applications for aid. Keep a record of who you talked to at each school; ask for their name, or better yet, their business card.

30. Ask your questions directly and consistently. Do not get caught up in the financial aid jargon.

31. Find out whether your application/need for aid affects the probability that you will be admitted. If so, how?

32. Find out if the college offers merit aid. If so, how many merit scholarships does it give? How are they determined, and who determines the recipients?

33. If you are thinking of applying for Early Decision/Early Action, ask if the aid policies/opportunities would be different. Some institutions do not offer merit awards or better need-based packages to early applicants. (Note: This is primarily a private college process.)

34. Ask how $3,000 in outside aid would change your aid package. You can use any amount when you ask this question, but use the same amount at each school. That way you will get consistent answers about how outside aid might affect your package.

35. Read everything you receive from the university. Failure to read or understand due dates, penalties, and institutional policies will not relieve you of the obligations relating to this information.

36. Study the administrative guides, catalogs, and class schedules. Students who understand how their college operates will have a competitive advantage in every area, from financial aid to course selection. Take advantage of every technological shortcut possible, from electronic deposit of financial aid to early Web registration for classes.

37. Talk to sophomores in college. They will know how best to take advantage of administrative rules and exceptions, from possible early disbursements for study abroad to early registration for working students.

The Application Process

38. Do not get intimidated by financial aid forms. If you need help, please see your counselor. If your counselor cannot help you, they can refer you to someone who can.

39. If your child has not yet been admitted, you should apply for financial assistance as soon as you have all the necessary income documents for the calendar year prior to the fall in which your child will start school. For example, if your child is starting college in August or September 2008, in January or February of 2008 you should have all your financial income information from 2007 in order and apply for need-based financial aid assistance as early as possible. You can do this even if your child has not yet applied for admission to a particular college.

40. Pay attention to deadlines. All schools have grant aid available to those students who qualify, but many have limited funds. Students who pay attention to deadlines have an advantage over those who don't. Even if you have to estimate your figures on your FAFSA or institutional applications, you should do so. The sooner you file your application, the better your chances of receiving aid. Also, you should file your income taxes as early in the year as possible.

41. Establish your filing date, and if necessary, make corrections later. A needy student can lose thousands in grants each year by applying after the published priority date.

42. Financial aid is an annual event. You must reapply every year.

43. Complete a FAFSA. For those who have never applied for aid before, the primary methodology used to apply for financial aid assistance is the Free Application for Federal Student Aid, commonly referred to as the FAFSA. This document can be filled out on line at www.fafsa.edu.gov or with a paper document. The application process is free, and the information can

be made available to all colleges and universities that your child is interested in attending. The FAFSA is the primary document for establishing eligibility for need-based federal financial aid, and frequently it is used for state financial aid and institutional scholarships as well.

44. The Free Application for Federal Student Aid (FAFSA) must be submitted each year after January 1.

45. Students and parents should register with the U.S. Department of Education for the purpose of securing PIN numbers. This will allow you to sign the Free Application for Federal Student Aid (FAFSA) online. Such action will speed up the processing of the FAFSA. Go to www.fafsa.edu.gov.

46. If you are also applying for a bank loan, know your expected college graduation date. Expected date of graduation refers to the date you expect to graduate from college (not high school). For example, most freshmen entering a bachelor's degree program in the fall of 2008 should expect to graduate in 2012. Why do lenders want to know this date? Many loans (federal and alternative) are deferred (payments don't have to be made) while the student is in school. Lenders use the expected date of graduation to put borrowers into this deferred status. So if you use your high school graduation date instead of your expected graduation date, you may be asked to start repaying your loan immediately.

47. For bank loans, calculate what your total loan cost will be. There are many online calculators that can tell you not only what your payment will be, but also how much you will pay in interest over the life of the loan. [See www.petersons.com.]

48. Borrow through the same lender each year. By doing so, you avoid having to make payments to multiple agencies once you begin repayment. It also helps simplify the management of your loans.

49. When borrowing through a bank, do not be afraid to call the lender no matter what the circumstances. They want you to be successful in managing and repaying your student loans, so it is in their interest to hear from you.

50. The normal expectation of the needs analysis process is that parents have primary financial responsibility in assisting their children paying for college. Even if you feel that your financial obligation to your children ends when they go to college, becoming an independent student directly from high school is almost impossible. Only a very tightly defined group of individuals, such as orphans or students who are parents themselves and are providing support for their own offspring, qualify as independent students.

51. Always tell the college financial aid office about any awards. If your child has been given a scholarship by a local community organization, her eligibility for aid will probably be affected. In most cases all forms of resources available to the student, whether they are coming from the parents or from a scholarship that a student has secured from an outside agency, will be taken under consideration in any need-based financial aid award. Request that, if a reduction in aid is required, it be taken from loan awards.

52. Re-Apply! Just because the student does not qualify for aid one year does not mean they will never qualify. Student and family situations change, which could change eligibility status.

53. If you were denied assistance when your first child started attending college, there are two very important reasons to reapply for financial aid assistance for your second attendee. First, the results of the need analysis calculations are substantially different when you have two or more children in college compared to only one child in college. Second, regulations change on a frequent basis, and you may have established eligibility for new or changed financial aid programs.

54. Complete your aid application materials completely. Blanks make financial aid officers crazy; if the answer is zero, use 0, don't leave it blank.

55. Parents, when you are completing the financial aid forms, remember to fill out your student's name, your student's birth date, and your student's Social Security number in the spaces provided, not yours.

56. Use completed federal income tax returns when completing the FAFSA when possible. However, if tax returns are not available prior to meeting deadlines for your state or institution, estimate your income and complete the form. You can make changes to the application information later, but you cannot change the application date if you file late.

57. Keep copies of everything you use to complete forms when you apply for aid. Your school may ask for documentation to support the data you supply.

58. Be on time. Refer to the deadline materials you have compiled to be sure you are meeting the right deadline for each school to which you are applying. Make a checklist, record when you sent materials, and keep copies of everything. Do as much online as possible. If you have questions about what is required or if something has been received, ask, don't assume.

59. When mailing items that have a deadline, request a Certificate of Mailing from the post office. This receipt will usually be honored by the institution should your materials be delayed or lost in the mail.

60. Be Proactive! Contact the financial aid office at your selected college to make sure your file is complete and no documents are missing. Check and double-check on a regular basis.

61. If you have special circumstances you want the aid office to know about, send them a letter apart from your application. Financial aid is about numbers, so if there are extra expenses you want to have considered, be sure to give the figures—less words, more figures is good!

62. Always let your financial aid counselor know of any unusual circumstances and/or expenses. Examples include: extraordinary medical expenses; expenses to care for the elderly, handicapped, or special need persons; child-care expenses (some institutions consider private education expenses, especially for areas of low performing public schools); bankruptcies and back taxes; large one-time payments; lay-offs, retirements, and resignations; and cost of attendance adjustments for travel, books and supplies, or living expenses.

Decision Time and Evaluating Financial Aid Awards

63. Know the difference between *NEED*-based aid and *MERIT*-based aid. Need-based aid is based on the financial need of the family. Merit-based aid is based on the student's grades and test scores.

64. Use the financial aid information to evaluate the colleges to which you want to apply but do not use it to exclude a college you really want to attend.

65. Have a financial safety school. This is one you can afford no matter what. Having a financial safety school frees you up to apply to schools that may seem to be out of range financially.

66. Know how colleges award funds. Many out-of-state public colleges will only award out-of-state students with loans and work programs, no matter how large the unmet need gap. In contrast, most private colleges meet full need and do not gap. Therefore, when wishing to attend out-of-state colleges, in the majority of cases it is actually cheaper to attend a high-cost private versus a low-cost public.

67. If you need to borrow, remember the terms and conditions of educational loans can vary. Make sure you understand the terms and the costs (i.e., interest rate, loan fees, and repayment schedule) of each loan you are offered.

68. There are a variety of loans that may be awarded as part of a financial aid package. In some cases, interest accrues while the student is attending school. If interest is accruing, consider paying the interest as you go to reduce your payments when your loan goes into repayment.

69. The first time a student accepts a loan as part of a financial aid package, there are additional requirements to be met. A student must participate in first-time borrower loan counseling either in person or on the Web, depending on the Institution. The student must also sign a promissory note. Failure to attend to these details will delay the disbursement of the loan.

70. Bank loans and federal direct loans (as part of a financial aid package) include an origination fee of 3 percent. Therefore, if your loan award is $1,000, you will actually receive $970. The origination fee is charged each time you receive one of these loans. When you repay the loan, you will repay the gross amount, in this case, $1,000. This is important when estimating the monies needed for college. Note: Some banks may not charge any origination fee.

71. Make a chart with each school's billed fees (tuition, fees, room and board). Add your estimated travel cost and then subtract any gift aid and student loans offered to come up with what you will actually have to pay to the college. Compare these bottom-line figures to determine which award is the most attractive. Beware: Some schools will put parent loans in an aid award—don't count these as aid at this point. Also don't count any work study since these funds are normally paid directly to the student as they are earned.

72. Compare the different packaging philosophies and awarding criteria at each school you are considering. If your child has been accepted at many highly selective institutions and has received numerous different financial aid packages and you are trying to decide which one to attend, compare the packaging philosophies. When you do this, one effective methodology is to calculate what the out-of-pocket costs will be, how much of the award package will be in grants or scholarships versus loans, and particularly what is the expected renewability of scholarships and grants. Understanding the differences in costs and the renewability of scholarships and

grants will give you a true picture of the comparative value of each of the awards. Finally, you must balance the value of the award package with the education your child will receive.

73. There is an abundance of loans available to assist families in their quest for higher education. All institutions have federal loan programs available to both students and parents, but in addition to the federal loans, there may be institutional or alternative private loans available. Often universities have unadvertised loans for the neediest students or for emergencies. You should request in-depth information regarding loans from your counselor. Most loans may be deferred until the student is no longer enrolled at least half-time. Counselors often recommend student loans over parent loans due to the repayment options and interest rates.

74. If there is a large discrepancy in offers among your selected schools, go back to the information you collected about each school; perhaps one award is merit and one is based on need.

Appealing a Financial Aid Award

75. If you feel that an aid award is not sufficient, you should contact the aid office immediately to discuss your concerns and ask for reconsideration. Start with the aid office at the school you most want to attend if you can work things out with them, you will be set. If not, go to your second choice and so on. Do not try to get into a bidding war, these are rarely productive.

76. Always try first to contact the Financial Aid Office directly, not the Admissions Office, not an alumna, and not the president of the school! If you have trouble getting through, keep trying because it's a busy time. But if you can't get in touch within a week, talk to the Admissions Office and see if they can help facilitate contact.

77. Another reason for filing an appeal is that some private colleges have an appeal policy that they will meet or match any award offer from a similar college.

78. Have copies of all your documents on hand when you do talk with the aid officer. If you have updated information, such as a more recent tax return, have that available as well.

79. If you have lost your job since you completed the needs analysis document and wish to inquire about additional aid, inform the college or university that your child is planning to attend about your economic situation. You can expect that the institution will require documentation verifying your current income. Most institutions have standard policies in place that allow for the use of projected income. Hopefully, this will increase your financial assistance.

80. If you have substantial credit card debt, the needs analysis process does not give consideration to credit card debt in the typical calculations. Your best course of action is to complete the Free Application for Federal Student Aid (FAFSA) as this document requests information. After your application has been sent to the appropriate financial aid office, establish a relationship with the university's financial aid office and explain your situation. Different institutions have different policies on how they will respond to these situations.

81. You should include information about better awards. But first be sure they are in fact better and also comparative. Don't send a merit award to a school that only does need-based aid.

82. Don't expect an answer on the spot, but do ask when you might expect a decision and how that decision will be communicated. Assuming you contact the office in a timely manner, you should expect an answer to an aid appeal prior to the May 1 reply date. If you don't get one by then, ask for an extension to the reply date.

83. Be prepared to also talk about financing options. But only discuss this after you have determined that there is no more grant aid available.

84. Approach an appeal as a fact-finding exercise, not a negotiation. Always consider the person you are talking to. Aid officers have families and kids in college, bills to pay, and choices to make. They may not respond well if you insist that your vacation home is a necessity! They value you and will work hard to help you come to their school. However, ultimately they are constrained by federal and institutional policy just as you may be constrained by what your family is willing to pay. If you can't come to an arrangement that works for you, then you need to move on to your next choice of school.

Cash Flow and Savings

85. Campus work is available. Most colleges employ significant numbers of their own students. They understand that college students are motivated, reliable, and smart employees.

86. Remuneration for on-campus work is priceless, especially for new students. Invaluable campus contacts, mentoring, and organizational smarts all become benefits to the real insider, the employee.

87. Make sure you arrive on campus with financial instruments that allow you to take advantage of bargains and early decisions. Local checking accounts, electronic transfers from financial aid, and credit cards can make early discounts available to you. The media love trumpeting stories of students in credit trouble, but college students are savvy consumers and are one group very likely to pay credit cards off each month.

88. Many apartment owners and landlords will discount if paid in advance for a full semester.

89. Buy books early, buy from other students directly, and check local bookstores. Many books can be borrowed from local libraries and kept for entire semesters.

90. Ask if your university provides rental of textbooks rather than purchase. Rental is generally less expensive than outright purchase. If you purchase textbooks, be aware of the refund policy. Usually there is a date after which you cannot return a book for a refund. Is there a sliding scale for refunds on returned books? The earlier you return a book, the greater your chance of a refund.

91. Will the bookstore buy your books back at the end of the semester? How are returned books valued? Is the condition of the book considered? Asking these questions could maximize the refunds or resale monies for which you are eligible.

92. Be cautious about the use of credit cards. It's the most common way that college students create a poor credit history. It only takes one 90-day delinquency to mar your credit report. These items stay on your report for years and can prevent you from being able to get other types of credit in the future, such as auto loans, alternative loans for education, and mortgages. Credit checks are often run prior to getting an apartment, and some employers require a credit check before they will hire you. Many lenders would rather lend to someone with no credit than to someone with bad credit.

93. Know tuition due dates and the penalties for not paying by those dates. Many institutions charge late fees for payments after a certain date or registration after a certain date. Paying on time and registering on time can save you money.

94. If paying tuition by credit card, be aware of any additional costs charged by the university or a third-party service to cover the costs they incur for accepting credit cards. The fee may range from 1 to 3 percent of the amount charged and is in addition to the interest charge on your credit card bill.

95. If paying tuition with a credit card in order to receive frequent flyer miles, compare the interest you will pay for charging the tuition versus the value of the free miles. If you decide to charge $5,000 of tuition and pay it off in one year at an interest rate of 1.25 percent per month, you will spend approximately $406 in interest. Are the frequent flyer miles worth $406?

96. Read and understand any contract you sign for campus housing. Are there penalties if you change your mind concerning where you want to live? Do you have to maintain a certain credit load to be eligible for campus housing? Are you allowed to change rooms without financial penalty?

97. A portion of tuition costs may qualify as a tax credit for parents and/or students contingent upon income and the method of payment. The Hope Scholarship Credit allows deductions on a per-student basis for the freshman and sophomore years of postsecondary education, while the Lifetime Learning Credit is used on a tax-return basis and covers a more expansive timeframe and array of educational courses. Tax-free grants, scholarships, and employer-education assistance used to meet educational expenses are not eligible for either tax credit. Education expenses paid for with loans are eligible. If you want to take advantage of either of these credits, contact your tax preparer.

98. Be aware of financial aid penalties for withdrawing from classes. These are in addition to tuition penalties. If a student who received Title IV (federal) financial aid withdraws from all classes before the 60 percent point in the semester, the student may be required to repay some or all Title IV financial aid. This is dictated by a federal formula. Check with a financial aid counselor before withdrawing from classes and ask specifically about Title IV.

Things to Consider

99. Avoid offers of guaranteed monies that you have to pay for. Never pay for any service that you can discover on your own for free.

100. Free financial aid seminars are not always free. These invitations often come from promoters seeking unreasonable fees to provide consulting advice.

101. Federal regulations protect the privacy of the student. If a parent or guardian needs financial information regarding a student (i.e., balance of a student's account, payments made, etc.), check with the institution concerning its policy on student privacy. At some schools, students may stipulate that another person may have access to their financial information. Knowing the policy in advance will facilitate making payments and receiving needed information.

EARLY COMMITMENT PROGRAMS

A recent paper published by the Western Interstate Commission for Higher Education explains that "an early commitment of aid can provide a strong incentive for students to complete a college-prep curriculum and for families to encourage and support their children's aspirations."[11] As a joint effort by the Pathways to College Network, the College Board, The Education Resources Institute, and the Western Interstate Commission for Higher Education, Blanco produced the report as a resource to help people learn about early commitment financial aid programs and describes current programs. Essentially, early commitment financial aid programs focus on reaching students from low-income families as early as middle school with a guarantee of financial aid if the students meet certain requirements. Blanco cites a number of requirements that include:

- Student commitment.
- Graduation from a high school in the state.
- Achievement of a minimum grade point average.
- Successful completion of a core curriculum or specific coursework.
- No use of illegal drugs or alcohol or involvement in criminal activity.
- Application to a public, and sometimes a private, postsecondary institution in the state.
- Submission of a federal and state financial aid application form.
- Participation in support activities for students selected to be in the early commitment program. (p. 14)

One purpose of early commitment financial aid programs is to ease the students' and their families financial concerns about going to college so there can be more encouragement and desire to focus on academic preparation. Our experiences with American Indian and Alaska Native postsecondary access and achievement (successfully completing a college program) has found that these students who early on in their schooling develop postsecondary intentions and commitments are inclined to think about ways of preparing for and finishing college.

SOURCES OF FINANCIAL AID

Each year, the Indian Resource Development (IRD) in Las Cruces, New Mexico, publishes a book that lists sources of financial aid available to

American Indian students.[12] Funded by the State of New Mexico, the 2006 version was compiled and edited by Angel Charley and provides a wonderful overview of some basic steps to follow to finance the rising cost of going to college. Although not a complete listing of financial resources available to Native students, it is a good start and easy to read. Visit IRD's web site at www.nmsu.edu/~ird.

The American Indian College Fund provides a series of online guides[13] titled, "Developing Your Vision While Attending College," which is comprised of four handbooks co-published by the American Indian College Fund and the National Endowment for Financial Education (NEFE). Book Two, "Paying for a College Education," indicates that there are scholarships for Native students. A Web site hosted by Red Lake Net News (www.rlnn .com/ArtNov05/AmericanIndianScholarships.html) found that an Internet search using the terms "Native American Scholarships" will yield close to 300,000 returns; the site provides a list of nearly 100 sources of scholarships for American Indians and Alaska Natives. While there are many scholarship opportunities, many scholarships for American Indian and Alaska Native students will require proof of tribal enrollment.

FINAL COMMENT

With financial aid comes financial responsibility. Remember that every dollar is precious as it will help you value your education in ways that are not simply monetary. Every dollar is the dream of your ancestors that they did the right thing when signing the treaties and giving up their lives to defend your right to maintain your tribal identity. Every dollar is the hope of your community that education is important. Every dollar represents the prayers of your family that you achieve your dreams. Every single dollar is more than what it can buy. Spend it wisely.

A Student's Voice

When I left the reservation to attend college after graduating from high school, it was with limited financial resources. That is another way to say I was poor. On top of that, I was not too good about managing my money, so I spent the little I had in the first few weeks of the semester. My financial situation became more precarious when the BIA financial aid check was running late. Without a meal ticket, the hunger soon set in, but I was not ready to go home. Instead, late one night I went to the local park to hunt those tame fat ducks. Spent my last dollar on a loaf of cheap white bread and set up a trail of bread crumbs that led around a group of bushes where I was waiting with a long stick. The plan was working perfectly. The ducks were attracted to the bread I spread on the shore, followed the trail to where I was prepared and when I was ready to swing the stick I heard a voice behind me, "I hope you aren't going to do anything to those ducks, young man."

Startled, I turned to see a uniformed police officer. My head went down along with the muttering of "Now I am in trouble." I looked up and said quietly, "Officer, I was hoping to get two or three of those ducks. You see, I came here from a reservation to go to college. I ran out of money and have been starving. I didn't want to go home, feeling like I let everyone down." The officer thought for a minute or two then said, "Well, right now you have not broken any laws. Where do you live and do you need a ride home?" I took him up on his offer, and on the way he stopped by a sandwich shop to pick something up for me, saying this would be better than those ducks I had in mind. When he dropped me off, he gave me $20 and said he hoped it held me over. It did. From that day on, I promised myself to be more responsible with my money. I wasn't always more responsible right away. However over time, I got better. You will, too.

CHAPTER 4

Spiritual, Mental, and Physical Well-Being

CHiXapkaid

A Student's Voice

School is hard, no doubt about it. Everything's so different, and it's hard to stay healthy. I think it's really important to do some of the recreational things you did at home at school. . . . If you played basketball, play basketball. I was always walking in the woods, so at school I try to go hiking whenever I can. It helps me stay grounded, gets me back to nature, lets me feel the wind and hear the birds and be away from the cars and people. I try to go home for all the breaks, too. . . . I find that going home for a little while keeps me grounded, and helps me remember what's important in life. It's not the classes, the grades, etc. (even though those are important to a degree). . . . It's the people and the place that I know, the people and the place that knows me. It reminds me of the big life picture, and makes me happier.

COMMUNITY LONGING OR HOMESICKNESS

I have been around many American Indian and Alaska Native undergraduate and graduate students while going to college and as a faculty member in higher education institutions. Personally, the feeling of homesickness affects everyone, and it still affects Native college students today. There are many

Web sites addressing homesickness, and most appear driven by clinical approaches that treat the psychological symptoms and minimize the cumulative affect on a person's college-going experience. Nearly all these resources can be helpful to (a) become aware of the symptoms and (b) take steps to prevent or overcome homesickness. For example, Hampden-Sydney College's Counseling Web site (www.hsc.edu/counseling/selfhelp/stress_periods. html) provides a helpful breakdown of stress periods, month by month, beginning with homesickness followed by adverse reactions to stress-related experiences. The State University of New York at Buffalo Student Affairs Web site (ub-counseling.buffalo.edu/adjusting.shtml) offers "Tips for Adjusting to University Life and Resources at the Counseling Services."

What helped me and has helped other American Indian and Alaska Native students was another explanation of homesickness that was rooted in our ancestry. There are many Native communities and families that have some kind of activity to support tribal members going to college. I have attended countless tribally sponsored graduation banquets at every grade level (preschool, middle school, high school, and higher education), and these events are rewarding in terms of bringing the community together to celebrate individual academic achievements. Many traditional societies across the country hold a wide range of ceremonies to recognize the honor American Indian and Alaska Native people bring on themselves when they are successful in school; being an invited speaker to many of these traditional ceremonies has demonstrated to me that there is no conflict between traditional and contemporary education. It has been humbling to attend countless family dinners to witness the glowing pride that the extended family gains when one of their own has done well in school.

A Student's Voice

Several elders talked with me prior to my leaving the reservation to attend a university about an hour's drive away. They explained that over their lifetime, many tribal members had left the reservation to attend college, and most came back home within the first year and never really went back. Feelings of loneliness and wanting to come back home were too much to stay and cope with going to college. After praying and holding a particular ceremony for me, the elders offered some insight and advice. I will tell it just like the elders told me.

It was explained that our people were genetically tied to the pulse and rhythm of the environment. Our clocks were the seasons and the celestial elements. Our first teachers, the plants and animals, reacted to the seasons. In the fall season, the animal people can be seen flocking, herding, or schooling together, and we have done the same while moving from our individual summer fishing and gathering camps to live together in the great longhouses during the fall and winter. We are genetically tied to the pulse and rhythm of the environment, and that cannot be bred out of us, they told me, no matter how civilized we become. At the very time of year that there is an instinctive desire to gather as a community, there are many American Indian and Alaska

Native people who are moving away from their communities to start college; community longing or homesickness can set in even when the college is only an hour away.

My elders pointed to the blanket that was gifted to me during the ceremony and reminded me to wrap myself in it when I started to feel lonely because it had all their prayers of support embedded within the blanket's fibers. If the stress got too much to handle, they held up a bundle of cedar limbs and instructed me to brush myself off and light some of it for incense to guide my dreams in a positive way. Then they said that there was no shame in coming back home if college was not for me. However, they hoped that I would try my best to finish. And finish I did. I still have that blanket and have burned cedar incense many, many times.

For American Indian and Alaska Native students to be successful in college, it is clear to me that one of the most sacred elements is the support of family. There is beauty in honoring and including the extended family in the college-going experience. Many students have told me that an important factor contributing to their college success is that at least one adult cared about the student's college experience. This is not surprising. Most efforts to embrace a family approach to serving American Indians and Alaska Natives in higher education have a well-meaning focus on improving institutions in lieu of speaking to students and their families.[1] However, the institutional approach is helpful to identify common principles that can be modified to speak to individual students and their families when working with college staff. For example, all American Indian and Alaska Native students and their family members should

- approach every contact with college staff with a sense of equality and respect;
- feel comfortable explaining to college staff that it is important to support the growth and development of all family members—adults, youth, children, and extended family;
- share that American Indian and Alaska Native families are resources;
- put in plain words that college student support services must affirm and strengthen Native cultural identity; and
- talk to college staff about the need to be flexible and responsive to emerging family and community issues.

YOU SAY YOU WANT TO PARTY?

A Student's Voice

Oh, that's a big one. The thing about college is almost everyone parties, and lots of people party pretty hard. I think it's especially tough for

Native students, because normal "college culture" is all about drinking and sex, and we're going through culture shock to begin with. . . . I've seen the negatives of drinking at home, and I know the effect it can have on people and families, but I still partied and drank too much at school. A couple of my friends were date raped at big parties, and a lot of really bad things can happen in those situations. Honestly, all it did was get me into trouble and make my grades go down and get me fat . . . plus, my parents could tell. Once after I got in some trouble my mom said, "Nothing good comes of alcohol," and I could see for myself that she was right. So I just quit going out, and that made a huge difference. . . . The trick is to find friends whose lives don't revolve around parties, and to find other fun things to do with your time. It takes discipline for me. But everyone knows it's easier just not to drink than it is to quit drinking. Nobody wants to hear it, especially if they're partiers, but it's true.

I am not going to cite statistics with regard to American Indian and Alaska Native alcohol or drug abuse. People might think it is more of a problem for Native people than other individuals from other cultures or that Native people are more susceptible to becoming addicted to alcohol or drugs than other racial and ethnic groups. I don't think so. I have been on enough campuses to know that abusing alcohol is a problem for every student group on most of America's college campuses (see www.collegedrinkingprevention.gov). Believe me. Just check out some of these facts.

- Death: 1,700 college students between the ages of eighteen and twenty-four die each year from alcohol-related unintentional injuries, including motor vehicle.[2]
- Injury: 599,000 students between the ages of eighteen and twenty-four are unintentionally injured under the influence of alcohol.[3]
- Assault: More than 696,000 students between the ages of eighteen and twenty-four are assaulted by another student who had been drinking.[4]
- Sexual abuse: More than 97,000 students between the ages of eighteen and twenty-four are victims of alcohol-related sexual assault or date rape.[5]
- Unsafe sex: 400,000 students between the ages of eighteen and twenty-four had unprotected sex, and more than 100,000 students between the ages of eighteen and twenty-four report having been too intoxicated to know if they consented to having sex.[6]
- Academic problems: About 25 percent of college students report academic consequences of their drinking, including missing class, falling behind, doing poorly on exams or papers, and receiving lower grades overall.[7]
- Health problems/suicide attempts: More than 150,000 students develop an alcohol-related health problem,[8] and between 1.2 and 1.5 percent of students indicate that they tried to commit suicide within the past year due to drinking or drug use.[9]

- Drunk driving: 2.1 million students between the ages of eighteen and twenty-four drove under the influence of alcohol last year.[10]
- Vandalism: About 11 percent of college student drinkers report that they have damaged property while under the influence of alcohol.[11]
- Property damage: More than 25 percent of administrators from schools with relatively low drinking levels and over 50 percent from schools with high drinking levels say their campuses have a "moderate" or "major" problem with alcohol-related property damage.[12]
- Police involvement: About 5 percent of four-year college students are involved with the police or campus security as a result of their drinking,[13] and an estimated 110,000 students between the ages of eighteen and twenty-four are arrested for an alcohol-related violation, such as public drunkenness or driving under the influence.[14]
- Alcohol abuse and dependence: 31 percent of college students met criteria for a diagnosis of alcohol abuse and 6 percent for a diagnosis of alcohol dependence in the past twelve months, according to questionnaire-based self-reports about their drinking.[15]

All of us can add another couple of pages of stories about alcohol and drug abuse that are just as sad and have death, dying, and loss as the moral. Going over these discouraging details reminds me that there is something far better for American Indian and Alaska Native students than a bottomless pit of drugs and alcohol. There *is* a way to enjoy college life as a Native without drugs or alcohol abuse.

CULTIVATING RESILIENCE

Before you even step on a college campus or enroll in a course, start with believing in yourself. You got this far, and you can go further. There are many American Indian and Alaska Native people who advocate that you have a strong history of resilience. We need to keep up this tradition. For Native people, resilience is the ability to address adversity and overcome challenges to earn accomplishment in our lives. A publication called *Helping Children at Home and School II: Handouts for Families and Educators* includes a very readable chapter by Virginia Smith Harvey that provides a framework for developing resiliency.[16] Harvey says, "Those who manage to become personally and professionally successful despite severe adversity are called 'resilient.' While we marvel that some people overcome seemingly overwhelming childhood adversity, resiliency is actually a normal trait that comes from inborn tendencies to adapt" (p. S5-79). That would definitely describe the ability of American Indian and Alaska Native peoples to overcome the historical colonization and constant affronts to our desire to maintain ancestral identity. Native college students can further cultivate resiliency by addressing their attitudes and emotions, academic competence, social competence, and physical health.

Attitudes and Emotions

We can clearly enhance resilience with positive attitudes, positive emotions, and the ability to appropriately express all emotions, even the negative ones.

American Indians and Alaska Natives embody this belief through what is commonly referred to as "Indian humor" or the ability to find something to laugh about in any situation. It is our inbred ability to see the positive side of life, make fun of ourselves, and feel good about stuff. There's nothing ˙gical about it—just allow yourself to laugh. Once you have taken that ˍall but significant step, you open a very wide door to the world of exhibiting a positive attitude and coping with a full range of emotions.

Being optimistic, encouraging, determined, and a problem solver are traits of our ancestors. These are personal characteristics that you should practice because it will be essential to your college success. More important, these are the traits that we look to be exemplified by Native leaders to inspire our communities to overcome hardships and celebrate their lives. Just as the sun greets us every morning, a positive attitude conveys to other American Indian and Alaska Native college students the feeling of warmth, looking forward to another great day, enjoying life, and feeling important. It sends the message to all that you are doing the right thing by going to college. This is one reason why many (if not all) Native peoples pray to the east each day.

A positive attitude leads to an optimistic outlook on life. If you try, you can learn, do well in college, and be successful in your life's pursuits. To many tribal elders, trying is as simple as getting out of bed and as difficult as confronting fears. However, what we do must be done by ourselves, and it will require a degree of effort.

A Student's Voice

Nothing ever really comes easy, like wishes that magically come true. Whenever somebody on our reservation said, "I wish _____" (fill in the blank), my grandmother would say while laughing, "Wishes are not what you need. Put all the wishes that come true in one hand and all the bullshit you hear in the other hand, and see which one fills up first." Her point was not to be crude but more that Native people need to be *real* about what their situation is in life and deal with it upfront. You might as well be positive while doing so.

American Indian and Alaska Native peoples are powerful when being positive together. You can see this and experience it in the cultural celebrations and the fact that there is an inclination to make new friends at gatherings of Native people. It is not because you have a greater opportunity to snag a sweetheart. It is how we want to be remembered and how we should strive to be in the eyes of our Native youth, just as you look back and remember the people who encouraged you in life. There will always be somebody positive in your life, and you can do that for someone else if you step forward to be a positive person. That is a direct outcome of a philosophical outlook that is circular and interconnected. Life is conceived as being (a) more circular rather than linear, and (b) everything is interconnected rather than separated or unaffected by everything else. These are two foundation beliefs of many Native people.

A Student's Voice

Elders within my traditional society taught me certain prayers that foster positive emotions. One in particular generally goes, "I want to think about all that is good in the world. I want to see all that is good in the world. I want to hear all that is good in the world. I want to pray for myself, my family, and all that is good in the world." You should talk or pray like this more than you criticize each other or other people within your community, be it at college or home. It will most certainly foster trust and appreciation in your relationships while being sensitive to the needs of other people. Within the interrelatedness of life, positive emotions that you convey will cause others to be like-minded, which will in turn help you ward off depression and negative reactions to adversity.

Positive emotions—interest, enthusiasm, laughter, empathy, action, curiosity, love, caring, gratitude—produce a sense of involvement that promotes within us the tendency to see the beauty of life. It is what our natural environment shares when the wind whistles through the trees, when the sun sparkles on the water, when we smell the sweet fragrance of blooming flowers, and when we see the laughter of our children. We are part of the environment as well. Positive emotions in college will motive us to learn more about the cultures and histories of our brothers and sisters from other Native communities. We will yearn to be more active with our Native student organizations while we all strive to and enjoy making things better. This latter point is especially important because positive emotions are stimulated by our ancestral desire for enjoyment and unity.

> Learning to forgive others and oneself for playing a part in causing adverse circumstances fosters resiliency. Forgiving is not the same as forgetting, pardoning, condoning, excusing, or denying the harm that one person does to another. It is a process in which the person becomes less angry, resentful, fearful, interested in revenge, or remorseful. . . . Forgiving increases well-being and improves interpersonal relations. In forgiving, an injured person can develop empathy and come to understand even an abuser's needs and motives. Empathy can enable a person to accept imperfections in all people, including themselves. Forgiving persons choose to experience, appropriately express, and then let go of negative feelings of anger, guilt, and retaliation.[17]

Positive and negative emotions are polarities. We cannot get rid of one and keep the other. Ultimately, our positive and negative emotions need to be integrated. The negative emotions are useful as motivation for moving away from what one does not want; yes, this may mean not going to college. The positive emotions are useful as motivation for moving towards what one does want. Virginia Harvey draws on the work of Gottman, Declaire, and Goleman[18] to explain that we need to become more aware of all our emotions, and each emotion is an opportunity for intimacy and teaching. We are encouraged to listen empathically and validate our feelings and to describe our emotions in words we, ourselves, can understand. In this way, we teach ourselves and others appropriate ways to solve a problem or deal with an upsetting issue or situation.

Academic Competence

The easiest road to feeling academically competent is to experience a moment of success in college. American Indian and Alaska Native college students need to experience academic success to deal with any other adversity they may face. Think about the type of courses you take (don't load up on all core required courses or the most demanding classes at one time). Know when the best time is for you to take classes (e.g., are you a morning person? have weekend responsibilities?). Select instructors wisely (know something about the instructor, meet the instructor, get a copy of syllabus, etc.).

A Student's Voice

I remember like it was yesterday. I was midway through my first semester of college, fresh from the reservation. Things had started out rough, personally and academically. I stuck things out only because I decided to get some academic assistance from the learning center on campus. Upon our first meeting, the tutor got to know where I was from and then requested a two-page paper about something I enjoyed doing on the reservation. That sounded easy enough. I chose to write about learning traditional songs and dances, which was fine with her. She asked me to spend the next hour and half writing the paper; when it was done, she asked to look it over and for me to return the next day.

I was nervous upon my return the next day. Not sure why I was nervous. Just was. That is, until I looked over the comments she had written on my paper. "Hey, this is a nice paper. You are a good writer. I enjoyed what you had to say. Why don't you fill out the introduction a bit more and tighten up the conclusion with the few suggestions I made. Let's talk about some punctuation and grammar rules; nothing too extensive, just some basic ideas that everyone needs to keep in mind." I was really happy at that moment. She liked my paper! We talked about sentence structure, organizing ideas, grammar, and other basic writing concepts in a way that made it interesting to me.

It was a fun semester. We met every other day for seven weeks, and she made it fun while assisting me on how to enjoy writing and setting myself up for success. Anyway, look at your own academic success and what it will take for you to perform at a level that makes it fun. Know right away whether you are going to need help in a particular subject area; for me, it was any class dealing with science, math, reading, and

---

writing. I know, what else does that leave? Well I was good at art and PE. Anyway, I found tutoring right away through a university academic assistance center, and they guided me through some pretty difficult semesters. They can help you, too.

Some degree of academic success essentially means passing classes with reasonable grades. However, success can become more about a feeling of enlightenment regarding social causes, community planning, organizing people, and serving Native communities. Eventually, for you, a sense of purpose will grow and be a source of motivation to further your intellectual development. Develop your academic schedule so that you can be successful most of the time, or at least try. Harvey believes that your "academic success is increased by the use of different types of teaching strategies that meet varied learning styles. It is also fostered by recognizing and understanding cultural and other differences among the students."[19] She is right. For a quick online assessment of your learning style, go to www.metamath .com/lsweb/dvclearn.htm and take Catherine Jester and Suzanne Miller's DVC Learning Style Survey for College. Your survey is scored immediately, and you are given a helpful guide explaining how to use the results of your survey.

This will sound simple, but let me say it anyway: to be successful in college you have to show up for classes on time and complete all assignments in a timely manner. However, doing this is your decision. Part of going to college is to experience a high degree of personal responsibility. You may feel the need to skate through the semester, showing up for class on "Indian time." It may be even mildly entertaining to test your intelligence by seeing how many lame excuses you can give to your instructors so they accept overdue assignments. *Not.*

It is much better to find a quiet place and workable times per week to study for around twice the number of credit hours you are taking (i.e., if enrolled in twelve credit hours, then schedule twenty-four hours per week, if enrolled in sixteen credits then schedule for thirty-two hours of studying). You can get away with fewer hours of study, but it will be important to schedule adequate time during the weeks prior to mid-terms and finals as well as when papers or class assignments are due. Native student centers are valuable resources to identify support when needed and have a list of academic support programs available within departments, colleges, and the university.

All American Indian and Alaska Native students, regardless of how gifted and talented you are, will benefit from fully developing your college-level study strategies. One of the best online college study guides and strategies that I have found is authored, developed, and maintained by Joe Landsberger as an educational public service (www.studygs.net). Use it freely (he grants permission to copy, adapt, and distribute individual study guides in print format in noncommercial educational settings to benefit learners) and give him credit for doing a great job. As shown in Table 4.1, Landsberger's site provides an array of resources to help you improve your postsecondary experience before you enroll in class, while you are in class, and by approaching different methods of demonstrating your learning.

Some American Indian and Alaska Native people are not aware of their strengths and talents due to negative feedback and judgmental relationships in public schooling. However, everyone has strengths and talents that can be developed to higher levels of effectiveness, efficiency, and excellence. These represent the areas where a person has the greatest potential

Table 4.1. Joe Landsberger's Approaches to Study Guides and Strategies

Preparing	Learning	Studying
• Learning to learn • Scheduling and setting goals (interactive day and weekly planner) • Managing time • Managing stress • Avoiding procrastination • Thinking critically • Thinking like a genius • Motivating yourself • Adaptive decision making • Making decisions/solving problems	• As student-athlete or student-performer • Visual learner • Mapping information for learning • Adult learner • Distance education and learning • Thinking aloud/private speech • Problem-based learning • With ADHD • Exploring your own learning style	• Effective study habits • Concentrating • Memorizing • MURDER—a study system • Index—a study system • Studying with multiple sources • Vocabulary-building exercise • "Study" bibliography • Addition study skills Web sites
Classroom Participation	**Learning with Others**	**Project Management**
• Preparing for the classroom • Influencing teachers • Taking notes in lectures • Guided notes • Paying attention • Classroom discussions	• Collaborative/cooperative learning • Active listening • Studying in groups • Tutoring guidelines • Conflict resolution • Peer mediation	• Developing case studies • Organizing projects • Developing spreadsheets (creating/developing budgets) • Presenting projects/speeches • Public speaking • Interviewing for class projects • Consent form
Reading Skills	**Preparing for Tests**	**Taking Tests**
• Reading critically • Prereading strategies • Taking notes from a textbook • Reading/understanding essays • Reading difficult material • Speed and comprehension • Marking and underlining • SQ3R reading method	• General test preparation • Anticipating text content • Review tools for tests • Overcoming test anxiety • Organizing for test taking • Cramming • Emergency test preparation • Testing bibliography	• Ten tips for terrific test taking • True/false tests • Multiple-choice tests • Short-answer tests • Open-book exams • Oral exams • Essay exams • Essay exam terms/directives

(continued)

Table 4.1. Continued

Writing Basics	Writing Types	Research
• Basics of writing assignments • Prewriting and drafts • Revising • Proofreading • Transitional words and phrases • Modifiers and commas • Spelling (American) • Print bibliography for writing • Internet bibliography for writing	• Writing under deadline • Writing for the Web • The five-paragraph essay • Essays for a literature class • Expository essays • Persuasive essays • Position papers • Writing strategies learned (by Stephen Wilbers)	• Writing research papers • Researching on the Internet • Organizing research with computers and avoiding plagiarism • Organizing research with note cards • Citing Web sites
Math	**Science and Technology**	**Web Truth**
• Solving linear equations • Solving math word problems • Evaluating algebraic expressions (order of operations/PEMDAS) • Math tests • Math bibliography (Web sites with online help)	• Writing lab reports and scientific papers • Writing white papers • Following the scientific method • Lab safety • Sudoku	• Evaluating Web site content • Netiquette • Developing Web sites • Accessible Web site design • Making your Web site "popular" • Web design bibliography

Source: Adapted from Joe Landsberger, "Studies Guides and Strategies." Available at www.studygs.net.

for growth. When fully developed and used, strengths and talents can produce a person's most rewarding fulfillment. Developing your talents occurs best within the context of healthy, loving relationships; most people enjoy the process of developing their strengths because it has a motivating effect and seems to generate hope and optimism about the future. Edward C. Anderson and Scott McDowell recommend being proactive and practicing because it takes time and involves several steps until your strengths and talents become natural.[20]

1. Identify your talents and strengths,
2. Affirm your talents and strengths.
3. Celebrate your talents and strengths—really feel good about the talents and strengths you have.
4. Develop your talents and strengths. Training and instruction can help you develop your talents and strengths. But remember the following principles of strength development:

   • Strengths develop best in the context of a trusted relationship where you express your intentions and progress in developing your strengths.
   • Strengths develop by being intentional. Decide which talent or strength you want to develop and focus on one at a time.
   • Talents and strengths develop best by practicing and frequently using them in as many settings as possible.
   • Reflecting on your experience always enhances development. Therefore spend focused time thinking about your experiences and the development of your talents and strengths.

5. Applying your strengths. This is the ultimate. You must actively apply and fully use your strengths in the area where you want to achieve and reach levels of excellence. This may take considerable thought and creativity. But this is exactly what the "best of the best do." They invent ways of applying their strengths in the areas where they want to achieve.

- Be active, creative, and inventive as you apply your talents and strengths.
- Don't wait until your talents and strengths are fully developed to begin applying them—in reality, applying talents and strengths helps develop them.
- Think about how you can combine two or three strengths to produce a powerful way to increase your effectiveness.

Social Competence

Social competence is about developing positive relationships and positive personal life choices, all of which result in increased resiliency. I discovered this by coming in contact with people who cared about my success in higher education institutions. True, I got the sense that there were some people who were indifferent about the Native presence in the higher education arena and some who were quite hostile. Focus on the fact that there are caring and wonderful people who are compassionate and helpful. You will find these individuals among the faculty, staff, administrators, students, and college community. The supportive people are, if you choose to see them, all over the place. Once you identify a network of resourceful people, be smart about using that support in your own academic plan to be successful.

The college experience is a great place to develop new friendships and get into lifelong relationships. One of the best ways to meet people and adjust to college life is getting involved, on or off campus. Start with locating and supporting any Native student organization or frequently visiting the Native student center if there is one on campus. If no Native student programs exist, at the start of each academic year there are activities around campus you can attend, or just go where student activities are housed to identify groups that might be of interest to you. Most likely you'll find a new club or organization that sounds interesting. In other words, don't just sit around and expect not to feel bored. Make a point to develop social relationships because it fosters resiliency. American Indians and Alaska Natives know this from the cultural outlook of extended family. As such, branch out to come in contact with other groups of students. Plus, we know that students who feel connected to different groups of people on campus are more resilient and even have fewer medical problems.

Your college experience is much more likely to be successful if you have clear and consistent expectations that are supported by some degree of structure in your life. The latter is generally carried forth with a day planner for the semester and academic year and complemented by a program of study that charts out the courses you will take to complete a degree. Once you have established a schedule of classes, you will want to build in things like study time, work time, recreation and leisure, and sleep. Have your schedule close to you (carry around your day planner in hard copy or electronic form) and use it; don't ignore or forget to it.

A Student's Voice

Can I just say that my day planner saves my life! I am naturally unorganized, and a day planner (though I resent it running my life, similar to wearing a watch) really allows me to stay on top of what I need to have done by when, and where I'm supposed to be next, and so on. I finally got over the fact that I had to bend around time at school, and that I should use this "unnatural constriction" of a day planner to get things done. I felt like greater American society seemed to value time more than people (which it generally does) and not using a planner was a passive aggressive way for me to hold out against the man. But once I decided that me succeeding would sock it to the man a lot more than not using a day planner, I started to use one. Now I can't live without it! My grades went up, too.

For your schedule to work, you need to set clear expectations for yourself. You are the one who has to do this because ultimately you have to exercise a great deal of personal responsibility for your life. Expectations may be about the level of effort you put forth, how serious you are about doing well in college, or how you want to be a great role model for American Indian and Alaska Native people. If you do not have clear expectations, you may decide to drop out, fearing the schedule will work against your other interests. It is also important you do not make personal promises to yourself that you cannot keep. Be realistic and set yourself up for success by revisiting your schedule and expectations to see how you are doing. Here it may be useful for you to ask other American Indians and Alaska Natives to provide examples of their schedules and expectations that have been successfully met.

Deborah Spaide shares that there is a reciprocal benefit to helping others because it is also healthy for us personally.[21] She cites Allan Luks and Peggy Payne,[22] who explain that people who help others experience an increase in energy, warmth, euphoria, and other physical and emotional responses that then evolve into a sense of calm characterized by a sense of emotional well-being with increased self-worth, greater happiness, and optimism. American Indians and Alaska Natives have an inherent purpose in helping others; for many Native peoples, it is described as a charge given to the humans by the Creator to watch out and care for all that existed prior to their creation. You can feel it in your biological makeup and need to feed the spirit of your ancestral empathy by trying to alleviate the suffering of Native communities. Often this comes about through acts of charity. Here are a few ways I have adapted Spaide's work to foster unity and kindness among American Indian and Alaska Native students.

- Native college students should encourage each other to plan kind deeds for each other.
- Native college students should have meetings to establish community caring goals.
- Native college students should create a community values totem pole or graphic (i.e., medicine wheel, dream catcher, etc.).
- Native college students should treat negative and hateful language as you would four-letter words.
- Native college students should write a story together that chronicles what you do to help each other and others.
- Native college students should hold meetings to discuss a charity event and brainstorm ways you can all help.
- Native college students should invite anyone of your community to call a meeting if they witness an injustice.
- Native college students should choose one or more students and ask all members of the community to think of nice things they can do for that person or persons.

Whatever you do to help others, do it together with other American Indian and Alaska Native students, make it hands on, keep it simple, grow memories, make it fun, strive to involve others, be good role models, convey caring, raise money with a purpose, and know the difference between empathy verses pity.

The Hopi people believe that all people should strive to make the world a more peaceful place. Susan V. Bosak provides an amazing kit to peace building as part of the Legacy Project.[23] She explains that people can feel a sense of liberation and cultivate hope when working together to build peace. The historical struggles that Native peoples have experienced and continue to experience call for a sense of healing that comes from feeling liberated and hopeful. Peace building is important for American Indian and Alaska Native college students because Bosak shares that

> education means listening, asking questions, and seeking to understand the nature of a problem. It means looking at the problem from your own perspective as well as the perspectives of others. It means learning skills and using them creatively, balancing a concern for yourself with a concern for the larger community. It means building on the past while finding new ways for people to live together peacefully in an increasingly shrinking world.

Bosak advises people interested in peace building to be aware of the need to

1. address emotional issues (emotional recovery must come first, and it can be a very long, slow process);
2. model effective conflict resolution (help people learn from conflict and resolve disagreements constructively rather than destructively); and
3. develop communication and thinking skills (be able to communicate and think rationally, insightfully, and creatively).

Many organizations, Web sites, and books related to peace building are listed in the resources section of Bosak's online kit. She brings our attention to several organizations and Web sites: the Association for Conflict Resolution; CDR Associates (www.mediate.org); Creative Response to Conflict; Educators for Social Responsibility; the Institute for Public Accuracy (www.accuracy.org); Pathways to Peace; the Peace Education Foundation; PeaceJam (www.peacejam.org); Tolerance.org (www.tolerance.org); the Workable Peace Project (www.workablepeace.org); and the World Peace Project for Children (www.sadako.org).

Physical Health

Historically, American Indians and Alaska Natives placed a premium on being in good physical health. Our ancestors knew from experience that being strong of mind and spirit was also being strong of body. Our diets, daily routine, and outlook on life produced a sense of joy from being able to endure physical hardship, feeling powerful, warding off the little aches and pains, overcoming extreme environmental conditions, and looking good. First we need to eat well—cut down on the fast food, sugary drinks, and bad eating habits. If we can, we should strive to eat natural/organic foods in healthy portions and drink the recommended amount of water. Water was a sacred drink to our ancestors and should be so to us today. Combine this with adequate physical workouts and exercise that you enjoy. You will need all the energy that comes from being in good physical health and the necessary neurological development that comes from taking care of yourself. Virginia Harvey[24] lays out some pretty helpful advice dealing with medical care, exercise, adequate sleep, positive stress control, and good prenatal care.

Vaccinations, vision and hearing evaluations, and seeking medical care for illness increases resiliency by improving academic performance. Along with it you may want to consider short-term medication, such as antidepressants or anti-anxiety drugs, which can be helpful in breaking the cycle of negative emotions. There are also long-term medications, when appropriately prescribed and monitored for disorders such as bipolar disorder or schizophrenia, that are essential for the resiliency of individuals with chronic conditions. Be willing to look after one another; often it is a massive psychological shock to leave our homes and families, so be prepared to support one another.

Any physical activity improves resiliency thorough good physical and emotional health. Students who get outdoors, move around, and enjoy the feeling of gulping air deal better with anxiety, anger, or depression that can result from adversity. Native students who are out-of-shape or not excited about exercising on their own can be encouraged to regularly exercise with others. Some of the best times of your collegiate experience may be when you all get on an Indian intramural team or run, walk, and hike together.

Sleep fosters resiliency. However, this simple little activity can be a problem for American Indian and Alaska Native college students during midterms and finals, given the conflict between sleep needs and the demands of class, student activities, and work. So you should schedule time to sleep.

That sounds weird, I know. Think of it though—this makes so much sense. You get the rest you need, and you feel capable of doing more and doing it better. Or you stay up all night, feel like dirt in the morning, mix it with coffee grounds, shrug off to class, sleepwalk through the day, manage to open a book to put over your eyes to ward off the glare of daylight, tell yourself you'll get to your homework tomorrow, but manage to rally for another night of fun. . . . Maybe not. Turn out the lights, and go to bed. Wake up refreshed.

Controlling stress encourages resiliency. This is what waking up to greet the sun is all about. The ancestors of many Native cultures were there to watch the sun rise because this is a powerful time to meditate. Some of us take swims in cold water early in the morning because it helps us control our breathing. The same thing is true for those who practice yoga, exercise, and focus on developing talents and other relaxation responses. Do not abuse alcohol, drugs, or tobacco to reduce stress. Not only are you making things difficult for yourself; it often means that you are spending precious money that could be used in far more important ways.

A Student's Voice

In regard to stress, I think it's important to do normal things outside of school, like going to movies, hiking, fishing, playing cards, hanging out with friends, et cetera. I got a dog and took her to school with me, and that helped a lot. You know, we chased squirrels and rabbits, barked at groundhogs every day, that kind of thing. Very stress relieving! Going home to where things were "normal" helps refresh me, too. I go home every chance I get. If it's schoolwork that's stressing you out, just buckle down and plug away at it. Not procrastinating and taking the bull by the horns always makes you feel better. Organize a study session with friends, you'll have fun and get stuff done at the same time. Having friends outside your department is important as well, because they remind you the world doesn't consist within the vortex of this test, that research project, or your huge paper due tomorrow. They always know that Earth will get along quite nicely without you. It puts things in perspective. I'm big on perspective.

I have seen many American Indian and Alaska Native women who had children while they were in college. Whenever we bring in the next generation of Native people, let's all help the mother eat well, take vitamins, see a physician, practice positive stress control, and avoid diseases, drugs, alcohol, and tobacco. Cultivating a healthy prenatal environment gives the unborn child and all of us a chance to turn the cycle of despair around. We want to promote our future health and learning, not create future health and learning problems.

Let's all achieve a high degree of resilience for the sake of ourselves, our communities, and future generations. Imagine a world that we actively create that allows us to prosper, develop, and fully experience the joy of life. We don't need to struggle. We don't need to feel the pain of our past. We don't need to suffer. We don't need to conspire to drag each other down. We should flourish. We should laugh all the time. We should enjoy each others' company. College is as good as place as any to experience this joy.

CHAPTER 5

Getting Prepared to Ensure Success in College

A Student's Voice

First off, be okay with asking for help, even if you don't want to! I know a lot of Native people hate to ask for help, or speak up to professors, often just out of respect. . . . But it's important to be willing to grow and change, and sometimes that means being brave enough to ask for help or speak up in class discussions. The funny thing is that in college the professors usually want us to talk. I had a professor pick on me for a long time, until I figured out that he just wanted me to say what I thought in class. It was a very strange experience. After college I know more about myself, and I learned how to move around and be successful in another world. I can go between home and everywhere else pretty smoothly now.

WHAT MATTERS MOST

A great deal is known about what matters most to cultivate college student success. One of most concise and informative tables was prepared by Alberto F. Cabrera and Helen Caffrey.[1] Their original table presented the academic stages of a student from seventh grade through the junior year in college, along with factors/predictors, outcomes, and intervention strategies.

Their original table has been separated into two tables. Table 5.1 looks at these academic stages keeping in mind factors and predictors of college success along with anticipated outcomes. Table 5.2 looks at these same academic stages keeping in mind outcomes and intervention strategies that are designed to further the outcomes. These two tables have proven invaluable to us when giving formal presentations to high schools, colleges, and communities and informally while discussing options and strategies with American Indian and Alaska Native students of all ages.

Table 5.1 shows that as early as seventh grade, when we begin develop predispositions about college, parental roles are primary factors predicting

Table 5.1. The Path to a Four-Year Degree in Terms of Factor/Predictors and Outcomes

Academic Stages	Factors/Predictors	Outcomes
Predispositions: Grades 7–9	Parental expectations, encouragement, and support Parental savings for college Parental involvement in school activities Socioeconomic status Student ability Parental collegiate experience Information about college	Career and educational aspirations Planning for college Enrollment in curriculum in reading, writing, math, critical-thinking skills, and competencies important to the preparation for college
Search: Grades 10–12	Parental encouragement, support, and involvement in school activities Educational and occupational aspirations Planning for college Socioeconomic status Student ability Saliency of potential institutions Preparation for college	Listing of tentative institutions Narrowing list of tentative institutions Securing information on institutions Taking pre-SAT and pre-ACT
Choice: Grades 11–12	Educational and occupational aspirations Planning for college Student ability Parental encouragement Perceived institutional attributes (quality, campus life/majors, availability/distance) Perceived ability to pay (perceived resources/ perceived costs) Preparation for college	Awareness of college expenses and financial aid Awareness of institutional attributes and admission standards Attaining scholastic aptitudes, attitudes, and competencies Support from family and friends Institutional commitment Submission of college applications Application for financial aid Preregistration Attendance
Enrollment: College Freshman-Junior Year	Preparation for college Parental encouragement and support	Gains in: • Personal development • Problem solving

Academic Stages	Factors/Predictors	Outcomes
	Collegiate aspirations	• Critical thinking
	Campus and classroom climate	• Understanding science
	Collegiate experiences	and technology
	• Out-of-classroom	• Appreciation for arts
	• Quality and intensity	• Career maturity
	of instruction	• Occupational awareness
	• Counseling	• Professional and
	• Interactions with peers	occupational competencies
	and instructors	• Ability to work in teams
	Engagement with the academic	• Tolerance and openness
	and social components of	to diversity
	the institution	• Work ethic
	Intensity and quality of	Persistence to graduation
	curriculum	Pursuit of graduate studies
	Working on campus	Incorporation into the
	Effort spent in academic	labor force
	related activities	
	College GPA	
	Financial assistance	

college success. Imagine American Indian and Alaska Native parents and adult relatives who voice expectations along the lines of, "It is the right of every Native person to pursue and be successful in college; we are people of aspiration and vision." Maria Reyes's study involving successful Eskimo college students found that sometimes it only takes one family member to make a difference.[2] Encouragement can come in many forms (smiling at child going to school, affirmative nodding when they come home from school, positive words about doing well in class, etc.), and the important element is sincerity.

Parents and adult relatives, alone or together, can put forth as little as $1 a day to contribute to college saving plans and send a powerful message of postsecondary commitment to young family members ($1 × 365 days × 5 years = $1,825!). Although it makes sense that high socioeconomic status is a predictor of college success, remember that sometimes wealth in Native societies is not always measured in terms of material objects or money; rather, identity, pride, integrity, and sense of commitment to the well-being of our people are more appropriate.

As for student ability, put this saying wherever American Indians and Alaska Natives might read it and where you can see it every day: "Education dates back to a time when every American Indian and Alaska Native child was identified as gifted and talented. That is our vision for educating our children today." Ability is something that can be cultivated, and every American Indian and Alaska Native needs to believe they have the ability to be successful in college. Some went to college and some have graduated, whereas others have not had the opportunity to attend. On one level, those who did go to college might be better able to provide postsecondary advising.

This may not be true, even while admitting that personal experience is a great teacher.

What matters most among American Indian and Alaska Native people are adults who are willing to share whatever stories they can with youth about making wise choices for their future. Then our schools need to have grade level–appropriate reading material about going to college. This guide can be useful along with Internet resources cited throughout the guide. When put all together, it helps American Indians and Alaska Natives in junior high school begin to develop aspirations, plan for the future, and understand what classes they need to take now to be successful in college.

When students are in high school, positive parental and adult influences continue to have an important influence, and it helps Native youth embark on the search process of naming particular institutions. In addition to the conversations and involvements that were important in junior high, the college-going vision can be clarified by identifying real institutions that have specific information important to survey (academic programs, tuition, type of institution, makeup of student body, etc.). At the same time, take certain pretests used by college admission personnel in making admission decisions. This kind of information becomes increasingly important in the final stages of the high school experience as you shift from searching to choosing and applying to college and taking the real standardized tests, of which results are generally required as part of most college applications.

Then apply to at least several colleges and wait for acceptance letters. The best advice is apply to a range of institutions (i.e., affordable, highly desirable, and/or dream colleges) and choose the best one based on your acceptance letter, finance aid package, and personal choice. Outcomes that you want to cultivate deal with your awareness of different types of postsecondary institutions, your particular academic strengths and interests, family support, how committed particular colleges are to Native success, submitting all financial aid and college applications well ahead of the deadline, getting preregistered and visiting the chosen campus(es) or making contact with college admission personnel, and keeping up with your high school attendance.

Then comes the most rewarding part for those American Indians and Alaska Natives wanting to be successful in college—actually enrolling and taking classes. The real college-going experience can seem like a constant journey of trying to become better prepared to do well (improving our writing, reading and comprehending more, gaining higher levels of understanding, etc.). Success depends on and inspires parental support. At the same time we experience success in college (making new friends, learning different things, being excited and humbled by the opportunity, etc.), our aspirations become clearer and increase.

Many successful American Indian and Alaska Native students took an interest in creating a campus and classroom climate that is conducive to Native worldviews and respect. They strove to engage in positive activities that define their collegiate experience in a powerful way, preferring to think back on what they learned outside the classroom, the depth of knowledge gained through formal coursework, the people that took an interest in their lives, and the time they took to interact with others.

Anybody receiving financial aid never forgets the relationship between passing grades and receiving aid because quite simply, passing classes is crucial to receiving aid. They laugh at and reminisce about how they managed to balance external commitments with classroom demands, even when it meant surviving all-nighters preparing for tests or writing that paper that put itself off until the last minute. They speak of the different odd jobs they held; many American Indian and Alaska Native students need to work and sought financial aid in the form of a work study position.

After completing a college degree program, the whole range of gains American Indian and Alaska Native students experience matter the most. It is what compensates for the time expended, money invested, choices made, and everything that went into getting a college degree. There is the possibility of becoming a better person with a greater appreciation of life and the world in which we live. It was important to learn and hone the skills, abilities, and knowledge that enables a person to apply the intellectual vision and creativity to address issues affecting American Indian and Alaska Native people. College can be a place where "critical" does not mean "demeaning" but becomes part of the thinking process to gather information from observations, experience, reasoning, and our interaction with other people to achieve clarity and fairness.

The college campus is an educational environment that encourages all of us to reach higher levels of understanding in subject areas such as science and technology while developing an appreciation for the arts. Value is placed on the ability to work in teams, and tolerance and openness to diversity is brought to life by a wide range of socially conscience and sensitive activities organized by members of the campus community. To be successful means to develop a good work ethic of starting class assignments in manner that allows for adequate completion time, a skill that will help you in life.

The latter part of your collegiate experience is a place where career maturity meets up with occupational awareness and results in a clear career path for you. Approached with a sense of purpose, you will strive toward professional and occupational competencies within your chosen field, particularly when American Indian and Alaska Native communities are in need of well-trained Native people in all areas of employment. All of this—learning, values, work ethic, life aspirations—facilitates resiliency and determination. That is what will help you persist to graduation and then transition into the labor force or graduate studies and beyond.

Nobody is expected to naturally grasp the implication of academic stages and outcomes. Some do; most of us don't. As Table 5.2 lists, be grateful and know that there are many intervention strategies to help you along the way. In junior high school, career education, learning how to make wise decisions, academic assistance, and curriculum planning are part of preparing to be successful in the future. Nobody can afford to walk into the next five or ten years of their lives ignoring what American Indian and Alaska Native ancestors conveyed throughout their lives, and that is to be prepared. Go visit colleges, expect your teachers to have high expectations of you, and involve the family in your educational plans, particularly when it deals with going to college.

Table 5.2. The Path to a Four-Year Degree in Terms of Outcomes and Intervention Strategies

Academic Stages	Outcomes	Intervention Strategies
Predispositions: Grades 7–9	Career/occupational aspirations Educational aspirations Planning for college Enrollment in college-bound curriculum Reading, writing, math, critical thinking skills, and competencies (preparation for college)	Career exploration and decision-making workshops Academic tutorial sessions Assessing academic potential and identifying gaps Curriculum planning Parental involvement Visitations to postsecondary institutions Field trips to workplaces for different occupations High teachers' expectations Parental workshops on college and ways to finance it
Search: Grades 10–12	Listing of tentative institutions Narrowing list of tentative institutions Securing information on institutions Taking pre-SAT and pre-ACT	Counseling on postsecondary programs Collecting and disseminating information about postsecondary institutions Academic tutorial sessions Participation in college orientation activities
Choice: Grades 11–12	Awareness of college expenses and financial aid Awareness of institutional attributes and admission standards Attaining scholastic aptitudes, attitudes, and competencies Support from family and friends Institutional commitment Submission of college applications Preregistration Attendance Application for financial aid	Assistance in filling out FAFSA form Assistance in filling out college application forms and meeting requirements Collecting and disseminating information about sources of financial aid Tutorial session and summer programs to enhance student academic ability and exposure to college
Enrollment: College Freshman–Junior Year	Gains in: Personal development Problem solving Critical thinking Understanding science and technology Appreciation for art Career maturity Occupational awareness Professional and occupational competencies Ability to work in teams	Pre-entry assessment and placement according to needs Study and learning workshops Active learning and collaborative pedagogies in and out of the classroom Faculty mentorship programs Learning communities (cluster programs) Orientation and academic programs to enhance the freshman year experience

Academic Stages	Outcomes	Intervention Strategies
	Tolerance and openness to diversity	Co-curricular activities
	Work ethic	Recognition of student enclaves and their inclusion in campus governance
	Persistence to graduation	Counseling and advising for job placement, summer programs, internships
	Pursuit of graduate studies	Career exploration activities
	Incorporation into the labor force	Networking with alumni and potential employers
		Scholarships
		Financial aid planning and debt advising
		Work study programs
		Multicultural education
		Workshops and training on learning styles
		Use of validation strategies in and out of the classroom

American Indian and Alaska Native students in high school should be exposed to activities that nurture higher education aspirations, intentions, and commitment through postsecondary counseling, getting information from specific colleges, and gaining a good understanding of college life. It is always helpful to have assistance available to fill out financial aid forms and college application forms. Don't wait until the last moment. Seeking help early is the easiest and best thing people looking to be successful in college can do, and it is generally free. If you are a first-time college student, make sure to explore any summer academic bridge programs or find ways to maintain or enhance your academic abilities (i.e., read, write, do math problems, get involved in art projects, etc.).

There are so many things to do to prepare yourself to make the college experience more rewarding and fulfilling. If available, take advantage of any pre-entry assessment and placement to match your learning needs to course selection. Similarly, orientation and academic programs during the first year can enhance the freshman experience. Study and learning workshops and training on learning styles give you keen insight about how to manage your time and tailor activities to complement your learning style. Active learning and collaborative pedagogies in and out of the classroom give you an important means to foster engagement in your overall college education.

Use of validation strategies (seeing if things make sense or work) in and out of the classroom will increase your tendency to be a problem solver and critical thinker. Faculty mentorship programs are designed to work intimately with instructors, and if there are no formal programs available, feel free to seek out teachers to work with or get to know. Get involved in learning communities or start one with other American Indian and Alaska Native students to make learning a group experience. Make the college experience fun by setting aside time for co-curricular activities. Recognize that student enclaves like the Native student organizations are an important part of campus life and play a personal role in making sure the American Indian and Alaska Native student body is included in campus governance.

It is important throughout your college experience to seek out scholarships, know about financial aid planning and debt advising, and identify work study programs. As you approach your final two years of an undergraduate program, career counseling and advising for job placement, summer programs, and internships become interesting ways to see yourself doing something after graduation. Make it even more rewarding by taking advantage of career exploration activities while networking with alumni and potential employers.

While examining the intervention strategies, you should take note that institutions should embrace the responsibility to provide a range of student support services that will meet the needs of students. However, considerable responsibility to take the first step rests with the student. You need to approach the challenge of pursuing a college education with the mindset that it will require making sufficient time available to put forth an honest effort. We know that there are people who will say this puts too much responsibility on you as a student and the institutions and society should do more to ensure postsecondary success. We agree.

A Student's Voice

I think it's important to remember that the big stuff is people. . . . Not grades, or theories, or knowing more or less than anyone else. At home there's a story about a mouse, and how it lived in a boot. And it thought it was the biggest thing in the world, because it could touch the sky and all four corners of the Earth (because its world was the boot!). Until one day it climbed out of the boot, and realized that everything else was bigger and different than it ever could have imagined. . . . It's important to stay grounded in who you are, to be humble, and to put your abilities to good use. Learn, like the mouse, that the world is pretty big and contains amazing things, and you can explore it. Also, I really think education is a responsibility. . . . Responsibility to my family and community. I think that is what matters most.

ACADEMIC AND SOCIAL PREPARATION

A Student's Voice

My mom was a teacher, and I think that helped me a lot preparing for college. But you know, a lot of people show up at school, and they really aren't prepared for the level of work, especially math and writing, that college expects. I see three kinds of people at school. The first kind was really prepared academically and succeeded without putting in a whole lot of effort (depending on their majors). The second kind wasn't really prepared, and started off doing poorly, but was proactive about getting help from the tutoring centers and professors in order to succeed and improve, and was genuinely interested in school and what they were learning. The last kind usually weren't there for long: they got to school and weren't prepared, but either they didn't know where to go for help or decided just not to get help. They often partied a lot, too, and they usually flunked out the first year. I guess the motto of the story is: Be as prepared as you can be, but don't let your precollege education stop you. There are lots of resources at school to help anyone who wants to grow and succeed if they put in the work. And it does take work!

The concept of academic and social preparation is closely aligned to the idea of integration. That is, how students integrate into the college academic and social environments influences the likelihood of college departure or completion (e.g., lack of integration often leads to departure before graduation, and experiencing integration promotes completion). Researchers have devoted considerable attention to assessing the concept of academic and social integration, generally with the intent of offering their own idiosyncratic input.[3] We want to address this issue only to say American Indian and Alaska Native peoples need to prepare for multiple challenges in their lives. One of the most challenging efforts that you undertake might be pursing a college education.

It is important to note that beyond the tribal colleges and universities, few (if any) of the mainstream higher education institutions in the United States make a profound effort to alter the institutional environment to accommodate the needs of American Indians and Alaska Natives. For example, on most campuses there are not a whole lot of Native faculty members. Many non-Native instructors do not take into account Native learning styles when developing curriculum or incorporating instructional styles. Student services generally have limited budgets, and programs for American Indians and Alaska Natives are often lacking due to competing interest to accommodate the broader student population. While we continue to reform higher education, it seems prudent to prepare yourself in the best way possible. It is not fair (socially, economically, culturally, spiritually), but together we can make things different for future generations; we are convinced of that possibility.

Academic Preparation

Clifford Adelman, a senior research analyst in the U.S. Department of Education authored a recent study to determine aspects of formal schooling that contribute to completing a bachelor's degree.[4] Although the national data set used does not always allow for detailed analyses of students by race and ethnicity, the findings make intuitive and practical sense and thus could be of interest to American Indian and Alaska Native students who want to consider ways to prepare for successfully complete their college education. Adelman posits that to be academically successful in college, one should consider taking a rigorous course load while in high school. For the most part, he is right.

A rigorous course load means taking several classes of English, mathematics (particularly the highest levels), science (with labs), languages, social studies, and technology-related courses (i.e., computer science). Don't count remedial courses (do these during the summer or after school). Enroll in Advanced Placement courses. Shop and trade classes are fine for a vocational track but will not give you the foundation for learning in college. After you have developed your rigorous course load, then see where you can afford to take extracurricular classes. However, if you do have extra time, take extra and higher level math classes.

The ACT has a similar position detailed in a 2005 policy report.[5] They "identified the college preparatory course sequences that contributed most to college readiness: English 9–12; Algebra 1, Geometry, Algebra 2, and one (or more) upper-level mathematics course; and Biology, Chemistry, and Physics. Taking a foreign language enhances the benefits of the English sequence, and the upper-level mathematics and science courses have cross disciplinary benefits" (p. 9). Of course, additional analysis by race and ethnicity do not reflect well on American Indians and Alaska Natives: only one-third take the courses to best prepare for college-level science, are less likely to take a complete college preparatory course sequence in mathematics, and most likely of all racial/ethnic groups to take less than algebra 1, geometry, algebra 2, biology, chemistry, and physics. Consider these findings as benchmarks; things will get better, and you can make a difference. As for foreign languages, take classes on your own Native language first.

Overall, the drawback here (and Adelman recognizes it) is that some schools serving American Indians and Alaska Natives may not be offering an array of rigorous or college preparation courses. If that is the case, considerable pressure needs to be placed on the school board and administration to ensure an adequate number of willing and capable teachers who can teach college prep courses. At the same time, students of all ages should explore what is available through other means, for example, community colleges or distance education when accessible. Remember, however, that nobody is taking the position that you will fail to graduate from college if you don't take an intense load of college preparation course in high school.

If you don't take college-level prep classes, then be clear about the fact that you may not be as academically prepared as some of your other classmates in four-year colleges and find other ways to prepare yourself academically. There are lots of ways to challenge yourself—read more, write more, take tests, be a creative problem solver, critique literature, look at reports produced by your tribe or about American Indians and Alaska Natives, share your views, expand your vocabulary, learn traditional songs, study your tribal history, learn the scientific and traditional names of plants, look at the mathematics inherent in art. These are just a few of the vast number of ideas you can embrace to expand and develop your intellectual capabilities.

For those graduating from high school, strongly consider going to college as soon as you can and take as many credits as you can to maintain momentum (i.e., twelve credits or more per semester and aim for more than twenty credits completed within the first year). If you graduated from high school some time ago but want to go to college, then start the process of getting a college education now and do not wait any longer. Come on, go for it! Waiting isn't helping you, and we have seen too many working single heads of households who have made it to know that when there is clarity of aspirations, anything can be accomplished. Go to college part-time as a last resort. If that is your only way to stay on the college track, then please do so.

Continuous enrollment is far better than stopping and starting. There are many American Indian and Alaska Native students who have stopped out for a while to work or find themselves and returned to complete their college degree. Nonetheless, most Native students who did stop out for more than a year generally did not return to complete their degree program, some for good reasons. Whatever the reason for stopping out, please remember that going to college is a personal choice. Some students choose to move around and go to college somewhere else. Adelman found that "formal transfer from a community college to a four-year college and formal transfer from one four-year college to another were positively associated with degree completion, but wandering from one school to another was not" (p. xxi).

Putting in the necessary work and making time to get the best grades possible at all levels of your schooling contributes to postsecondary completion. Don't be discouraged if you get lower grades than expected early in your educational experience. Progressively getting better grades over time is a positive and significant indicator of eventual completion. Avoid abusing and carelessly taking advantage of institutional policies that allow you to drop and repeat classes without penalty. At times it is unavoidable, but too many students will get into the habit of taking advantage of these institutional policies as an easy way out. You do yourself no favors by taking the easy way out in life. All the advice and support means very little unless you respond to it in a grateful manner. Be thankful that people care.

Social Preparation

Social preparation may be the hardest part of preparing for college. Think about it. The academic stuff is pretty much straightforward, making it easier to develop and follow strategies. Social preparation is different. First of all, a considerable amount of your college experience might be considered social, which is essentially outside of the class and beyond your academic responsibilities. It entails things like finding housing and selecting roommates, being in charge of your own personal schedule, deciding what and when to do what is fun and relaxing. You've got to meet new people and let them get to know you, from professors to other students. For the most challenging social part of succeeding in college:

- Develop a schedule and establishing priorities.
- Enjoy your college experience and don't get overwhelmed by the pressures.
- Be confident, humble, and have fun.
- Develop friends that will become your family.

We are sure there is more that you will discover. Preparing socially for college is one of those areas of life where tribal elders might smile and say, "Don't stay up too late because morning comes soon enough as it is."

A Student's Voice

What has been important to me along my journey is getting involved in a lot of activities while in high school and college. These are essential to developing leadership skills that I have been able to use throughout my life and career. I was a three-sport athlete in high school, and I also earned a full-ride college football scholarship. Through sports, I was able to learn how to work as a team toward a common goal. I also learned communication skills, hard work, and how to plan and achieve goals. In high school, I also served as the student body vice president. I was able to learn social skills, budgeting skills, how to facilitate and plan meetings, among other things. In addition, every summer I attended a summer camp, including the National Youth Sports Program (NYSP), as a participant. When I was in college, I continued my participation with NYSP but I worked as a youth counselor to help the youth develop their leadership skills. I was also involved with Native student activities on campus when I had time outside of football. These activities included organizing student potlucks and helping out with the annual pow wow. Through this I was able to develop and utilize my leadership and social skills.

Of all the skills that I learned from participating in these activities, probably the most important skill I learned is the ability to network. I believe networking is absolutely essential to success in college and *beyond* because it is so true that it is not what you know, but who you know. I have seen far too many people, including Native students, who lack this social skill, and it hurts them in the long run. Many Native students may appear shy or reticent, but I don't think that's entirely true. I used to be very shy in my classes as a college student. It was like everything I had learned in high school was lost due to the strange environment. I felt like I had to learn everything all over again. You would not hear a peep out of me. I would just sit there and observe the professor's behavior or draw pictures in the margins of my books. I was scared and lacked confidence. So my method of communication was through writing and/or drawing. One day my English professor came up to me and said, "You're an excellent writer, why don't you speak up in class?" His compliment immediately lifted my spirit and gave me the confidence to believe that I was college material and that I do have something to contribute. From that day forward, I have gained more and more confidence by talking with people from backgrounds completely different from my own. This has increased my social capital and has paid huge dividends in my life.

The ability to network has opened doors that I never thought were possible. Through networking I was able to land a job working on my home reservation as a coordinator of a program that allowed community members to earn an associate of arts and sciences degree that transfers to a four-year college. Later on, I was able to secure a graduate assistantship through networking and am now working toward a Ph.D. Looking back on my life, all of the activities that I participated in have prepared and equipped me with the ability meet and interact with people from all walks of life, build friendships, and adjust to new environments. These are the most important things I have learned during my college journey.

MATRICULATION AND THE CRITICAL PERIODS

Being successful in college will not be easy, and there will be barriers that require you to develop persistence. Believe that you are the type of person who will not quit and acquires a sense of pride from overcoming obstacles in life. For many American Indians and Alaska Natives, pursuing a college degree was not always about getting an education but also, drawing on the spiritual strength of their ancestors to realize the ultimate in survival as a people, to prosper—not prospering financially or materially, although that may be a secondary outcome, rather prospering spiritually and feeling a sense of purpose and accomplishment.

There are similar themes in persistence studies of American Indian and Alaska Native college students. For example, Aaron Jackson, Steven Smith, and Curtis Hill found the following themes[6]:

- **Family support:** "Students talked about the strong encouragement and support they received" and as found in other studies it "was positively related to commitment to academic achievement" (p. 553).

- **Structured social support:** "Students talked about the positive effects of Native American clubs, multicultural offices and other groups organized to provide social support for to Native American students" (p. 553).

- **Faculty/staff warmth:** "Students talked about the positive experience of being greeted and contacted warmly by faculty and staff" (p. 554).

- **Exposure to college and vocations:** "Students indicated some previous positive experience with the college environment" (p. 554).

- **Developing independence and assertiveness:** Students "experienced an existential shift toward being more independent and outgoing . . . becoming more willing to ask for help and more comfortable speaking in social situations" (p. 555).

- **Reliance on spiritual resources:** "Traditional spirituality varied considerably, for some students it was a significant source of strength in completing their academic work" (p. 555).
- **Dealing with racism:** "Student saw this as an inherent aspect of their experience that they had to manage" (p. 556).
- **Nonlinear path:** "None of the students reported a linear path to academic success. Each of them had attended at least three schools in the process of getting their degree. . . . Likewise, most of them had periods over the course of their academic career, when they struggled academically" (p. 557–58).
- **Paradoxical cultural pressure:** "Students discussed conflicting pressures to (a) be successful in college and (b) maintain their identity as a member of their reservation community" (p. 558).

Maria Elena Reyes's story of Alaska Native students at the University of Alaska Fairbanks shared that students know that college will require working hard and persisting through the difficult times.[7] Students place a high importance on commitment to community and remind us all that we can be deeply motivated to do well in college with the goal of helping Native people. Our internal aspirations are cultivated by even a small measure of family support along with adequate financial assistance, and this indicated that all Native students need to communicate with family and apply for financial aid in a timely way. The results of Reyes's study indicate that Native students welcomed developmental (remediation) classes and student support services. These same students shared that they overcame the lack of institutional support while in high school, financial barriers, racism against Alaska Natives, concerns for the safety of their children, and the fear of speaking up in class. Although uncomfortable with being labeled "successful," every one of the students had advice to offer Native students going to college:

- "Just keep going."
- "Get to know what resources are available. . . . You can do it."
- "College is so different from high school [much better]. . . . Find the resources. Get involved; the more people you talk to, the more you find out about things that can help you."
- "Set goals and plan your expenses. Look for scholarships. Stay determined. Find supportive friends and family. Look at it as your job; it is your job to get these grades, to get through."
- "Take all the college prep courses you can in high school. Prepare for college. Ask people how to prepare for it while you are still in high school. Get good grades."
- "Ask yourself, 'What do I want?' Make sure that this is what you want, not just what your parents want for you. If you have to work, that's okay. Take your core first, and find an advisor you can trust."
- "Make use of the Writing Center, Counseling Center, both have been helpful to me. Get to know the library. Don't be afraid to speak up." (p. 155)

Florence McGeshick Garcia's study illustrates an incredible ability to do well in all kinds of settings, educational or otherwise.[8] The insights of twelve American Indians who received their doctorates tell all of us that achieving in America's finest universities can strengthen our cultural identity and reinforce deeply rooted ancestral beliefs. The intrinsic gift of spirituality keeps you on the right path, and praying to the Creator and your ancestors will remind you of the humble journey you walk when in service of the people's welfare. In the end, giving back still means something to every American Indian and Alaska Native who chooses to pursue a college education. You become role models and mentors, setting an example that achieving in a good way is an ancient and time-honored tradition.

It is helpful to understand and place into some meaningful context the influence that going to college has on American Indian and Alaska Native students. You will find that knowing about the emotions that you may experience can help you deal with what Terry Huffman refers to as estrangement and transculturation.[9] *Estrangement* describes the emotions of students who experience intense alienation or isolation in college and generally do not do well socially or academically. *Transculturation* depicts students who prevail over acute alienation and usually have successful college experiences. As shown in Table 5.3, Huffman describes a four-stage process that students move through that can help you be aware of potential pitfalls and understand how you can prepare for overcoming any psychological and social barriers that get in the way of your desire to enjoy the college experience.

Almost every American Indian and Alaska Native student may experience some degree of alienation in their college experience—particularly those students who grew up in a tribal community and those immersed in the traditional culture of urban Indian communities. This even may be true for those students who attend a tribal college or university. It seems to be a normal rite of passage. You should be prepared for some kind of personal questions that go something like, "What am I doing here? Am I supposed to be here? Aren't there better things that I can do with my life than suffer through college?"

Table 5.3. Process of Estrangement and Transculturation in American Indian College Students

Stage	Process of Estrangement	Process of Transculturation
One	*Initial Alienation*: Feelings of alienation or little with which to relate in the college experience.	*Initial Alienation*: Feelings of alienation or little with which to relate in the college experience.
Two	*Disillusionment*: Strong perception of college as agent of assimilation; extreme alienation.	*Self-Discovery*: Discovery of personal strength emerging from Native cultural heritage.
Three	*Emotional Rejection*: Rejection of perceived assimilation; continued severe feelings of alienation.	*Realignment*: Learn to relate in both Native and mainstream cultural settings using traditionalism as an emotional anchor.
Four	*Disengagement*: Physical withdrawal from college.	*Participation*: Full use of American Indian culture and heritage as source of strength.

To transcend this sense of alienation, take comfort in the knowledge that you can overcome the initial alienation with the conscious decision to succeed in college because of your cultural background. This is the true essence of self-discovery that gives rise to strength and confidence. Then as you realign your focus on doing well in college, clarify and commit yourself to the core values, way of thinking, and vision of how a college experience will be helpful to you and the American Indian and Alaska Native people. Believe that you will settle into a positive routine that will facilitate the successful completion of your college education. Thousands of American Indian and Alaska Natives do it every year. You can, too.

CHAPTER 6

Develop Problem-Solving and Critical-Thinking Skills

Experiencing a high degree of academic success in most college degree programs may require you to master two important intellectual skills: (a) problem solving and (b) critical thinking. The National Postsecondary Education Cooperative (NPEC) produced an impressive volume that provides clear definitions of and suggestions leading to a greater understanding of these skills.[1] The following quotation offers a general definition.

> **Problem solving** is defined as a step-by-step process of defining the problem, searching for information, and testing hypotheses with the understanding that there are a limited number of solutions. The goal of problem solving is to find and implement a solution, usually to a well-defined and well-structured problem. **Critical thinking** is a broader term describing reasoning in an open-ended manner, with an unlimited number of solutions. The critical thinking process involves constructing the situation and supporting the reasoning behind a solution. (p. 11)

Although these two skills are practiced across various academic disciplines and used interchangeably, problem solving is often associated with math, engineering, and science-related fields, whereas critical thinking generally aligns with behavioral sciences disciplines.

PROBLEM SOLVING

"Problem solving is defined as understanding the problem, being able to obtain background knowledge, generating possible solutions, identifying and evaluating constraints, choosing a solution, functioning within a problem-solving group, evaluating the process, and exhibiting problem-solving dispositions" (p. 25). More important, gaining mastery with problem solving and critical thinking is helpful far beyond the classroom and is intended to be applicable in your personal and professional lives. The following series of tables (Tables 6.1 to 6.8) provide insights into specific problem-solving skills, such as

- Understanding the problem
- Obtaining background knowledge
- Generating possible solutions
- Identifying and evaluating constraints
- Choosing a solution
- Group problem solving
- Evaluation
- Dispositions

Each table then identifies areas you can develop to be proficient in a given problem-solving skill. In line with the spirit of this book, the narrative associated with each table has been constructed based on the fact that being successful in college is the solution to a problem you and others may want to address.

A Student's Voice

I remember being in grade school and generally getting along OK. OK, that is, until I had story problems in math. Then, for some reason, I couldn't get the problems right or even understand what they were asking me to do! I was always so frustrated until I realized we use problem solving every day. Diaper dirty? Where did I stash the clean ones? Where's the diaper bag? The Desitin? The wipes, the trash can, etc., etc., etc. . . . My ability to answer all of those questions in a way that lets me actually change the diaper within two minutes is an act of problem solving. And, as we go through higher education, we learn there are different kinds of problems we need to solve.

We learn to solve down-to-earth, see-and-do problems, like "Where do I get a parking permit?" and "How am I going to pay for this college education?" We also run into deeper, more abstract problems, like "If we hold to one of these styles of philosophy in our environmental regulations, how will each impact our river ecosystem, in the sense of water rights and sustainable salmon harvest, 50 years down the road?" You can see the different approaches needed in each case. The thing the different questions have in common is (A) they are asking something worth considering, and (B) they all have answers. Sometimes more than one! So whether it gets you a slot in the yellow lot, a three-thousand-dollar scholarship, or an "A" on a test, problem solving is what you need to get by. If you're having difficulty coming up with the solution to a problem, academic or otherwise, you need to get help to figure it out. Find your resources and use them. You are entitled to all the help offered to you, if you are working on figuring stuff out. Problem solving is the nuts and bolts of education, and of life. Otherwise we all might still be in dirty diapers!

In Table 6.1, to understand the problem, an essential first step is to recognize that there *is* a problem. After doing so, your next step is to find out more about the problem and what is known and what is not well understood. In your case, it might be discovering that a particular career you are interested in requires a college degree or the way you want to help your tribe will require a college education. Whether conceptually large or small, it is important to develop the ability to sum up the problem and communicate your understanding to other people. For example, there is a lack of American Indians and Alaska Natives in professional fields like medicine, law, science, and so on, and you feel that one way to alleviate the problem is to pursue a college education that allows entry into those and other fields of interests.

Being able to look at any given problem from all sides or different perspectives is germane to the traditional concept of things being interconnected. Gain a good understanding of why American Indians and Alaska Natives are underrepresented in college. Ascertaining characteristics of the physical environment and determining influences from social constructions like schools often places a problem in its proper context. Often we find that the quality of schooling and the socioeconomic conditions of our communities make it difficult to develop the support systems necessary

Table 6.1. Understanding the Problem and Potential Areas of Development

Problem-Solving Skill	Areas of Development
Understanding the Problem	• Recognize that the problem exists. • Determine which facts are known in a problem situation and which are uncertain. • Summarize the problem to facilitate comprehension and communication of the problem in clear and concise descriptions. • Identify different points of view inherent in the representation of the problem. • Identify the physical and organizational environment of the problem. • Describe the values that have a bearing on the problem. • Identify time and financial constraints associated with solving the problem. • Identify personal biases inherent in any representation of the problem.

for postsecondary aspirations. However, you become part of the solution when aspiring to enter into and graduate from college because you transform yourself into a positive role model for other American Indians and Alaska Natives. It is that simple.

Understanding and being able to describe values that affect the problem can increase your ability to factor in how ideals or standards play a part in creating or affecting the perception of what is or is not a problem. This is critical because non-Natives at times can impose their own value orientation on American Indian and Alaska Native peoples. This might be in the form of overt expressions of doubt (i.e., "You can't make it in college. Don't even try.") or more covert (i.e., "Going to a university may be too much for you, why don't you enroll in a local certificate program instead?"). Always take the opportunity to identify how much time there is available (i.e., weeks, months, years) and fiscal resources needed to solve a problem. Finally, we all need to distinguish to what extent our personal preconceptions and prejudices affect our ability to identify and define a problem.

Obtaining background knowledge, as addressed in Table 6.2, builds on the skill just mentioned in that it expresses the importance of getting sufficient background information to seek a solution. A helpful step is to tap your own prior experiences or those of other Native people in solving a variety of problems (i.e., how did they decide to pursue a postsecondary degree and choose a college?). A useful strategy among American Indian and Alaska Native peoples is to design a visual representation of the problem that

Table 6.2. Obtaining Background Knowledge and Potential Areas of Development

Problem-Solving Skill	Areas of Development
Obtaining Background Knowledge	• Determine if you have the background information to solve the problem. • Apply general principles and strategies that can be used in the solution of other problems. • Use visual imagery to help memorize and recall information. • Identify what additional information is required and where it can be obtained. • Develop and organize knowledge around the fundamental principles associated with a particular discipline. • Develop and organize knowledge around the fundamental principles associated across functions or disciplines. • Use systematic logic and organize related information into clusters. • Evaluate arguments and evidence so that competing alternatives can be assessed for their relative strengths. • Recognize patterns or relationships in large amounts of information. • Use analogies and metaphors to explain a problem. • Identify people and/or groups who may be solving similar problems.

allows you to record your increased understanding of the issue. Creating such visual illustrations can also guide your efforts to determine whether additional information is needed, and, if so, where you can obtain it.

Start with a symbolic representation of yourself entering college and graduating. Now fill in more detail that maps out how you are going to succeed in college. Note that as you become more familiar with your particular chosen area of study, you will be able to apply concepts and strategies you are learning to the problem-solving process.

Whatever strategies you employ, being somewhat systematic, logical, and organized can help clarify and demystify the extent of certain problems that confront Native people. Note that being systematic and logical is not always at odds with being organic and spiritual. This is particularly true when being systematic and logical allows you to evaluate arguments and evidence counterproductive to the aims of Native people and communities. So many arguments and evidence weigh against Native interests that it is helpful for you to be able to develop ways to scale down or organize the complexity of massive amounts of information. The use of metaphors to explain problems is a traditional Native method to break down the complexity of information that is rooted in storytelling. Sadly, the prevailing story is that many of the same or similar problems are present across many tribal communities and urban Indian enclaves, and solutions need to align together to better address prevailing issues.

Problem solving is as much about developing a solution as it is about having the ability to generate a variety of possible solutions to choose from (see Table 6.3). Too long and too often, Native communities have endured a solution paternalistically forced onto them because there was little effort to incorporate the creative possibilities inherent within the communities. That is why you have to be flexible and entertain numerous possibilities without critique as embraced in brainstorming. American Indian and Alaska Native peoples typically have an inherent systemic worldview (seeing the whole) and at the same time the ability to conceive of the various elements (components) within the system to determine individual influences.

Table 6.3. Generating Possible Solutions and Potential Areas of Development

Problem-Solving Skill	Areas of Development
Generate Possible Solutions	• Think creative ideas while listing several methods that might be used to achieve the goal of the problem. • Be flexible and use common brainstorming techniques to generate possible solutions. • Divide problems into manageable components and isolate one variable at a time to determine if it is the cause of the problem. • Develop criteria that will measure success of solutions. • Determine if cost of considering additional alternatives is greater than the likely benefit.

Criteria are important to establish the benchmark of what you are willing to accept and what you will find unacceptable. Factoring in costs is essential, and you will engage in this aspect of problem solving while making the determination of whether going to college is worth it. For example, you might ask yourself, "Does the increased wage earnings and opportunity to make a difference associated with a college degree outweigh the financial aid debt incurred while getting the degree?" Yes.

As shown in Table 6.4, identifying and evaluating constraints is an important problem-solving skill. Here you must engage in an effort to list factors that conspire to prohibit solving the problems. Among American Indian and Alaska Native communities, there are internal and external factors that you have to identify. Inquiring about your own conjectures (i.e., assumptions) is essential because a history of colonization by non-Native societies can taint our perspectives. For example, some Natives believe that going to college is a "white" thing to do. It is not, because when we make well-informed decisions, we control our own destiny.

Nevertheless, problem solving endeavors to recognize the constraints associated with possible solutions because going to college is not going to be a panacea (i.e., universal remedy). In our quest to be creative, we must keep in mind ancestral teachings that are still widely applicable to contemporary circumstances. Many past Native leaders encouraged future generations to see that it would not be guns but the pencil, books, and paper that would be the means to offset the encroachment threatening the existence of Native peoples.

Choosing a solution, as in Table 6.5, requires you to look back on the choices that are available; in the case of college choice, it represents the range of options to pursuing a college degree and the various postsecondary institutions to attend. You have to have something to support the solution you choose (i.e., decision to go to college and the school you select). Being able to ground this decision in what you know works for yourself and others is a wise step. Moreover, map out the positives and negatives, particularly how you might resolve the negative as in choosing to attend an out-of-state institution and figuring out additional travel costs to and from home. This is part of your problem-solving plan that continually has you revisiting why you chose to pursue a college degree and attend a particular school. In the end, be able to share your insights with your family, peers, or

Table 6.4. Identifying and Evaluating Constraints and Potential Areas of Development

Problem-Solving Skill	Areas of Development
Identifying and Evaluating Constraints	• List the factors that might limit problem-solving efforts. • Question credibility of one's own assumptions. • Recognize constraints related to possible solutions. • Apply consistent evaluative criteria to various solutions. • Use creative thinking informed by ancestral teachings to evaluate constraints.

Table 6.5. Choosing a Solution and Potential Areas of Development

Problem-Solving Skill	Areas of Development
Choosing a Solution	• Reflect on a wide range of possible alternatives before choosing a solution. • Use established criteria to evaluate and prioritize solutions. • Draw on data from known effective solutions of similar problems. • Evaluate possible solutions for both positive and negative consequences and how negative consequences can be resolved. • Analyze alternatives to determine if most effective options have been selected. • Explain and justify why a particular solution was chosen.

those interested in knowing how you made the wise choice to be successful in college.

The last point made in Table 6.5 in regard to sharing insights is an integral part of group problem solving, a point reinforced in Table 6.6. This is particularly evident among American Indian and Alaska Native high school students or among similar-age friends at a point in their lives where wanting to pursue a college degree is increasingly important for upward mobility and career stability. Some people may not be very supportive of going to college, and that is where a sense of patience and tolerance allows you to respect their decision without derailing your own aspirations and intentions. Be open to discussing how you see college fits in your life, and be attentive to how it may not fit into other peoples' lives.

Many American Indians and Alaska Natives encounter a certain resistance to seeing a college education as a solution to the problem of where

Table 6.6. Group Problem Solving and Potential Areas of Development

Problem-Solving Skill	Areas of Development
Group Problem Solving	• Identify and explain thought processes to others while delivering the message that everyone will work on collaborative projects as a member of a team. • Be patient and tolerant of differences by understanding there may be many possible solutions to a problem. • Use discussion strategies to examine a problem and pay attention to feelings of all group members while listening carefully to others' ideas. • Channel disagreement toward resolution by being able to identify and manage conflict. • Fully explore the merits of innovation and integrate diverse viewpoints by stimulating creativity rather than conformity. • Identify individuals who need to be involved in the problem-solving process.

Table 6.7. Evaluation and Potential Areas of Development

Problem-Solving Skill	Areas of Development
Evaluation	• Choose solutions that contain provisions for continuous improvement. • Revise and refine solutions during implementation. • Frequently measure progress toward a solution. • Seek alternative solutions if goals aren't being achieved.

they want to go in their lives or how they want to help their communities. Resentment may arise out of a reaction where someone might say that a person is going to college because he or she thinks "they are better than everyone else." To ensure that you don't carry this emotional baggage into your college experience, channel such a differing opinion by being resolved to explain that it has nothing to do with feeling better about anybody else but more about how you might better help others. See the value of recognizing the many American Indians and Alaska Natives who choose to pursue other important life paths, particularly those who see the value of working, continuing subsistence activities, or learning about and maintaining traditional culture. Nevertheless, for you to be successful in college, it will be important to involve everyone—family, friends, and teachers—who can provide the necessary support to ensure that you do well.

Your ongoing evaluation of the solution, showcased in Table 6.7, is an indispensable step in the overall problem-solving process. In the college-going experience, it is much like how you should strive to involve yourself in campus activities, improve study skills, and become more educated about the topics in which you are interested. For some of you, it might mean altering the direction of what major to pursue, the advisor to work with, or schedule of classes. Whatever you do, take time out of your day to check in with yourself about how well you are doing and what you can do to improve. If things are not working out, it may mean switching institutions, changing majors, developing a different schedule, or any number of workable alternatives (besides just giving up).

The focus of Table 6.8 is that, as with any aspect of being an effective problem solver, how successful you are in college will be affected by your own disposition or, put another way, your temperament. Be the type of person

Table 6.8. Dispositions and Potential Areas of Development

Problem-Solving Skill	Areas of Development
Dispositions	• Learn from errors. • Work within constraints. • Actively seek information. • Take personal responsibility for your solution to a problem. • Remain creative, adaptable, and flexible when implementing solutions. • Search for outside expertise for solutions.

who learns from what did not go right and work with constraints instead of feeling boxed in or limited. You have to engage in self-directed learning that has you looking for ways to make things go well and take on a high degree of personal responsibility for your success. Your way of relating to the world should embrace creativity, adaptability, and flexibility because these qualities are very much in line with Native ways of knowing and worldviews. If things are beyond the scope of your aptitude, then seek solutions from experts in counseling, housing, employment, financial aid, academic advising, academic support, student involvement, your major area of study, and life in general because postsecondary institutions generally have a range of professionals to help make sure your solution of going to college will work for you.

CRITICAL THINKING

Critical-thinking skills are both embedded in and distinct from problem solving.[2] Tables 6.9 through 6.15 provide an overview of individual skills

A Student's Voice

The trick to good critical thinking is to really understand what is being asked, and then figuring out how to address it. If you can do that, you can find answers to big questions. If you don't know the answer (and once you get to certain levels of academia sometimes there is no single right answer, or maybe no answer at all!) then you figure out how to find it. That's a good three-quarters of the battle. You ask other people, you hash it around your brain at breakfast, with classmates, and through your textbooks. I purposely look at things from a "within the box" view, then force myself to turn around and play devil's advocate on what I've come up with, to find the holes and weaknesses in my own thoughts and views. I have to be OK with my thoughts sometimes being wrong!

Sometimes the answer the instructor is looking for does not exist in my perspective, so I have to temporarily "adopt" another to discover it. If looked at with wisdom, this does not negate my perspective, but allows me to understand others' perspectives (like my professors' or classmates' perspectives) better. In doing so I understand them better as well. Do not be shy, do not be silent. Be active, initiate, and cast around until you find a good answer. Whether it gets you a good class discussion or a working model of riparian habitat as found in the boreal forest, you'll need to use critical thinking to get by in education. Don't sit on your duff and take information point blank as truth. Scratch your head, scratch your beard if you have one, and look at as many angles and possibilities as you can when evaluating new theories and information. Do not just accept or reject! Soak in, mull around, toss, turn, and give things extra time for reflection. Listen, hear, see, think, feel, and taste and smell as appropriate! And don't let any overriding sense block out the others.

Table 6.9. Interpretation and Areas of Development

Critical-Thinking Skill	Areas of Development
Interpretation	*Categorization* 1. Formulate categories, distinctions, or frameworks to organize information to aid comprehension. 2. Translate information from one medium to another to aid comprehension without altering the intended meaning. 3. Make comparisons; note similarities and differences between or among informational items. 4. Classify and group data, findings, and opinions on the basis of attributes or a given criterion. *Detecting Indirect Persuasion* 1. Detect the use of strong emotional language or imagery that is intended to trigger a response in an audience. 2. Detect the use of leading questions that are biased toward eliciting a preferred response. 3. Detect "if, then" statements based on the false assumption that if the antecedent is true, the consequence must be true also. 4. Recognize the use of misleading language. 5. Detect instances where irrelevant topics or considerations are brought into an argument that diverts attention from the original issues. 6. Recognize the use of slanted definitions or comparisons that express a bias for or against a position. *Clarifying Meaning* 1. Recognize confusing, vague, or ambiguous language that requires clarification to increase comprehension. 2. Ask relevant and penetrating questions to clarify facts, concepts, and relationships. 3. Identify and seek additional resources, such as resources in print, which can help clarify communication. 4. Develop analogies and other comparisons to clarify meaning. 5. Recognize contradictions and inconsistencies in written and verbal language, data, images, or symbols. 6. Provide an example that helps explain something or removes a troublesome ambiguity.

that define critical thinking: interpretation, analysis, evaluation, inference, presenting arguments, reflection, and dispositions. "Within each of these categories are skills and subskills that concretely define critical thinking" (p. 11). As with the previous section on problem solving, go over each skill in the context of succeeding in college. For example, within Table 6.9, the critical-thinking skill of interpretation has the subskill of categorization that would aid you in managing information about various colleges.

The subskill of detecting indirect persuasion is helpful for critically examining the marketing and recruiting material that individual colleges develop. Under clarifying meaning, these items give you great direction on what type of questions to ask of college representatives.

The essence of critical thinking is being able to engage in a high level of analysis that involves examining ideas and purposes as well as detecting and analyzing arguments (see Table 6.10). From the perspective of going to college, you may find that being involved in organizing Native-related events in campus activities requires an ability to examine ideas and purposes. This can be particularly relevant when speaking out about seasonal issues like Columbus Day and prevalent issues like using Native images for mascots of athletic teams. These and other opportunities will challenge you to determine exactly how you want to alter society's perception of American Indians and Alaska Natives.

Your ability to detect and analyze arguments can assist you in classroom discussions and interactions with students out of class that deal with the validity of treaties and the legal relationship between tribes and the federal government. There are many who do not agree with the sovereign status of tribes, question the right of tribal members to exercise their aboriginal rights to subsistence hunting and fishing, and lament the fact that tribal governments can establish casinos and other economic development opportunities. Those who oppose many of the legal and cultural interests of American Indians and Alaska Natives are operating under inaccurate, incomplete, or even no sound information. Their arguments against Native positions lack sound conclusions, fail to establish background information, and demonstrate a determined avoidance to recognize unstated assumptions. All in all, you should hang in there and develop your critical-thinking skills to stand resolute with the greater goal to overcome people who have, are, and will

Table 6.10. Analysis and Areas of Development

Critical-Thinking Skill	Areas of Development
Analysis	*Examining Ideas and Purpose* 1. Recognize the relationship between the purpose of a communication and the problems or issues that must be resolved in achieving that purpose. 2. Assess the constraints of the practical applications of an idea. 3. Identify the ideas presented and assess the interests, attitudes, or views contained in those ideas. 4. Identify the stated, implied, or undeclared purpose(s) of a communication. *Detecting and Analyzing Arguments* 1. Identify the main conclusion(s) of an argument. 2. Determine if the conclusion is supported with reasons, and identify those that are stated or implied. 3. Identify the background information provided to explain reasons that support a conclusion. 4. Identify the unstated assumptions of an argument.

continue to undermine your inalienable right to retain your Native identity and your tribe's political sovereignty.

The critical-thinking skill of evaluation, as shown in Table 6.11, first allows you an opportunity to determine if you want to expend any energy and time attending to a specific argument. You might be required to engage in class discussions even when the argument has no merit (i.e., American Indians and Alaska Natives are intellectually inferior). Then it becomes more important that you develop an ability to determine credibility, accuracy, and reliability of information sources. The chances are you will be able to skillfully uncover untenable assumptions that seem to have a life of their own, sort of like urban myths. Being well read and informed about issues, Native and non-Native, enables you to know when and how to use new information or data in discussions that characterize the rich exchange of ideas conducive to the college going experience.

It is always an option to ask other people if their observations are based on anecdotes or reliable information. If you choose to attend a mainstream, predominately white postsecondary institution, you are likely to encounter prejudice against American Indians and Alaska Natives that is not well reasoned. In these and other situations, you can take comfort in the fact that most of these tainted points of view rarely use clear and consistent language, terminology, and concepts (regardless of how widely held the beliefs might be, as in the opposition to diversity initiatives to admit or hire American Indians and Alaska Natives).

Table 6.11. Evaluation and Areas of Development

Critical-Thinking Skill	Areas of Development
Evaluation	1. Assess the importance of an argument and determine whether it merits attention.
	2. Evaluate the credibility, accuracy, and reliability of sources of information.
	3. Determine if an argument rests on false, biased, or doubtful assumptions.
	4. Determine how new data might lead to the further confirmation or questioning of a conclusion.
	5. Determine if conclusion(s) based on empirical observations were derived from a sufficiently large and representative sample.
	6. Assess bias, narrowness, and contradictions in points of view.
	7. Assess degree to which the language, terminology, and concepts employed in an argument are used in a clear and consistent manner.
	8. Determine what stated or unstated values or standards of conduct are upheld by an argument and assess their appropriateness to the given context.
	9. Determine and judge the strength of an argument in which an event(s) is claimed to be the result of another event(s) (causal reasoning).

You will find in college and in your career that knowing about core values of your community and how these differ from society at large will enable you to understand why certain conflicts arise. For example, there may be a conflict with responding immediately to question prompts in classrooms when in many Native cultures the concept of time is more extended, and the idea of giving someone some moments of reflection before responding to a question is warranted. Imagine that a professor asks you a question, at which point you pause, think about it, and after five or ten seconds you are ready to respond; but it's too late, the professor has already moved on to someone else, thinking you don't know the answer. Don't let these and other value differences influence your feeling of belonging. If there is not a lot of congruence (i.e., similarity) between you and the institution leading to a decision to leave, ask yourself this question: What is the strength of an argument that you don't belong versus the argument that you do not *want* to belong? Look at the answer to this question critically if ever faced with this kind of issue.

Table 6.12 shows that the critical-thinking skill associated with inference has you collecting and questioning evidence, developing alternative hypotheses, and drawing conclusions. These areas are fun to develop, and not just because it will make you a person who people like to be around when watching a forensic science TV series or reality-based dramas. It will be fun because you can become the kind of team player who can focus energy within group projects. Professors will love you for being astute and intellectually driven to explore topics while sharing these insights in class and lab assignments or tests. Imagine being the kind of person that others can depend on when they want to better understand the choices inherent in any given situation or that you can feel the sense of creativity that comes along with seeing things from multiple perspectives.

Being highly skilled at inference will help you hand in well-reasoned written assignments and classroom presentations. In turn, possessing the ability to articulate well-developed hypotheses provides you an added advantage to examine or test logical or empirical consequences. Why is this important? American Indians and Alaska Natives have been subjected to nearly 500 years of half-baked, ill-conceived, and outright irrational solutions to what non-Natives argue is a problem to be solved. Don't go get a college degree and add to this miserable past. Instead, become a highly informed critical thinker grounded in the wisdom of your ancestors; these concepts are not mutually exclusive.

You can finish a college education and return to a tribal community or work for Native-oriented organizations demonstrating the ability to draw good conclusions by reasoning with divergent points of view in formulating an opinion on an issue or problem, especially with views that seem at odds (i.e., traditional and contemporary). Often, you can turn to your Native community's cultural core values as criteria for making judgments that are reliable, intellectually strong, and relevant to the situation at hand. Here, too, you will find it advantageous to be familiar with multiple strategies to address any issue at hand, including means-ends analysis, working backward, analogies, brainstorming, and trial and error. Develop the opportunity to network in college, and later in life you will be inclined to seek various

Table 6.12. Inference and Areas of Development

Critical-Thinking Skill	Areas of Development
Inference	*Collecting and Questioning Evidence* 1. Determine the most significant aspect of a problem or issue prior to collecting evidence. 2. Formulate a plan for locating information to aid in determining if a given opinion is more or less reasonable than a competing opinion. 3. Combine disparate pieces of information that when combined offer insight into a problem or issues. 4. Judge what background information would be useful to have when attempting to develop a persuasive argument. 5. Determine if one has sufficient evidence to form a conclusion. *Developing Alternative Hypotheses* 1. Seek the opinion of others in identifying and considering alternatives. 2. List alternatives and consider their pros and cons. 3. Project alternative hypotheses regarding an event, and develop a variety of different plans to achieve a goal. 4. Recognize the need to isolate and control variables to make strong causal claims when testing hypotheses. 5. Seek evidence to confirm or disconfirm alternatives. 6. Assess the risks and benefits of each alternative. 7. After evaluating the alternatives generated, develop (when appropriate) a new alternative that combines the best qualities and avoids the disadvantages of previous alternatives. *Drawing Conclusions* 1. Reason well with divergent points of view in formulating an opinion on an issue or problem. 2. Develop and use criteria for making judgments that are reliable, intellectually strong, and relevant to the situation at hand. 3. Use multiple strategies in solving problems including means-ends analysis, working backward, analogies, brainstorming, and trial and error. 4. Seek various independent sources of evidence to provide support for a conclusion. 5. Note uniformities or regularities in a given set of facts, and construct a generalization that would apply to similar instances. 6. Employ graphs, diagrams, hierarchical trees, matrices, and models as solution aids.

independent sources of evidence, rather than just a single source, to provide support for a conclusion.

While in college, practice the ability to note uniformities or regularities in a given set of facts, and you will find it can help construct a generalization that would apply to all these and similar instances. Often this will scale down the complexity of the college-going experience and assist you each year. A good example is applying for financial aid, where the uniformity or regularity of applying each year is enhanced by having a manageable record-keeping system that in fact helps you in other areas of your life. Also, cultivate your natural artistic talents (everyone has artistic talents) to create graphs, diagrams, hierarchical trees, matrices, and models as solution aids because these tools are the most effective way to present large amounts of or complicated information in an attractive and concise manner. It is a good thing to practice these skills in college before you go out in the real world.

So there you are, faced with presenting a line of reasoning or case about something. What do you do? As shown in Table 6.13, you should lay out your supporting reasons and evidence for your conclusions. You then experience the very real possibility that other people don't agree; you should be able to negotiate fairly and persuasively. Presenting things succinctly to convey the crucial point of the issue may prevent you from being side-tracked or drawn into unnecessary and unrelated drama. This will be extremely important if you choose to work for Native people. In college, you will find that professors admire and peers envy an ability to cite relevant evidence and experiences to support your position. This skill will be helpful after college as well. In the end, develop the ability to illustrate central concepts with significant examples and show how these concepts and examples apply in real situations. This may not help you cook fried bread, but it will help you do well in your classes.

Table 6.14 provides several suggestions to develop the critical skill of reflection. It is a significant process to look at your own ideas and bases of understanding. Sometimes the lived experience of being American Indian and Alaska Native colors your perception of the world in a way that is unsupportable. In such cases, you will find a sense of freedom in correcting your own reasoning and outlook on life. Doing this allows you to develop critical-thinking skills that closely subject thought and action to a critique based on what drives one's interests, beliefs, and assumptions. Your intellectual capacity increases when self-examination presents yet another opportunity to expand and correct your understanding of issues and life in general.

Table 6.13. Presenting Arguments and Areas of Development

Critical-Thinking Skill	Areas of Development
Presenting Arguments	1. Present supporting reasons and evidence for conclusions that address the concerns of the audience.
	2. Negotiate fairly and persuasively.
	3. Present an argument succinctly to convey the crucial point of issue.
	4. Cite relevant evidence and experiences to support your position.
	5. Illustrate central concepts with examples and show how these concepts and examples apply in real situations.

Table 6.14. Reflection and Areas of Development

Critical-Thinking Skill	Areas of Development
Reflection	1. Analyze and evaluate your own argument(s) to confirm and/or correct reasoning and results. 2. Critically examine and evaluate vested interests, beliefs, and assumptions in supporting an argument or judgment. 3. Make revisions in arguments and findings when self-examination reveals inadequacies.

It is a wonderful way to live life when your disposition is oriented to curiosity and wondering (see Table 6.15). At the same time, you are able to facilitate higher experiences of learning by exercising some semblance of order and focus, even in the most artistic endeavors. Over time, you should cultivate a habit of perseverance that enjoys overcoming periods of intense challenge or drudgery that can be common throughout your college experience. It is good practice for life after college. Nothing seems to remain consistently easy or constantly hard, so you need to be able to ride the waves and go with the flow by being adaptable and resourceful.

Despite the attraction to only use insights informed from Native worldviews, a hallmark of college life is exploring the diversity of perspectives

Table 6.15. Dispositions and Areas of Development

Critical-Thinking Skill	Areas of Development
Dispositions	1. Be curious and inquire about how and why things work. 2. Be organized, orderly, and focused in inquiry or in thinking. 3. Willingly persevere and persist at a complex task. 4. Be flexible and creative in seeking solutions. 5. Be inclined to arrive at a reasonable decision in situations where there is more than one plausible solution. 6. Apply insights from cultures other than your own. 7. Be honest. 8. Monitor your understanding of a situation and progress toward goals. 9. Find ways to collaborate with others to reach consensus on a problem or issues. 10. Be intellectually careful and precise. 11. Value the application of reason and the use of evidence. 12. Be open-minded; strive to understand and consider divergent points of view. 13. Be fair-minded; seek truth and be impartial, even if the findings of an inquiry may not support one's preconceived opinions. 14. Willingly self-correct and learn from errors made, no matter who calls them to your attention.

advanced by other cultures. Welcome the opportunity to be honest; it will help nurture the integrity so important in the academic arena and society. Be willing to take the pulse of how things are going and see how well you are achieving your educational goals. You can't and shouldn't feel compelled to go it alone (for any reason), so develop the propensity to work with others to solve problems through consensus.

Being careful and precise is about how to be conscientious and accurate in taking care of business and doing what needs to be done, in and out of class. Don't think that reason and use of evidence are solely concepts of Western civilization, because these are time-tested skills that allow Native people the ability to deduce the importance of harmony and balance. Use the college experience to further develop your ability be open-minded and fair-minded; it is not a pleasant experience to suddenly realize that you disagree with an idea or approach just because it was not your own. You should be willing to self-correct and learn from errors, no matter who points them out. Somewhere out there some American Indian and Alaska Native brother or sister could still be with us or could have avoided some measure of misfortune by heeding advice offered by someone else. Take it to heart and hope that someone cares enough to bring to your attention the need to focus more on your education, live healthy, pray for your people, and appreciate life and the opportunity to improve yourself that comes with pursuing a college education.

CHAPTER 7

Internet Resources

There are vast number of Web sites dedicated to promoting postsecondary access and achievement (nearly 1 million hits of one type or another!). The problem is not finding resources on the Internet that can help to guide you along the postsecondary journey; the real issue is filtering through and identifying helpful Web sites that are easy to navigate and utilize. This chapter presents an overview of selected Web sites that might be of assistance to you and your family. The following sections are organized along three themes: general Web sites dedicated to improving postsecondary access and achievement, Web sites dedicated to improving Native postsecondary access and achievement, and state-supported Web sites that often have links dedicated to assisting parents and students. The Web sites listed are truly a cross-section of the many helpful Web sites that you can visit to find information to ensure that you prepare for, stay in, and graduate from college. The Web sites listed in this chapter were selected for a number of reasons: (a) they were hosted by established organizations promoting postsecondary access and achievement, (b) easy to access and navigate, and (c) provide critical information that can help you learn about important information to ensure your success in college.

GENERAL WEB SITES DEDICATED TO IMPROVING POSTSECONDARY ACCESS AND ACHIEVEMENT

Pathways to College Network (pathwaystocollege.net)

The Pathways to College Network is one of the premier Internet resources committed to using research-based knowledge to improve postsecondary education access and success for the nation's underserved students. The site explains that "the Pathways to College Network is an alliance of 38 national organizations and funders committed to advancing college access and success for underserved students, including those who are the first generation in their families to go to college, low-income students, underrepresented minorities, and students with disabilities." There are six guiding principles:

1. Expect that all underserved students are capable of being prepared to enroll and succeed in college.
2. Provide a range of high-quality college-preparatory tools for underserved students and their families.
3. Embrace social, cultural, and learning style differences in developing learning environments and activities for underserved students.
4. Involve leaders at all levels in establishing policies, programs, and practices that facilitate student transitions toward postsecondary attainment.
5. Maintain sufficient financial and human resources to enable underserved students to prepare for, enroll, and succeed in college.
6. Assess policy, program, practice, and institutional effectiveness regularly.

These principles are complemented by four priorities to meet the needs of all underserved students and speak to the needs of American Indian and Alaska Native who aspire to pursue a postsecondary education.

1. Encourage schools to make a rigorous college-prep curriculum the standard course of study for all students, so they will have the skills and knowledge they need to be successful in both postsecondary education and the workplace.
2. Improve the effectiveness of college access marketing campaigns that aim to influence the college-going behavior of underserved students.
3. Encourage early financial aid commitments and early notification programs for underserved students.
4. Persuade postsecondary leaders to take steps to improve the retention and graduation rates of underserved students.

The link for Publication and Resources is extensive and targets students, parents, teachers, counselors, and researchers. The link for the National Outreach Program Database is a free online database of precollege outreach programs for seeking specific programs and makes available a publication from the College Board and TERI, a repackaged *Outreach Program Handbook*. This particular site is in constant construction to bring you the latest information to improve college student access and achievement, and current links are being established for

- Academic preparation and support
- Access
- College success
- Financial aid

National Academic Advising Association (www.nacada.ksu.edu)

The National Academic Advising Association (NACADA) is an association of professional advisors, counselors, faculty, administrators, and students working to enhance the educational development of students. NACADA's mission is to

- Champion the educational role of academic advisors to enhance student learning and development in a diverse world.
- Affirm the role of academic advising in student success and persistence, thereby supporting institutional mission and vitality.
- Anticipate the academic advising needs of twenty-first-century students, advisors, and institutions.
- Advance the body of knowledge on academic advising.
- Foster the talents and contributions of all members and promote the involvement of diverse population.

NACADA's Native American and Tribal College Interest Group is intended to bring together both Native and non-Native students, advisors, faculty, and other student service personnel (www.nacada.ksu.edu/InterestGroups/C36/index.htm). The forum is designed to address the needs of Native American students and transfer students from tribal colleges and to engage the greater advising community in Native educational issues. Students will also want to visit NACADA's Clearinghouse, which has an amazing array of helpful articles and links.

The Education Trust (www2.edtrust.org/edtrust)

The Education Trust mission is to work "for the high academic achievement of all students at all levels, pre-kindergarten through college, and forever closing the achievement gaps that separate low-income students and students of color from other youth. Our basic tenet is this—All children will learn at high levels when they are taught to high levels." The Education Trust is involved in national and state policy debates, "maintains a relentless focus on improving the education of all students, and particularly those students whom the system has traditionally left behind." Among the many helpful tools and presentations is the College Results Online data tool (www .collegeresults.org). User-friendly and simple, this remarkable resource will allow American Indian and Alaska Native students to search most of the four-year colleges and universities in America to

- Examine overall graduation rates and see how those rates have changed over time.
- Learn about universities' records in graduating diverse groups of students.
- Compare the graduation rates of similar institutions—colleges and universities that share many characteristics and serve similar student populations.

National College Access Network (www.collegeaccess.org/NCAN)

NCAN has 161 member organizations, and all use their resources "to help motivated, academically capable, low-income young people enroll in and graduate from college. . . . Many members provide last dollar or gap scholarships to students who have been accepted into college but whose financial aid packages fall short of enabling the students to actually attend." There is an amazing Resources Library, oriented to professionals but of high interest to American Indian and Alaska Native students and parents. It includes information on

- Access
- Adult learners
- Early awareness
- Financial aid and affordability
- Minorities in higher education
- Persistence and success
- Policy
- Reference
- Resources available from the U.S. Department of Education
- Workforce development

Lumina Foundation for Education (www.luminafoundation.org)

Lumina is a "private, independent foundation, [that] strives to help people achieve their potential by expanding access and success in education beyond high school . . . and addresses issues that affect access and educational attainment among all students, particularly underserved student groups, including adult learners. The Foundation bases its mission on the belief that postsecondary education remains one of the most beneficial investments that individuals can make in themselves and that society can make in its people."

GEAR UP (www.ed.gov/programs/gearup)

This Web site describes that GEAR UP (Gaining Early Awareness and Readiness for Undergraduate Programs) is a discretionary grant program designed to increase the number of low-income students who are prepared to enter and succeed in postsecondary education. GEAR UP provides six-year grants to states and partnerships to provide services at high-poverty middle and high schools. GEAR UP grantees serve an entire cohort of students beginning no later than the seventh grade and follow the cohort through high school. Funds are also used to provide college scholarships to low-income students. One of the best state GEAR UP Web sites can be found in Montana (www.gearup.montana.edu). Its site starts off with the statement "that postsecondary education is possible for all Montana students, regardless of economic background, and strives to empower them to realize that ambition. Montana GEAR UP brings this message to middle and high schools, students, their parents, and the community through early college and career awareness activities, scholarships, financial aid information, and improved academic support to raise the expectations and achievement of all." Their On-Line Resources for college and career preparation are particularly helpful and include the following resources listed here.

- **Pathways to Success** (Montana Guaranteed Student Loan Program; www.mgslp.state.mt.us). This interactive planning tool is an excellent resource to use with middle school and high school students. The presentation features information about choices after high school and how to get to college.

- **Montana Career Information System** (Student Assistance Foundation of Montana; www.safmt.org). The Student Assistance Foundation (SAF) is a nonprofit entity dedicated to helping students finance their education. The Department of Labor and Industry allows SAF to provide access online for self-assessment and career and college planning.

- **College Is Possible** (American Council on Education; www.collegeispossible.org). College Is Possible is the American Council on Education's K–16 youth development program that motivates middle and high school students from underserved communities to seek a college education.

- **Bridges Transitions Co.** (www.bridges.com). Bridges is a provider of products and services used by schools, universities, and agencies to help people achieve education and career success. Other Bridges planning and exploration products give students and adults in transition assistance in exploring all their options, setting goals, and making plans to get there.

- **College Answer** (Sallie Mae; www.collegeanswer.com). College Answer (formerly known as Wired Scholar) is a site designed to prepare students and parents for the world of continuing education. The site has interactive tools and resources to help through all steps of postsecondary planning.

- **ACT** (www.act.org). ACT is a not-for-profit organization that helps people achieve their education and career goals. They are best known for the ACT test. The site offers extensive resources, links to products, and planning tools for students, parents, and educators.

- **College Board** (www.collegeboard.com). The College Board is a not-for-profit membership organization committed to excellence and equity in education. Among its best-known programs are the SAT, the PSAT/NMSQT, and the Advanced Placement Program. Their Web site features action plans for middle school and high school students and their parents.

- **Career Resources Network** (Montana Department of Labor and Industry; mcis.dli.state.mt.us). The Montana Career Resources Network is the state of Montana's resource for career and education decision making. The site features numerous resources (available for download) to use in lesson plans and activities related to college and career preparation.

- **Say Planning** (www.plansforme.org). This site features life event planning guides, including guides for college and career planning and college savings.

- **Decades of Decisions** (College Parents of America; www.collegeparents. org). College Parents of America (CPA) is a national membership association for current and future college parents. Decades of Decisions is one service CPA provides; it is a quarterly e-mail reminder for parents of seventh graders through college and offers information about what students and parents should do to plan ahead. CPA also offers an Ask the Experts column, a weekly e-newsletter about trends and education-related issues, and special discount deals with national partners for its members.
- **First Gov for Kids** (Federal Citizen Information Center; www.kids.gov). This is a U.S. government interagency kids' portal that offers links to federal kids' sites and is grouped by subject, including career information and activities.
- **Think College** (U.S. Department of Education; www.ed.gov/thinkcollege). This U.S. Department of Education site has special sections for parents whose children have not yet entered high school, high school–aged youth and their parents, and adults seeking to return to school.
- **Mapping Your Future** (www.mapping-your-future.org). General information on college admissions and financial aid, with a special emphasis on student loans. Developed by a coalition of state and private student loan guarantors.
- **National Association for Student Financial Aid Administrators** (www .nasfaa.org). Information on preparing for college academically and financially from campus financial aid administrators.
- **Preparing Your Child for College: A Resource Book for Parents** (U.S. Department of Education; www.ed.gov/pubs/Prepare). This very popular book is now available only online.
- **Developing Your Vision While Attending College** (American Indian College Fund and National Endowment for Financial Education; www .collegefund.org). Four books are available for download (in PDF format): *Making the Decision to Attend College*, *Paying for a College Education*, *Managing Your Money*, and *Choosing Your Path*.
- **National Association for College Admission Counseling (NACAC)** (www .nacac.com). The NACAC aims to support and advance the work of college admission counseling professionals as they help students realize their full educational potential, with particular emphasis on the transition from secondary schools to higher education. This site features resources for students and educators about postsecondary planning.

CollegeView (www.collegeview.com)

This is a Web site from Hobsons that "brings together educational and corporate recruiters with the students they want to reach-worldwide." This easy-to-navigate site is full of helpful information. The sophisticated college search menu allows you to locate institutions by a variety of characteristics (i.e., location, major, etc.). The financial aid menu helps you understand financial aid, gets you through the process, and provides advice from lenders. The application menu walks you through selecting and applying to a particular college whether you are coming right out of high school, transferring, or a returning adult student. The menu on campus life enables students to learn about what to expect on campus. The majors and careers menu allows you to explore majors and careers and prepare for your future.

ACT (www.act.org)

ACT's mission is to provide information for life's transitions. They provide the kind of information that helps individuals make better choices and develop their fullest potential.

WEB SITES DEDICATED TO IMPROVING NATIVE POSTSECONDARY ACCESS AND ACHIEVEMENT

U.S. Department of Education Student Aid on the Web (studentaid.ed.gov)

Please do yourself a favor and visit the U.S. Department of Education's Web site on student aid. You will notice a pull-down menu under the title, "If you are a(n) . . . " and there is a link to Native American that is specifically dedicated to you, your parents, counselors, and mentors, and offers additional links to educational information for Native communities. It begins by saying "Welcome to your source for federal student aid and other college information," and offers a user-friendly presentation of resources laid out as follows:

STUDENTS
What can you do at this site?
Start by creating a MyFSA user name and password so you can use the site's interactive tools and save the results of your searches to your own private account.
Then you can:

- Explore colleges to help you decide where to go
- Search for scholarships (try a keyword search for "native" or "tribal" or "Indian")
- Learn about financial aid offered by the U.S. Department of Education
- Get information about repaying student loans
- And more! We hope you enjoy taking a look around. (And don't forget to check out the links we've compiled for you.)

PARENTS
Use this site to help you prepare for your child's college education:

- Watch a federal student aid video with your child
- Learn about savings plans and education tax credits
- See what classes your child should take in high school on the College Preparation Checklist

COUNSELORS AND OTHER MENTORS
Explore our resources just for you:

- Plan a financial aid night
- Find a TRIO program (Upward Bound, Talent Search, etc.)

- Order free publications (including our "We have a bright future" poster for Natives) and videos
- See what college fairs and conferences the Federal Student Aid team will be attending

LINKS TO EDUCATION INFORMATION FOR THE NATIVE COMMUNITY
Government scholarships:

- Bureau of Indian Education
- Morris K. Udall Scholarship Program
- Health Professions Pregraduate Scholarship Program
- Tribal Lands Environmental Science Scholarship Program
- Scholarship for Service Program
- NIH Undergraduate Scholarship Program
- Harry S. Truman Scholarship
- Robert Byrd Honors Scholarship—contact your state higher education agency
- Benjamin A. Gilman International Scholarship

Other links that might interest you:

- U.S. Department of Education Office of Indian Education
- Tribal colleges

The American Indian Higher Education Consortium (www.aihec.org)

This Web site describes AIHEC's mission to support the work of tribal colleges and universities while being engaged in the national movement for tribal self-determination. The mission statement identifies four objectives:

1. maintain commonly held standards of quality in American Indian education;
2. support the development of new tribally controlled colleges;
3. promote and assist in the development of legislation to support American Indian higher education; and
4. encourage greater participation by American Indians in the development of higher education policy.

AIHEC offers links with an impressive array of sites to visit that should fulfill the interest of high school students looking for financial aid to high-level policy makers seeking ways to support American Indian and Alaska Native postsecondary access and achievement. The link to the *Tribal College Journal* should be of interest to students at any educational level; many of the articles in current and past issues are accessible online. An essay written by Marjane Ambler (editor of the *Tribal College Journal* since 1995) is quite appropriate to this guide.[1] She begins by saying,

Tribal colleges and universities often are asked to demonstrate their success by inappropriate standards. Is a tribal college successful if all of its graduates move to the city and get good jobs? Is a student successful if he or she earns a 3.0 grade point average? The answer to both of these questions is "not necessarily." Tribal college administrators care not only about what happens to the student but also about how the community is transformed by their graduates. (p. 8)

A survey of tribal college students found a deep sense of wanting to help their Indian communities. "Apparently these Indian students have absorbed an inclination toward altruism either while attending college or before they arrived. They expect their colleges to provide them with skills, knowledge, and talents they can share with others" (p. 8). Success to tribal college administrators and faculty takes on different meanings:

- preparing graduates for basic survival and to take care of themselves and their families.
- helping Native communities be successful and understand the mainstream society and what is required for them to prosper in it.
- being connected to Native communities.
- understanding who they are and coping with their feelings.
- gaining a sense of pride and high self-esteem.
- developing the skills to recognize and address social injustice.
- being culturally competent, well versed in the cultural values of their tribe.
- becoming good citizens, familiar with treaties, federal laws affecting Indians, and reservation economics.

Tribal college students engaged in their own focus groups identified success as:

- successful transfer to a four-year school,
- employment in their field of study,
- sense of self-confidence/achievement,
- competitiveness in the workforce, and
- status as a role model in the community, a leader.

Tribal college students all feel a sense of responsibility to be involved in cultural preservation and knowledge while being able to integrate Western and traditional tribal epistemologies. "The students pointed out the difference between education and wisdom. 'Some things you cannot learn from books,' one student said. They wanted to be able to celebrate both selves: the college-educated and the traditional American Indian."[2] AnnMaria Rousey and Erich Longie explain that a tribal college creates a family support system.[3] Retention is an issue that administrators, faculty, and staff take into account by seeing students' personal and family concerns as being relevant to the overall educational experience. "Traditional values are family values. This is an essential fact that may be overlooked by non-Indian faculty . . . who fail to see the connection between the cultural mission of tribal colleges and Indian families" (p. 1498).

Alaska Native Knowledge Network (www.ankn.uaf.edu)

This is an Alaska Rural System Initiative "partner designed to serve as a resource for compiling and exchanging information related to Alaska Native knowledge systems and ways of knowing. It has been established to assist Native people, government agencies, educators and the general public in gaining access to the knowledge base that Alaska Natives have acquired through cumulative experience over millennia." This Web site has an amazing array of resources that deal with:

- *Native Pathways to Education* that include Native organizations, conferences, and educational opportunities; oral tradition and cultural atlases; spirituality; Alaska Native languages; Alaska Native math and science education; elder and cultural camps; Alaska Natives claims settlement action; culturally based curriculum resources; and articles, speeches, and papers.
- *Alaska Native Cultural Resources* that include material from: Aleut-Alutiiq-Unangan/s-Sugpiaq, Athabascan, Iñupiaq/St. Lawrence Island Yupik, Tlingit-Haida-Tsimshian, Yup'ik/Cup'ik, and Alaska Native languages.
- *Indigenous Knowledge Systems* that offer resources about Alaska Native Science Commission; Science in the North and IPY (International Polar Year); cultural research, documentation, and impact analysis; cultural and intellectual property rights; traditional ecological knowledge; subsistence way of life; traditional health, medicine, and healing; and ecology, environment, and education.
- *Indigenous Education Worldwide* that covers Aborigine of Australia, Indigenous people of Africa, Ainu of Japan, American Indian, First Nations of Canada, Inuit, Maori of New Zealand, Indigenous peoples of Russia, Saami of Scandanavia, Native Hawaiian, Indigenous higher education, as well as other Indigenous organizations and conferences.

What will the American Indian and Alaska Native student who wants to be successful in college get out of the Alaska Native Knowledge Network Web site? The student will gain everything dealing with better understanding the depth of our cultural roots, the tenacity of our creativity, the humility of our power, and love of our ancestors. Visit this site with the intent of spending years gaining wisdom.

American Indian Graduate Center (www.aigc.com)

This has grown to become more than just a source of scholarship funding for American Indian and Alaska Native graduate students. The AIGC's vision statement seeks a transformation that draws on the spirit and traditions to prepare us and future generations to participate in the constructive revitalization of our respective communities. AIGC's "ultimate objective is self-sufficiency and self-determination within all Indian communities. People who are self-sufficient and self-determined are free to find meaning in their lives, to build quality lives, and to leave a legacy of wisdom for all humanity." AIGC staff members set high expectations and provide a climate where great things happen with the idea of achieving excellence in any areas we choose to pursue.

The circle of AIGC stakeholders invigorate a sense of community from the ground up to cultivate American Indian and Alaska Native "leaders with vision and clarity, who have the focus and direction that comes from a sure internal compass. We need people who are generous, energetic, and know how to connect with and nurture others. These new leaders must have the extraordinary skills to move through the barriers that have so often kept Indian leaders from achieving community visions: barriers like pessimism, discouragement, and dependence on outside sources." AIGC promises to "help plan and produce the social, economic and political changes needed to ensure the long-term positive development of our communities" by providing extraordinary numbers of talented, highly skilled, and exceptionally trained professionals. AIGC offers a range of services and resources that include undergraduate and graduate scholarships, an All Native American High School Academic Team, other resources and funding opportunities, leadership development, professional development, publications, and an annual conference that brings together the best and brightest students with tribal leaders, traditionalist, and Native scholars.

Catching the Dream, Inc. (www.catchingthedream.org)

This site has the primary focus "to raise funds to provide scholarship funding for high-achieving American Indians in the fields critical to the economic, social, environmental, political, educational, and business development of Indian communities." To supplement the focus on scholarship aid, CTD has programs to help Indian students prepare more thoroughly for college-level studies and improve the educational resources and programs that prepare these students for college. You will find their links to other scholarships valuable and overall tenor of the message to be fulfilling and inspiring.

College Horizons (www.collegehorizons.org)

College Horizons prepares Native Americans for undergraduate and graduate school. It offers a five-day training staffed by expert college counselors teamed up with college admission officers to help you:

- Select colleges suitable for you.
- Complete winning applications and write memorable essays.
- Learn what turns an applicant into an admitted student.
- Become a test-prep "whiz kid."
- Find your way through the financial aid/scholarship jungle.

Participants in the training learn about different types of colleges and universities and have the opportunity to establish enduring personal relationships with admission representatives and college counselors.

American Indian Science and Engineering Society (www.aises.org)

This group has the mission "to substantially increase the representation of American Indian and Alaskan Natives in engineering, science and other related technology disciplines." AISES has an amazing array of programs that would be of interest to American Indian and Alaska Native students.

- National American Indian Science and Engineering Fair (NAISEF). NAISEF offers great opportunity for K–12 students through cash prizes and scholarships students can win. In addition, the exposure and experience students gain stays with them as they progress through their college and professional careers.
- Teacher Development. Currently, the K–12 department offers a Professional Teacher Development Day at the annual national conference. In keeping with the spirit of support for Indian education, this day is fee free and open to all teachers of American Indian students.
- K–12 Affiliated Chapters Program. The program is open to all K–12 schools that have American Indian students. Membership offers the opportunity to participate in the annual NAISEF. Membership also offers opportunities to participate in outreach programs, workshops, summer programs, and other special AISES events.
- College Relations. AISES currently has over 160 college chapters nationwide, including 23 tribal colleges. Over the past year or so, AISES headquarters has undergone a comprehensive initiative to collect in-depth information from its constituent chapters and has also implemented a streamlined process for new chapter applications. Over the past few years, AISES has gained seven new chapters.
- Student Representatives. AISES college chapters are divided into seven regions, with a regional student representative for each. Alaska is in Region 1; Canada is split among Regions 1, 5, and 6; Hawaii is part of Region 2; the Upper Peninsula of Michigan is within Region 5. The student representatives coordinate with the regional representatives. The national student representatives are nonvoting members of the board of directors.
- Scholarships. AISES administers five distinct scholarships, in partnership with various organizations, as well as its own memorial scholarship. AISES scholarships are intended to supplement the unmet financial needs of qualified American Indian students pursuing degrees in science, engineering, and technology. The scholarship programs were created to ensure that deserving American Indian students could actively pursue higher education.
- Internships. AISES provides opportunities for college students to intern at a variety of agencies. Placements are made in several locations, including Washington, DC, and Atlanta, Georgia, as well as regional placements across the nation and some areas of Canada. Some international placements are available. In the past few years, this program has expanded in scope, and numbers of students gaining hands-on experience doing work that is closely related to their field of study and major.

Please consider getting a subscription to *Winds of Change* magazine (www .wocmag.org), "the only American Indian–published and nationally distributed full-color magazine with a focus on career and educational advancement for Native people. Articles highlight cross-cultural issues of interest to both Native and non-Native people." *Winds of Change* also publishes the *Annual College Guide for American Indians*.

Expanding the Circle (ici1.umn.edu/etc/curriculum)

This curriculum resource (available through the University of Minnesota for approximately $57), is intended to help American Indian and Alaska Native students transition from high school to college. It focuses on their mental, physical, spiritual, and emotional well-being while helping them learn how to set goals, organize, communicate, self-advocate, problem solve, and work in teams. Native youth explore who they are, what skills they need, and what their options are for life after high school by following the curriculum that is organized in four themes:

1. The Discovery theme provides activities that engage students in exploring and learning about who they are, what kind of personal expectations they have for themselves, who the key members of their family/community are that act as a support system for them, and how they learn.
2. The Framework theme focuses on the foundational skills and information students need when making their own plan for the future.
3. The Choice theme builds on the previous two themes, and students explore various post–high school options.
4. The Reflection theme includes culminating activities to be used as reflection on the skills learned and concepts explored during the Discovery, Framework, and Choice themes.

Principles of the curriculum are

- the belief in the resilience in American Indian youth and their communities.
- the value of humor in American Indian culture.
- the importance of the product and the process. Some activities have products, and others are more reflective in nature. The authors of the curriculum believe that the process and reflection are just as important as the products that are created.
- the awareness of sensitive topic areas. There are some areas in the curriculum that some individuals may feel are too sensitive or controversial, yet without addressing these issues, the transition process would not be complete.
- the conviction that although not all of the postsecondary options may be appropriate for all students, the purpose of exploration is to develop educated consumers who can make informed choices.

The American Indian Business Association (www.unm.edu/~aiba)

The American Indian Business Association (AIBA) is a service organization dedicated to supporting and encouraging American Indian people in their academic, personal, and professional pursuits. The AIBA seeks to

combine the spirituality of the Native world with the culture of the professional world. A balance of opportunities is provided by membership from
diverse fields of study and experience. As a service organization, AIBA
holds the primary goal of increasing the graduation rate of American Indians
in their academic endeavors and serving as a role model by promoting the
values of a formal education.

The Association of American Indian Physicians (www.aaip.com)

The AAIP was founded in 1971 as an educational, scientific, and chari-
table nonprofit corporation. Today, the AAIP fosters forums where modern
medicine combines with traditional healing to provide care for American
Indian and Alaska Native communities. Its mission today is "to pursue
excellence in Native American healthcare by promoting education in the
medical disciplines, honoring traditional healing principles and restoring
the balance of mind, body, and spirit." This is realized through direct services provided and educational and advancement opportunities presented
to American Indian and Alaska Native people in the medical professions as
well as referral and mentoring sponsorship of youth entering the medical
profession. Another major goal of AAIP is to motivate Native students to
remain in the academic pipeline and to pursue a career in the health professions and biomedical research, thereby increasing the numbers of medical
professionals and improving access to quality health care.

The AAIP maintains headquarters in Oklahoma City, Oklahoma; however,
educational forums and conferences are hosted throughout the year in different regions of the United States. American Indians and Alaska Natives are
served through direct service programs such as preadmissions workshops,
annual AAIP meetings, and cross-cultural medicine workshops. Additionally, through information and referral services, the AAIP provides leadership in various health care arenas affecting American Indians and Alaska
Natives, such as diabetes mellitus, HIV/AIDS, domestic violence, and
traditional medicine. In addition, the AAIP supports the Native Research
Network to provide a forum for collaboration among health providers and
researchers and the Association of Native American Medical Students to
encourage and nurture graduate health profession students.

National Native American Law Students Association
(www.nationalnalsa.org)

The NNALSA is committed to the success of Native American law students, exposing the legal community and the greater public to the issues
that Native American people and tribal governments face under the law,
and promoting the study of federal Indian law, tribal law, and traditional
forms of governance.

The benefits of membership are long lasting and valuable. The NNALSA
provides its members with great networking opportunities with fellow
Native American law students, Native American attorneys, tribal leaders,
and many others who work within and outside of the Indian law field.

Members can expect regular communications concerning organizational events and other news.

Each year, NNALSA members have access to the annual Washington, DC, Job Fair where firms, government agencies, and nonprofit legal advocacy agencies recruit members; the annual NNALSA Moot Court Competition, held at William Mitchell College of Law, St. Thomas University, Hamline University, and University of Minnesota in February 2007; the annual NNALSA Writing Competition, coordinated by the UCLA School of Law; and the NNALSA annual conference held in conjunction with the Federal Bar Association's Indian Law Conference.

STATE-SUPPORTED WEB SITES AND LINKS TO ASSIST PARENTS AND STUDENTS

State Higher Education Executive Officers (www.sheeo.org/access/access-home.htm)

SHEEO is an organization comprised of chief executive officers serving statewide governing boards and coordinating boards of higher education. Their multifaceted objectives and mission are to develop higher education institutions that fully meet the needs of society. Although somewhat oriented to the professional and a bit on the technical side, this Web site has wealth of information in the form of in-depth views of higher education issues, projects to promote access and achievement, data resources, and links to a large number of organizations.

SHEEO's one-stop shopping will provide immediate access to all the Web sites mentioned here and more, and valuable resources for students—all American Indian and Alaska Native students and parents might find them of interest. The information in Table 7.1 was gathered using SHEEO access

Table 7.1. Web Site Addresses of State Higher Education Offices/Systems and Links of Interest to Parents and Students

State	State Higher Education Web Addresses	Links of Interest to Parents and Students
AL	www.ache.state.al.us	www.ache.state.al.us/Students&Parents/CollegePrep.htm
AK	alaskaadvantage.state.ak.us/	alaskaadvantage.state.ak.us/page/292
AZ	www.abor.asu.edu	www.abor.asu.edu/3_for_students/students_section.html
AR	www.arkansashighered.com	www.arkansashighered.com/student_site/students.html
CA	www.cpec.ca.gov	www.cpec.ca.gov/CollegeGuide/CollegeGuide.asp
CO	www.state.co.us/cche_dir/hecche.html	www.state.co.us/cche/students/index.html
CT	www.ctdhe.org	www.ctdhe.org/sp.htm
DE	www.doe.state.de.us/high-ed	www.doe.k12.de.us/high-ed/publications.htm
DC	seo.dc.gov/seo/cwp/view,a,1222,q,535237.asp	seo.dc.gov/seo/cwp/view,A,1225,Q,536504,seoNav_GID,1511,seoNav,/31238/.asp
FL	www.flbog.org	www.fldoe.org/student

State	State Higher Education Web Addresses	Links of Interest to Parents and Students
GA	www.usg.edu	www.usg.edu/studentp.phtml
HI	www.hawaii.edu	www.hawaii.edu/prospective
ID	www.idahoboardofed.org	www.boardofed.idaho.gov/academics/index.asp
IL	www.ibhe.state.il.us	www.ibhe.state.il.us/Academic%20Affairs/p16.htm
IN	www.che.state.in.us	www.che.state.in.us/student
IA	www2.state.ia.us/regents	www2.state.ia.us/regents/StudentInfo/ studentparentinfo.html
KS	www.kansasregents.org	www.kansasregents.org/financial_aid/index.html
KY	www.cpe.state.ky.us	cpe.ky.gov/forstudents
LA	www.regents.state.la.us	www.regents.state.la.us/Students/parents.htm
ME	www.maine.edu	www.maine.edu/faqstudents.html
MD	www.mhec.state.md.us	www.mhec.state.md.us/preparing/index.asp
MA	www.mass.edu	www.mass.edu/a_f/home.asp
MI	www.michigan.gov	www.michigan.gov/som/ 0,1607,7-192-29940_32270-60361--,00.html
MN	www.mnscu.edu	www.mnscu.edu/students/index.html
MS	www.ihl.state.ms.us	www.ihl.state.ms.us/Academic_Affairs1/p&s.htm
MO	www.dhe.mo.gov	www.dhe.mo.gov/students.shtml
MT	www.montana.edu/mus	mus.montana.edu/preparingforcollege.htm
NE	www.ccpe.state.ne.us/ PublicDoc/CCPE/Default.asp	www.ccpe.state.ne.us/publicdoc/ccpe/ studentsparents.asp
NV	system.nevada.edu	system.nevada.edu/Initiative/index.htm
NH	www.usnh.unh.edu	www.usnh.unh.edu/grc/index.cfm
NJ	www.state.nj.us/highereducation	www.state.nj.us/highereducation/njedge/prospect.htm
NM	www.hed.state.nm.us	www.hed.state.nm.us
NY	www.highered.nysed.gov	www.highered.nysed.gov/kiap/COLLEGIATE/ home.html
NC	www.northcarolina.edu	www.northcarolina.edu/content.php/students/index .htm?submenu=0
ND	www.ndus.nodak.edu	www.ndus.nodak.edu/students
OH	www.regents.state.oh.us	www.regents.state.oh.us/students_parents.htm
OK	www.okhighered.org	www.okhighered.org/student-center
OR	www.ous.edu	www.ous.edu/ps_home.htm
PA	www.passhe.edu	www.passhe.edu/content/?/audiences/students
RI	www.ribghe.org	www.ribghe.org/students.htm
SC	www.che.sc.gov	www.che.sc.gov/New_Web/Students&Parents.htm
SD	www.ris.sdbor.edu	www.sdbor.edu/sdcollegeprep
TN	www.state.tn.us/thec	www.state.tn.us/thec/2004web/division_pages/ student_pages/students.html
TX	www.thecb.state.tx.us	www.collegefortexans.com/default2.cfm
UT	www.utahsbr.edu	www.utahsbr.edu/acad01b.html
VT	www.uvm.edu or web.vsc.edu	www.uvm.edu/parents or web.vsc.edu/SpecialPrograms/ tabid/75/Default.aspx
VI	www.schev.edu	www.schev.edu/Students/Students.asp?from=students
WA	www.hecb.wa.gov	www.hecb.wa.gov/Paying/index.asp
WV	www.hepc.wvnet.edu	www.hepc.wvnet.edu/students/index.html
WI	www.wisconsin.edu	www.wisconsin.edu/accessforyou/students
WY	www.uwyo.edu or www.commission.wcc.edu	uwadmnweb.uwyo.edu/uw/admissions

to individual state higher education organizations. We then visited each state higher education Web site to locate links to resources intended to assist students and parents in the college access and achievement world. *Enjoy.*

CONCLUSION

This chapter presents a selected number of Web sites that might be helpful to explore as you prepare yourself for college. At the same time, these and other Web sites can be essential to your success in college. You will want to visit a cross-section of these Web sites for your own benefit and the benefit of other American Indian and Alaska Native students. Often, something that you come across and learn about will be helpful to someone else. It is important to take notes about what helps you so that you can advise and guide other Native students who aspire to successfully obtain a college degree. It is in this manner that you can make a significant contribution to helping American Indian and Alaska Natives become overrepresented and do exceedingly well in college.

CHAPTER 8

Exemplary Four-Year Institutions and Tribal Colleges and Universities

The higher education journey can take you in a variety of directions. If you decide to attend a four-year college or university, you will have over 4,500 accredited institutions from which to choose in the United States. Of course, you want to find a college that is suited to your lifestyle and interests. As previously mentioned, this means making decisions based on location (close to home, in state, or out of state), setting (rural, small town, or city), costs and available financial aid, majors and coursework offered, as well as social and recreational opportunities that exist on campus and in the surrounding area. You will also want to ensure that you feel comfortable on a particular campus. For many Native students, this means looking for a strong Native presence at the college and opportunities to connect with your Native identity. There are a number of programs across the United States that have taken the lead in connecting with Native philosophy and culture. Some of these programs can be considered exemplary or as models of achievement in moving toward the ideal of high levels of Native student success and respect for tribal sovereignty and Native identity.

In this chapter, thirteen exemplary colleges and universities are described. We have selected these institutions based on their holistic approach to Native student recruitment and achievement. These institutions have established programs that work with Native students as they transition into college, provide a variety of opportunities to connect with Native culture through coursework and tribal partnership programs, and promote scholarship and research to benefit Native communities. In addition, these institutions promote development of leadership skills for Native students.

The following descriptions are intended to provide examples of the types of programs that you might look for as you search for the college that best meets your individual needs. The descriptions provided are organized by institutional type—private, four-year, and research colleges and universities. Information included was drawn from institutional Web sites with Native student enrollment and graduation data coming from the U.S. Department of Education (2004). We conclude with an overview of tribal colleges and universities, institutions that we think serve as the institutional benchmark of any higher education institution that desires to meet the needs of American Indian and Alaska Native students.

PRIVATE INSTITUTIONS

Dartmouth College

Dartmouth College in New Hampshire is a four-year, Ivy League institution with roots firmly embedded in providing education for Native youth. In fact, its founding mission in 1769 directly stated that Dartmouth was to provide educational opportunities for the "youth of Indian Tribes." Although inclusion of American Indian students was limited during its early years, Dartmouth recommitted itself to educating Indian youth in 1970. At that time, a Native American Program was established to recruit and retain Native students, and it involved holistic student support services inclusive of emotional, personal, and spiritual dimensions. Demonstrating a continuing commitment to Native students, each fall Dartmouth holds a Native American Student Fly-In Program. Associated costs are covered so that students with a definite interest in enrolling can experience the Native campus community and learn about its resources firsthand. Students accepted for enrollment receive financial aid to cover 100 percent of their documented need for four years of undergraduate education, and efforts are made to limit loans for students coming from middle- to low-income families, so that they can complete an undergraduate degree with minimal debt.

A range of undergraduate and graduate programs are available at Dartmouth, including graduate school opportunities to study medicine, engineering, and business. Through the Native American Studies (NAS) program, students can obtain either an undergraduate major or minor. The NAS program allows students to examine historical and contemporary issues, knowledge, accomplishments, and the political status of Native peoples, inclusive of Alaska, Hawaii, and Canada. Courses are taught by both Native and non-Native faculty. To foster leadership development, Native students benefit from a mentoring program that regularly brings tribal elders and leaders to reside on campus. Students have the option to go off campus to complete internships, ranging from cultural projects at the Smithsonian Institution to involvement in language preservation projects on reservations. In addition, Native students benefit from Dartmouth's status as a center for Native scholarship and intellectual activity. The college regularly hosts symposia that bring in tribal scholars from across North America. Students have access to resources of the Native American Studies research library, as well as the regular campus library, which houses extensive holdings of pertinence to Native peoples. Dartmouth's current enrollment includes 157 Native students from over 50 different tribes. The graduation rate for Native students is 72 percent.

Contact: Dartmouth College, Native American Program, 201 Collis Center, Hanover, NH 03755; (603) 646-2110; www.dartmouth.edu/~nap

Stanford University

Stanford University in California is another private, four-year institution that has established a strong Native presence. This came about as the result of the efforts of Native student leaders in the 1960s and 1970s to work with university administrators in creating the Stanford American Indian Association, followed shortly by the opening of the Native American Cultural Center and a Native theme house. Today, the Native community at Stanford is inclusive of American Indians, Alaska Natives, and Native Hawaiians. Muwekma-Tah-Ruk, the resident theme house, serves as a focal point for on-campus cultural activities, such as hosting Native poets and authors, as well as for organizing off-campus trips to local events, such as the San Francisco American Indian Film Festival and Indigenous People's Day events at Alcatraz Island. The Native American Cultural Center provides student support, starting with transition and orientation programs for freshman. Throughout their enrollment at Stanford, students have access to academic advising and assistance and small group mentoring to ensure they are prepared to meet rigorous academic expectations. Peer mentoring is provided through a Big Sib/Li'l Sib program.

A Native American Studies program along with excursions to tribal reservations and Native Hawaiian lands provide formal learning opportunities. Students also can become active in Native student organizations at a variety of levels. They organize one of the largest pow wows on the West Coast as a major regional event. Students have the opportunity to be mentored through LEAD (Leadership through Education, Activism and Diversity) as they initiate activities that lead to social change on campus. They contribute to *Coming Voice*, the Stanford Native community newsletter. In addition to an undergraduate focus, Stanford specifically strives to recruit and retain graduate students. Various organizations orient themselves to graduate student interests, such as the Stanford Native American Graduate Students, the Native American Law Student Association, and Stanford American Indian Medical Students. Stanford recognizes the accomplishments of its Native graduates by inducting a new member into its Alumni Hall of Fame each year. Two hundred undergraduate and graduate students who are members of more that 50 tribes are currently enrolled.

Contact: Stanford University, American Indian, Alaska Native and Native Hawaiian Program, Clubhouse #12, 524 Lasuen Mall, Stanford, CA 94305-3064; (650) 725-6944; www.stanford.edu/dept.nacc

Antioch University

Antioch is composed of six campuses located in various geographic areas of the United States. The Seattle campus is the focus here due to its exemplary efforts in reaching out to meet the needs of Native communities. Antioch University Seattle (AUS), a private, liberal arts college, provides a flexible curriculum designed to fit the needs of nontraditional learners while promoting positive educational change. Through the First Peoples' Partnership established with Muckleshoot Tribal College in Auburn, WA, AUS offers bachelor's and master's degrees in education. The First Peoples' education program prepares teachers to infuse the culture and perspectives of Coast Salish peoples into the educational process. Emphasis is placed on collaborative learning; a number of Native instructors teach courses, such as oral history, tribal law, and leadership. As part of the curriculum, students complete research that addresses Native cultural issues.

AUS has taken the lead with another educational innovation that holds much promise for Native communities—early college high schools. Through its Center for Native Education, in partnership with the Bill and Melinda Gates Foundation and several additional private foundations, Antioch is working with other educational institutions and tribes to broadly apply the early college high school model in various parts of the United States. The model allows students to take coursework that meets high school graduation requirements while simultaneously receiving up to two years of college credit. To date, ten sites in Western states are participating in the initiative with assistance from Antioch. These sites are located on or near reservations or in urban Indian communities so that Native students can access higher education while remaining in their home communities. Partnership with a Native community in the planning, implementation, and governance of the school is required, along with a focus on Native culture. Antioch recently extended the early college high school model to include an intergenerational component so that adults can take courses alongside the high school students. With funding from the Lumina Foundation for Education, the intergenerational initiative will bring Northwest Indian College into the partnership to develop course curricula centered on Native perspectives.

Contact: Antioch University Seattle, Center for Native Education, 2326 Sixth Avenue, Seattle, WA 98121-1814; (206) 441-5352; www.antiochsea.edu

PUBLIC FOUR-YEAR INSTITUTIONS

Northeastern State University (NSU)

Northeastern State University (NSU) in Oklahoma enrolls and graduates the largest number of undergraduate Native students in the country. NSU is located in Tahlequah, the capital of the Cherokee Nation, and offers a bachelor's degree in Cherokee language, Native American studies, and a variety of other majors such as law enforcement, education, and business. The Center for Tribal Studies leads the university in contributing to quality of life for Native communities. Student organizations affiliated with the center are active participants in carrying out this mission. For example, through the Indian University Scholars Society, Native students take on leadership roles by partnering with tribes to advance the study of sovereignty, tribal governments, and issues of concern to tribal communities. The NSU chapter of the American Indian Science and Engineering Society (AISES) has been recognized by the university and nationally for its student leadership and innovation in community service. The Native American Student Association strives to mentor high school students and assist with transition of new Native students into NSU. The center also sponsors the Annual Symposium on the American Indian, an event that brings together scholars from across the United States.

To promote achievement, Native students can access personal, academic, and career support services through the Center for Tribal Studies. As an example, the ASPIRE (American Indian Student Pre-Medical/Dental Identification Recruitment Education) program supports Native students who are interested in professional health careers. Native students receive assistance in obtaining scholarships, tutoring for sciences and math coursework, and opportunities to network with Native professionals. Students in the ASPIRE program take coursework that links Native culture to the well-being and health of tribal communities. Financial aid available to NSU students includes an American Indian nonresident tuition waiver. Various scholarships are available, including the Trail of Tears Scholarship for students of Cherokee descent. The center facilitates summer internship placements for students in both public and private organizations. NSU enrolls a total of 1,985 full-time, undergraduate students and 83 graduate students yearly. Three hundred twenty-five students receive bachelor's degrees on an annual basis.

Contact: Northeastern State University, Center for Tribal Studies, 320 Academy Street, Tahlequah, OK 74464; (918) 456-5511 x4350; arapaho.nsuok.edu/~cfts/services.htm

Montana State University (MSU) Bozeman

MSU Bozeman has demonstrated a strong commitment to Native student achievement while serving as a model for partnering with tribes and tribal colleges in the educational process. American Indian Research Opportunities (AIRO), a consortium among the seven tribal colleges in Montana and MSU Bozeman, was formed to increase the number of students prepared for careers in science, engineering, and mathematics. AIRO provides summer research opportunities for high school students and their teachers through the Montana Apprenticeship Program. The Bridging Tribal College Students to MSU program facilitates the transition process from tribal colleges into biomedical and health-related fields. The Initiative for Minority Student Development, the Montana Network for Biomedical Research, and the Leadership Alliance are other MSU-affiliated programs that provide advancement opportunities for Native undergraduate and graduate students. At the national level, the MSU Native nursing education program has been formally designated as an exemplar. Through the Native American Nurses—Caring for Our Own Program (CO-OP) Native students are provided with a comprehensive support network encompassing academic and financial aid assistance, culturally responsive advising, mentoring by Native professionals, and leadership preparation.

Students at MSU can receive a minor or a master's degree from the Department of Native American Studies. With an interdisciplinary focus, these degrees provide in-depth study of Native culture and prepare students for careers in tribal affairs. Furthermore, the department has dedicated itself to playing a leadership role in Native language preservation by establishing an endowed chair devoted to this cause. Students can be involved in various student organizations at MSU, such as the American Indian Student Council and AISES. The American Indian Peer Advisors is an organization that was started and is run by students to provide support for each other. Multiple academic and need-based scholarships and fee waivers are available to resident and nonresident Native students. MSU enrolls 198 full-time Native undergraduate students and graduates 28 per year.

Contact: Montana State University Bozeman, Native American Studies, 2-179 Wilson Hall, Bozeman, MT 59717-2340; www.montana.edu/wwwnas

The University of Alaska Fairbanks (UAF)

The University of Alaska Fairbanks serves as a role model in providing multiple educational programs designed to simultaneously benefit Native students and their communities. At UAF students can access 170 different degrees, several of which are centered on Alaska Native cultures and languages. These include a bachelor's or master's degree in rural development that prepares graduates to assume leadership roles in specific areas, such as tribal administration or Indigenous knowledge and research. Students can also attain majors or minors in Alaska Native studies or in Eskimo languages (Central Yup'ik and Inupiaq), as well as associate's degrees and certification in tribal management or Native language education. UAF has become particularly renowned for activities associated with its Alaska Native Language Center (ANLC). In addition to supporting degree programs, the ANLC works with communities to research and preserve the twenty Alaska Native languages. The status of the ANLC is reflected in its ability to acquire substantial funding to support its efforts, such as a recent $1 million grant from the U.S. Department of Education to focus on preservation of Athabascan languages, all of which are considered to be near extinction.

Elders play an important role in education for students at UAF. The Alaska Native Studies Department sponsors an Elders-in-Residence program where tradition bearers live on campus for an extended time each semester, allowing students to access their rich knowledge base during formal and informal interactions. Elders also serve as key educators through the Alaska Native Knowledge Network. Through this network UAF promotes the contributions of Native knowledge systems to both traditional and contemporary life in Alaska. The network has produced numerous publications and curriculum materials that draw heavily from the knowledge base of Alaska Native elders. Additional support is available to Native students at UAF through the Office of Multicultural Affairs and a variety of student organizations, such as the Native American Business Leaders, Alaska Natives in Psychology, and Alaska Native Social Workers Association. Those with an interest in science, mathematics, or engineering can participate in the Alaska Native Sciences and Engineering Program, which makes available scholarships, tutoring, study sessions, and internships. Native arts are celebrated on campus during the student-organized Festival of Native Arts, as well as via ongoing exhibits at the University of Alaska Museum of the North. UAF enrolls a total of 1,558 Native students, of which 542 are full-time undergraduates and 19 are full-time graduate students. Forty-eight Native students receive bachelor's degrees each year.

Contact: University of Alaska, Fairbanks, Office of Admissions, P.O. Box 757480, Fairbanks, AK 99775; (800) 478-1823; www.uaf.edu/admissions/diversity/academics.html

New Mexico State University (NMSU)

NMSU in Las Cruces strives to create an environment where Native students become role models and active contributors to the peace and well-being of tribal communities and society. The American Indian Program (AIP) lies at the core of these efforts facilitating a variety of student organizations and activities. Through the United Native American Organization (UNAO), students work toward increasing unity across NMSU students of varying tribal backgrounds, as well as build their leadership skills through activities that are designed to preserve and share the cultures of Native peoples. As an example, UNAO sponsors educational and social events associated with American Indian Week, such as the Pueblo Throw, arts, crafts, dancing, and the Miss NMSU Pageant. Native students can also participate in a student ambassador program that provides opportunities for public speaking and assisting with student recruitment. Available AIP student services include peer mentoring, educational advising, career enrichment programs, tutoring, scholarships, and access to a wide array of internship opportunities. Recognizing the importance of physical well-being, AIP sponsors a variety of intramural sports opportunities. NMSU is fundraising for construction of a Native American Cultural Center, a priority of the current university administration. It is anticipated that this center will enhance the capacity to provide service to Native communities.

Students can obtain a variety of degrees through NMSU. An interdisciplinary minor in Native American Indian studies complements coursework in majors, such as law enforcement and business. Several undergraduate research mentoring opportunities are available, including the New Mexico Alliance for Minority Participation and the Undergraduate Research Scholars Program. This latter program is funded by the Howard Hughes Medical Institute and facilitates the transition of students from New Mexico tribal and community colleges to NMSU science majors through mentoring in the research process with an associated monetary stipend. In addition, the Center for Border and Indigenous Educational Leadership has developed the Model of American Indian School Administration. Native students in this program work toward a master's degree while preparing to serve schools enrolling high percentages of Native students. An induction component extends mentoring beyond attainment of the degree to support new administrators in capitalizing on educational opportunities. NMSU enrolls 339 full-time Native undergraduate students and 33 Native graduate students per year, with 48 students awarded bachelor's degrees each year.

Contact: New Mexico State University, American Indian Program, Garcia Annex Building, Room 136, P.O. Box 30001, MSC 4188, Las Cruces, NM 88001-8003; (505) 646-4207; www.nmsu.edu/~aip

Fort Lewis College (FLC)

Fort Lewis College (FLC) is a public liberal arts college located in Durango, Colorado. It focuses on providing undergraduate education. Situated in close proximity to three reservations, FLC seeks to honor American Indian culture both on campus and in its outreach to the surrounding region. Based on recognition of treaty obligations, all Native students at FLC receive a full tuition waiver from the state of Colorado. A degree in Southwest studies with an emphasis in Native American studies is offered. Through this degree students can participate in the publication of a Native campus newspaper, the *Intertribal News*. They also have the option to study the Navajo language. The Native American Center serves as a hub for student support and a variety of cultural activities. Center staff members provide Native students with academic advising, assistance in obtaining financial aid, and workshops to promote personal growth. In addition, faculty make themselves accessible to students through regular office hours held at the center. A tutoring program employing Native students serves the entire campus community by making services available to Native and non-Native students.

A variety of student organizations play a substantial role in heightening American Indian visibility at FLC. The Indian Student Organization, referred to as Wanbli Ota ("Gathering of Eagles"), invites involvement of all students on campus. As one of the most active student organizations at FLC, it hosts Hozhoni Days, a major three-week campus event involving a pow wow, speaker series, and basketball tournament. FLC serves as home to the Bala-Sinem Choir. This intertribal choral group focuses on performing traditional Native music as well as preserving it. Students interested in tribal economic development and business careers can become involved in the American Indian Business Leaders organization, which provides opportunities for mentoring, networking, internships, and leadership development. FLC also participates in the Colorado Alliance for Minority Participation (CO-AMP), a collaborative partnership among four tribes and eleven Colorado colleges and universities, which focuses in part on increasing retention of Native students in science and engineering fields. CO-AMP, a program funded by the National Science Foundation, integrates cultural components into its mentoring and internship opportunities and facilitates the transition into career paths. Achievement of Native students across various fields is recognized through involvement in the Native American Honor Society. FLC enrolls 730 Native students (17 percent of full-time FLC undergraduate students), and 109 bachelor's degrees are conferred to Native students each year.

Contact: Fort Lewis College, Native American Center, 1000 Rim Drive, Durango, CO 81302; (970) 247-7221; nac.fortlewis.edu

Northern Arizona University (NAU)

Northern Arizona University (NAU) in Flagstaff has set a goal to be a nationally recognized leader in educating Native students, as well as in serving Native American tribes and nations. This has led to the development of a variety of precollege and transitional programs for Native students interested in pursuing higher education degrees, such as Talent Search, Upward Bound, and the Nizhoni Academy, a residential academic summer program. Students continue to be supported through their higher education journey with an array of programs. The Native American Student Services are available to all Native students, whereas other programs, such as the Native American Forestry Program and the Multicultural Engineering Program, support students in particular disciplines. Accomplishments of the College of Education in graduating Native students are particularly noteworthy. Students interested in general and special education careers can participate in Bilingual Rural Inclusive Development for General and Exceptional Education. Students who want to go on to pursue graduate coursework have the option of enrolling in the Faculty for Inclusive Rural/Multicultural Special-Educator Training or becoming a Dine/Hopi School Administrators fellow. Specialized coursework and stipends are available through other programs, such as Hopi Teachers for Hopi Schools or Alchini Ba (For the Children), a program designed for Navajo students.

To address its goal of providing service to tribal communities, NAU offers the Applied Indigenous Studies (AIS) program, which prepares students for leadership in building Native community capacity in areas of particular need, such economic development, environmental issues, and cultural resource management. To extend this preparation, NAU partners with the Navajo Nation Archaeology Department to provide employment and training for AIS and anthropology undergraduate and graduate students. Students interested in environmental sciences can also participate in summer research projects that benefit Native peoples through the Institute for Tribal Environmental Professionals or an environmental science program sponsored by the National Science Foundation. New NAU students aspiring to go into health professions or environmental studies can participate in mentored research activities through the Native American Student Research Awards Program. The NAU Institute for Native Americans serves the university by building and sustaining the multiple NAU programs designed to benefit Native tribes. A full listing of educational opportunities offered by NAU is available in the *Native American Programs at Northern Arizona University Handbook*, which can be found on the university Web site. NAU enrolls 757 full-time Native undergraduate students and 106 full-time graduate students, with 164 Native students receiving bachelor's degrees each year.

Contact: Northern Arizona University, Institute for Native Americans, Blome Building (Bldg. 2), Room 103, P.O. Box 4085, Flagstaff, AZ 86011-4085; www.nau.edu/ina

PUBLIC RESEARCH UNIVERSITIES

The University of Minnesota (UM) Twin Cities

UM Twin Cities is a public research institution that creates a sense of Native community on campus through its Circle of Indigenous Nations. With a family-oriented focus, the Circle fosters academic excellence while centering its services on cultural identity. Students are supported in becoming self-directed learners and in advocating for themselves and their home communities. The Circle of Indigenous Nations works jointly with the Department of American Indian Studies, the American Indian Student Cultural Center, and various student organizations to promote Indigenous values and perspectives within the educational process. A leader in the study of American Indians, UM was the first postsecondary institution in the country to establish a department devoted to this area. The department strives to construct and explore theories and methodologies that are consistent with Native ways of knowing. In addition, the department is actively involved in revitalization of the Ojibwe and Dakota languages. Two student organizations, the Ojibwe Language Society and the Dakota Language Society, extend departmental language preservation efforts. UM reaches out to Native communities by offering language courses with associated university credit to high school students via an interactive television system.

In recent years UM has established the American Indian Cultural House, a residence for new UM students. The intent of this living and learning community is to facilitate transition into the culture of academic life at the same time that students are supported in connecting with Native cultural values and traditions. Students residing in the Cultural House enroll in two courses as a cohort, an introductory American Indian studies course and a college skills course. In addition, the residents work together with student organizations to bring in Native speakers and traditional storytellers, as well as to put on pow wows. The university provides further support to students and Native programs by facilitating consultations with the UM American Indian Council of Elders. Various scholarships and tuition waivers are available to Native students who choose to pursue one of a variety of undergraduate, graduate, and professional degrees at UM, including law, medicine, engineering, and journalism. UM enrolls 330 Native students, including 58 graduate students per year. Approximately 27 bachelor's degrees are awarded yearly.

Contact: University of Minnesota Twin Cities, Circle of Indigenous Nations, 125 Fraser Hall, 106 Pleasant Street SE, Minneapolis, MN 55455; (612) 624-2555; www.mcae.umn.edu/circle/about.html

Arizona State University (ASU)

Arizona State leads the country in scholarship pertaining to American Indian and Alaska Native education. Through the Center for Indian Education the university focuses on building a knowledge base of educational practices that work for Native students. ASU students benefit from associated resources, including the center's publication of the *Journal of American Indian Education*, conferences, colloquia, and professional preparation opportunities for those interested in becoming teachers. In addition, ASU provides a wide range of services, leadership programs, community events, and other resources for Native students. The American Indian Institute and the Multicultural Student Center are active in recruitment and retention efforts. In partnership with three nearby tribes, the center takes a holistic approach to enhancing the cultural, spiritual, physical, and academic growth of students participating in the Native American Achievement Program (NAAP). The tribes take responsibility for providing financial support for NAAP participants, and ASU is responsible for supporting students as they strive to achieve academic and career-oriented goals and develop leadership and life skills.

Academic offerings at ASU include an American Indian studies program dedicated to preserving Native cultural identity and integrity, as well as to supporting student research carried out in partnership with tribal communities. Students involved in research have access to the Labriola National American Indian Data Center, an extensive collection inclusive of Native peoples in the United States and Canada. Students can pursue undergraduate and graduate degrees in a variety of other disciplines, such as nursing, law, business, and social work. Each of these majors is associated with an active Native student organization. ASU students can participate in a range of events centered on Native culture, such as a pow wow, music, a marketplace, and an art workshop. Cultural immersion tours take students beyond the campus to experience life in Native communities. ASU's commitment to Native student achievement is exemplified by the involvement of the former chair of the Navajo Nation in a position as a special advisor to the president of the university. ASU enrolls 731 full-time Native undergraduate students and 95 graduate students. Each year, 124 Native students receive bachelor's degrees. Interested individuals can access the American Indian Resource Guide on the ASU Web site for detailed descriptions of resources available to students.

Contact: Arizona State University, American Indian Institute, Engineering Annex Building (ECANX) 100, P.O. Box 879909, Tempe, AZ 85287-9909; (480) 965-8044; www.asu.edu/aii

The University of California, Los Angeles (UCLA)

UCLA, located near one of the largest urban Indian communities in the United States, has been at the forefront of research and scholarship in American Indian studies. Through the American Indian Studies Center (AISC), UCLA has attracted Native faculty who provide leadership on both national and international scales in producing conferences, multimedia educational materials, and research publications, including the *American Indian Culture and Research Journal*. AISC activities and projects enhance student learning across undergraduate and graduate levels, as well as provide predoctoral and postdoctoral fellowships to those aspiring to become academic and professional leaders. Recent conferences hosted by the AISC have addressed topics such as gaming, repatriation, the Indian Child Welfare Act, and federal recognition of tribes. Project HOOP (Honoring Our Origins and Our

People), sponsored by the AISC, promotes cultural renewal and education through community-based Native theater at tribal schools and tribal colleges and universities across the country. Project Peacemaker involves collaboration with tribal colleges and universities to create curricula in tribal justice. Another project, the Helping Path, focuses on the development and evaluation of educational materials that address breast cancer in a culturally responsive manner.

In addition to opportunities for involvement in AISC projects and conferences, UCLA students can pursue undergraduate and graduate degrees in a wide range of fields, including engineering and law. Students interested in engineering will find a well-established support network comprised of the Center for Under-represented Engineering Students and the Minority Engineering Program that provide mentorship, tutoring, and family-oriented social events for Native students. AISES is particularly active on campus, organizing events such as the yearly pow wow. In addition to the option of pursuing a major, minor, or master's degree in American Indian studies, UCLA offers a degree that combines American Indian studies with law. The intent is to provide graduates with a comprehensive understanding of Indian law and an enriched ability to provide legal service to Native communities. The American Indian Law Student Association is one of many Native student organizations on campus. Others include the American Indian Student Association, Women of Indian Descent, Retention of American Indians NOW, and the American Indian Graduate Student Association. Each year UCLA enrolls 107 Native undergraduate and 48 graduate students on a full-time basis, with 39 receiving bachelor's degrees.

Contact: University of California, Los Angeles, American Indian Studies Center, 3220 Campbell Hall, Los Angeles, CA 90095-1548; (310) 825-7315; www.aisc.ucla.edu

Washington State University (WSU)

Washington State University (WSU) has committed itself to honoring tribal sovereignty by establishing a memorandum of understanding with nine tribal nations of the Plateau region. In partnership with these tribes, WSU has formed the Plateau Center for American Indian Studies. This center extends educational opportunities for Native students by promoting cultural revitalization and research, as well as making university resources more accessible to tribal members. The main event sponsored by the center, the Plateau Conference, highlights Native scholarship by bringing elders and other tribal leaders to campus to share their knowledge with the university community. WSU further reaches out to tribes through the Clearinghouse on Native Teaching and Learning. The clearinghouse compiles curricular materials and makes them available to university students, as well as to teachers who serve students in Native communities, through a Web site and a campus library. In addition, it serves as a resource supporting research on issues of relevance to Native education.

Students can pursue undergraduate and graduate degrees in various fields at WSU, including engineering, education, speech and hearing sciences, and nursing. All of these programs make specific efforts to recruit and graduate Native students. In addition, students have the option of obtaining a minor or certificate in American Indian studies. Academic and personal support, as well as the opportunity for leadership development, is provided through the Native American Student Center. The center serves as home to various student organizations, including the Palouse Falls Intertribal Drum Group, Ku-Au-Mah (Native American student group whose name means "cougar" in Nez Perce), the Native American Women's Association, the Native American Graduate and Professional Student Organization, and the Native American Alliance. Events sponsored by these groups include the Pah-Loots-Pu Celebration, a pow wow that honors Native students, and the Native Women's Roundtable, a forum for alumnae to interact with current students, faculty, and staff. Some scholarships are available to Native students, including the Future Teachers of Color Scholarships, Creighton Scholarships for Native American Students in Allied Health Professions, and Plateau Scholarships. Tribes also nominate their outstanding high school seniors to participate in the Regents' Scholars Program. WSU enrolls 200 full-time Native undergraduate and 32 graduate students on a yearly basis, with 57 Native students receiving bachelor's degrees each year.

Contact: Washington State University, Native American Outreach Coordinator, Admissions Office, 370 Lighty Building, Pullman, WA 99164-1067; (509) 335-1358; www.wsu.edu/~naschome/org.htm

Summary

The four-year higher education institutions reviewed in this chapter are considered exemplars because they have shown a commitment to reaching out to Native students and communities in multiple ways. These institutions recognize that student recruitment efforts are important but are also aware that their efforts must go further. Once students are enrolled, an environment that values Native culture must exist. This might be evidenced through courses taught by Native faculty with tribal elder involvement, the presence of culturally relevant content and teaching strategies in the curriculum, Native cultural organizations, celebration of traditional Native events, and support services specific to Native students. In recognition of tribal sovereignty, you could expect to see a means for tribes to be involved in establishing university policies, as well as partnership programs in which tribes determine directions for connecting with Native communities.

The institutions selected for review here represent only a small sample of those available to Native students. Each year the programs of 200 four-year colleges and universities are selected for inclusion in the *Winds of Change Annual College Guide*.[1] To be included in this review, each institution must enroll a substantial number of Native students and demonstrate that a high percentage of them graduate. As you proceed with your search for the college that best meets your needs, this guide will be a valuable source of information regarding additional college and university opportunities for you to consider.

TRIBAL COLLEGES AND UNIVERSITIES

"Tribal colleges are true community institutions—they are involved in almost every aspect of local community life, ranging from the provision of public services to the nurturing of traditional cultural values and beliefs that help develop a social and economic vision for the future."[2] Tribal colleges and universities (TCUs) represent one of the most important recent developments in higher education for American Indians and Alaska Natives. Since the founding of the first tribally controlled college in 1968, the total number of TCUs in the United States has grown to thirty-four with one additional college located in Canada (www.aihec.org). Student enrollment has increased steadily so that today 15,800 students are enrolled in TCUs, of which 82 percent are American Indian and Alaska Native (see Table 8.1). Native student enrollment at TCUs is growing at a much faster rate compared with Native student higher education enrollment overall, with 32 percent enrollment growth at TCUs and 16 percent enrollment grow in general.[3] It is obvious that TCUs are reaching out to meet the educational needs of Native students like no other kind of educational institution has done before.

Table 8.1. Number and Percentage of American Indians and Alaska Natives Enrolled in Accredited Tribally Controlled Colleges and Universities (Fall 2002)

Institution	Location	Total	American Indian/Alaska Native	Percent American Indian/Alaska Native
Bay Mills Community College	Brimley, MI	430	237	55.1
Blackfeet Community College	Browning, MT	418	402	96.2
Candeska Cikana Community College	Fort Totten, ND	160	157	98.1
Chief Dull Knife College	Lame Deer, MT	268	207	77.2
College of the Menominee Nation	Kashena, WI	530	409	77.2
Crownpoint Institute of Technology	Crownpoint, NM	283	279	98.6
D-Q University	Davis, CA	251	88	35.1
Dine College	Tsaile, AZ	1,822	1,764	96.8
Fond du Lac Tribal and Community College	Cloquet, MN	1,315	316	24.0
Fort Belknap College	Harlem, MT	158	136	86.1
Fort Berthold Community College	New Town, ND	249	233	93.6
Fort Peck Community College	Poplar, MT	443	353	79.7
Haskell Indian Nations University	Lawrence, KS	887	887	100.0
Institute of American Indian Arts	Santa Fe, NM	155	150	96.8
Lac Courte Oreilles Ojibwa Community College	Hayward, WI	550	421	76.5
Leech Lake Tribal College	Cass Lake, MN	244	226	92.6
Little Big Horn College	Crow Agency, MT	275	265	96.4
Little Priest Tribal College	Winnebago, NE	146	126	86.3

Institution	Location	Total	American Indian/Alaska Native	Percent American Indian/Alaska Native
Nebraska Indian Community College	Macy, NE	118	90	76.3
Northwest Indian College	Bellingham, WA	667	525	78.7
Oglala Lakota College	Kyle, SD	1,279	1,124	87.9
Saginaw Chippewa Tribal College	Mount Pleasant, MI	41	35	85.4
Salish Kootenai College	Pablo, MT	1,109	885	79.8
Sinte Gleska University	Rosebud, SD	787	787	100.0
Sisseton Wahpeton Community College	Sisseton, SD	285	238	83.5
Si Tanka College	Eagle Butte, SD	434	309	71.2
Sitting Bull College	Fort Yates, ND	214	190	88.8
Southwestern Indian Polytechnic Institute	Albuquerque, NM	777	777	100.0
Stone Child College	Box Elder, MT	83	78	94.0
Turtle Mountain Community College	Belcourt, ND	897	833	92.9
United Tribes Technical College	Bismarck, ND	463	423	91.4
White Earth Tribal and Community College	Mahnomen, MN	99	74	74.7
Total enrollment		**15,837**	**13,024**	**82.2 (average)**

Source: U.S. Department of Education, National Center for Educational Statistics, *Digest of Education Statistics, 2004* (forthcoming), based on Integrated Postsecondary Education System (IPEDS), Spring 2003.
These colleges are, with few exceptions, located on reservations. They are all members of AIHEC. The U.S. Department of Education, Office for Civil Rights maintains the U.S. Department of Education Minority Postsecondary Institution listing, which includes a listing of tribally controlled colleges.

What makes educational opportunities at a TCU different from those provided by other institutions? As shown in Table 8.2, a TCU is a tribally controlled postsecondary institution with the mission to provide educational opportunities for tribal members and other potential students that lead to various levels of college degrees. It is an enterprise operating under the sovereign authority of a particular tribal government or board of trustees largely comprised of Native people. All TCUs are increasingly recognized as being responsive to the dynamic educational and enduring cultural needs of American Indian and Alaska Native communities. The core values of a TCU include considerations for extended families living in a modern and changing world. TCUs place a high premium on recognizing the importance of education with an emphasis on culture and customs. Inherent to this position is the value and importance of the environment and the value of protecting it for future generations. TCUs are often positioned to provide supportive leadership in curricular planning for a wide variety of programs throughout the tribal community.

Table 8.2. Degrees Offered at Tribal Colleges and Universities

Institution Name	> 1-year Certif.	1-year Certif.	Assoc. Degree	2-year Degree	BA Degree	Post-Bacc.	Master's Degree
Bay Mills Community College	X	X	X	X			
Blackfeet Community College	X	X	X				
Cankdeska Cikana Community College	X	X	X	X			
Cheyenne River Community College		X	X	X			
Chief Dull Knife College		X	X				
College of Menominee Nation	X	X	X				
Crownpoint Institute of Technology	X	X	X				
D-Q University	X	X	X		X		
Diné College		X	X				
Fond du Lac Tribal and Community College		X	X				
Fort Belknap College		X	X				
Fort Berthold Community College	X	X	X				
Fort Peck Community College		X	X				
Haskell Indian Nations University	X	X	X		X		
Ilisagvik College		X	X				
Institute of American Indian Arts			X				
Keweenaw Baj Ojibwa Community College		X	X	X			
Lac Courte Oreilles Ojibwa Community College	X	X	X				
Leech Lake Tribal College		X	X				
Little Big Horn College		X	X				
Little Priest Tribal College	X	X	X	X			
Muckleshoot Tribal College	X	X	X		X		
Nebraska Indian Community College	X	X	X		X		
Northwest Indian College	X	X	X				
Oglala Lakota College			X		X	X	X
Red Crow Community College	X	X	X	X			
Saginaw Chippewa Tribal College		X	X				
Salish Kootenai College		X	X		X		
Sinte Gleska University		X	X	X	X		X
Sisseton Wahpeton College		X	X				
Si Tanka University			X		X		
Sitting Bull College	X		X				

Institution Name	> 1-year Certif.	1-year Certif.	Assoc. Degree	2-year Degree	BA Degree	Post-Bacc.	Master's Degree
Southwestern Indian Polytechnic Institute	X	X	X	X			
Stone Child College		X	X				
Tohono O'odham Community College		X	X				
Turtle Mountain Community College	X	X	X	X			
United Tribe Technical College		X	X				
White Earth Tribal and Community College		X	X				

There is a widening view within Native communities that a TCU can engage community members in the long-term continuation of their intellectual, emotional, physical, and spiritual growth. Perhaps most important, TCU curricula can extend beyond the institution to become a core element in all aspects of community functioning. A TCU offers a number of benefits along the following themes: (a) responding to community needs, (b) supporting individual community members' goals to pursue higher education, (c) preserving and revitalizing traditional language and culture, and (d) facilitating community healing.

Educational attainment is a concern among American Indians and Alaska Natives across the continent. Although overall enrollment in many postsecondary institutions is lagging, as mentioned previously, TCU enrollment has risen. National figures showing high dropout rates and low graduation rates reinforce the important role that a TCU can provide to American Indian and Alaska Native people. Without such services, we effectively curtail any opportunity to meet the needs of many Native students. The increased earning potential associated with greater amounts of educational attainment is unarguable, and the figures showing college-going characteristics are important to keep in mind for the success of Native students in postsecondary institutions.

North American society has experienced a shift to knowledge jobs that calls for workers who possess skills that extend beyond basic academics to include problem-solving, critical-thinking, interpersonal communication, occupational, and attitudinal skills. More than ever, a two- and four-year college degree, other postsecondary credentials, or on-the-job training are increasingly important for American Indians and Alaska Natives looking to secure a good job. Today, more than two-thirds of all workers in growing, well-paying occupations have postsecondary education (office jobs, education/health care jobs, technology jobs). It is obvious that the tribal community economic and civic well-being depends on significantly improving American Indian and Alaska Native student success along the educational pathways.

It seems difficult to imagine true economic diversification or community development if people do not want to pursue postsecondary educational opportunities. By getting a college education you can be of service to your community and to Native people in general. The consequence of not pursuing a college education is the risk of a reality where economic development and community stability remains nonexistent in your tribal communities and programs. The other scenario is that economic and community development outpace tribal members' qualifications and capabilities, leaving no recourse but to hire (non-Native) talent outside the boundaries of a Native community to maintain profitability.

TCUs are sending a message to you and other community members that higher education aspirations are attainable, affordable, and positive. This message cultivates hope for all community members, particularly when they need it most. When we talk about public safety and how more people are seeking treatment, there has to be something in their lives to replace the drinking and drug abuse or it will be all too likely that community members will return to that abyss and associated risky behaviors. TCUs provide new possibilities for changing patterns built on centuries of despair and hopelessness.

A common theme expressed by all TCUs is a high level of commitment to culture and community. TCUs draw on ancestral knowledge as a source of strength and insight in addressing the community issues of today. A walk through a TCU campus reveals buildings adorned with cultural symbols, artwork, images of tribal heroes, respected elders, and other tribal members who have made significant contributions to the well-being of the tribal community. TCUs further honor tribal ancestors by centering their curricula on cultural identity by creating courses emphasizing traditional ways of knowing, teaching Native languages and history, as well as bringing back art, music, and dance as legitimate areas of study. People find strength in the promise of a TCU; many Native people know how difficult it was to pursue postsecondary education opportunities before there was a TCU in their community. Times have changed, so it is entirely possible for you to get a college degree; through TCUs you are free to make and pursue this choice. This has not always been the case through much of the history of American Indian and Alaska Native peoples.

The benefits of a TCU are grounded in the community in which it exists. TCUs represent the ultimate manifestation of tribal self-determination with community members controlling all aspects of the school's operation. As such, TCUs demonstrate a shift in power from outside entities controlling local educational practices to the tribal communities controlling the mission, scope, and functioning of higher education. Marjane Ambler describes TCUs as being "of the community, by the community, and for the community."[4] She goes on to state that "tribal colleges . . . have a direct local connection to the fate of their communities. They are committed to transforming their communities, one graduate at a time" (p. 9).

The outgrowth creates educational opportunities that simultaneously allow tribal communities to build their community infrastructures and promote participation in the TCU movement and larger democratic society of the United States. Those associated with the development of TCUs see the need for a range of postsecondary educational opportunities to provide community members with knowledge and skills necessary to reconstruct community infrastructures essential to renewed prosperity and community well-being. The community-based nature of a TCU makes it optimally suited to serve as a resource for the people.

TCU students are the investments manifesting the long-term visions of American Indian and Alaska Native people. By looking at the goals, structure, outcomes, and the impact of a TCU, it is clear that an investment made in the college is more than just economic. True education costs money, which can be easily measured. The investment in education produces economic benefits to individuals and the community, but just as important are the noneconomic benefits that result from an educational investment in the people. In the past 300 years, life has changed dramatically for Indigenous people. Even though there has been little opportunity to completely recuperate from the atrocities of settler contact, genocide, disease, and assimilation, Native people continue to keep pace with the changes of the modern day. A TCU is committed to refining the strengths of the tribe and community by providing a place and space to maximize individual potential by defining the self, positively represent the tribe by opening doors to employment and further education, and promote tribal sustainability and self-determination through a culturally sensitive curriculum while envisioning and building a future that authentically serves the people of a tribal community.

Strengthening Identity by Learning Close to Home

TCUs are helping students strengthen their cultural identity by learning close to home. In the past, the distance from higher education institutions prevented potential students from pursuit of their dreams. Many TCU students who had experienced other colleges acknowledged that the distance between home and school forced them to separate their life in unnatural and ineffective ways. They felt a lack of ownership at other colleges and a lack of desire to fully invest and apply themselves; there was a sense of "being a number, not a name," and responsiveness to their cultural backgrounds was limited. In contrast, students attending TCUs have expressed a strong desire to apply themselves because of the engaging and relevant teaching methods and culturally adapted curriculum. Having a TCU located directly in a Native community ensures that a college education is available and accessible for community members who want to increase their potential. Additionally, many people have more clearly recognized the value of education because the tribe is supporting it wholeheartedly.

Welcoming, Encouraging Environment

TCU students often feel that a sense of family is created the moment they enter the school and this feeling is sustained long after graduation.

First impressions can last a long time. When new students come to the front desk of a TCU to get information and sign up, they regularly indicate that the college staff want them to have an experience of overwhelmingly positive significance. Many American Indian and Alaska Native students have not been enrolled in school for decades. This might be you or somebody you know. Maybe every educational experience you had in the past was isolating, alienating, and negative. Maybe you don't know what your potential skills and values are. Maybe someone else pushed you to enroll in college. Maybe other students came on their own volition, confident that their curiosity will lead them to success.

Regardless of the situation, how you approach the moment you enter college can make the difference in your success. A lesson learned from many TCU students experiencing apprehension on coming to campus is that it is comforting to relax by having a meal and taking a tour to see all that the campus has to offer. Your goal is to immediately immerse yourself as deeply as possible into the offices and classrooms, as well as meeting some of the people you will have contact with on a regular basis. As a new student, is important to feel like the college is there for you and to have no doubt that you can do it.

Personal Growth, Self-Development, and Self-Esteem

We have found that many TCU students had negative experiences in public schools and other colleges; they were humiliated, stereotyped, in the "wrong crowd," scared, made to feel dumb or stupid, felt alienated and lost and unaccepted, and many used alcohol or drugs to compensate or dull the pain. For many of these individuals, more education meant more grief. Historically, education has been used as a weapon against Native people; boarding schools mandated the assimilation of Native people into white culture through atrocious methods that denied the existence of a positive Native identity and modern public schools are not free of institutionalized racism. This is the legacy that TCU combats through patience and effort and you can take that attitude anywhere you go.

One of the most important aspects of a TCU is that every American Indian and Alaska Native student knows that the college was created for them; the staff try to get every student to recognize their importance and that they deserve and even need to be at the college. Due to the honesty of the staff of a TCU, the students know that they are not alone in their history and present obstacles, but instead they are welcomed, accepted, and embraced as they are. This encouragement is the prerequisite to confidence; when you are aware that you are believed in and supported, success becomes tangible and inevitable. We want you to succeed in college and in life and know that you can do it.

When you open the doors to pursing a college education, the metaphorical doors of life open as well. Through patience and an ever-present sense of humor, you can quickly dissolve fears and open avenues of possibility. The future becomes a beautiful landscape with infinite opportunities and possibilities; setting goals and pursuing dreams becomes second nature and a lifelong agenda. Of course, TCU students cite an incredibly immediate boost in professional skills and personal confidence once they begin a program; by taking personal responsibility, high standards are set for and by each individual. You can enjoy this as well.

Enroll in a college that shows you respect and it will cultivate your own self-respect, which leads to distinguished treatment of others. Developing the habit of going to school can create positive routines and effective habits. A college degree is at the center of many Native students' achievements. It is not by any means an end point but a center from which to expand exponentially in any direction you choose.

Being successful in college may mean cultivating a commitment to ongoing self-evaluation and lifestyle awareness. Because of your college enrollment, you may find your aspirations growing on a daily basis. Many Native students experiencing substance abuse have found the courage to enter substance abuse treatment centers so that they will be spiritually and emotionally equipped to continue on their postsecondary education. It may just be the time that Native students recognize that it is possible to be successful and feel good about oneself without drugs or alcohol. Moving beyond your current status of education to the pursuit of other dreams is the right thing to do.

Commitment to the Family

We have found that many TCU students express a desire for self-development and personal growth, but evidently students also wish to instill a sense of pride in their families. Some Native students express that they want their parents to be proud of them for activating their potential; they want their family to know that they did a good job of raising them—so good that they are continuing that job by bettering themselves. Other students want to show their children that education promotes more than just better economic opportunities: it instills a sense of pride. Those students who are in college for the sake of their children want to show their descendants that they can choose a path to better themselves at any age. That may be you.

You may be a sixty-two-year-old student who got a GED in part because you wanted to show your children that it is never too late to drop bad habits and adopt new strategies. You could be a young mother who wants her young son to say, "That's my mother!" which is something you may not have felt your child could always say with pride. The individuals who are in school for their children want to be positive role models for them, showing that at any point, even rock bottom, determination, desire, and dedication will lead them to the right path. Is that you or somebody you know?

Are you a middle-aged man who recently graduated from a TCU program, community college, or another college who wants your young daughter to be proud of her Dad? Do you want to show her that you know ways to successfully provide a good life for yourself and create a clear pathway for her? As your child grows older, be the type of father who knows that his daughter will be able to choose a path of self-improvement and stop the cycle of despair that has gripped Native families for generations. You want to be a source of knowledge and wisdom for her, and the Creator will guide you on this sacred path.

You could be experiencing the awakening that you are not getting any younger and have felt an intense sense of immediacy to pursue college-level studies. You are acutely aware of your limited time on this planet—your children are growing up quickly, and you want to be able to do more than just provide for them. It is all right to want your life work to be an example and a lesson to your children. When you tell them how much you care about them and their future, you want to be able to show all your children how and why you can experience success in college.

You might feel a sense of immediacy that is a response to environmental destruction that takes place on reservations and in villages across the country. Your ultimate goal could be to become a wildlife manager or involved in managing natural resources, a mainstay of many TCUs. You're the type of student who wants to be outside, protecting the resources that will guarantee a future of abundance for your people and forthcoming generations. At heart is the desire to instill in present and future generations the cultural values that will lead them to fully appreciate, utilize, and protect the natural world, and know that the best way to teach children is to lead by example.

You might be a person who dropped out of high school in her junior year to take care of her sick grandmother; at the time, nothing else mattered besides helping her. After she passed away, you could not get the nerve to go back to school. Years later, with encouragement and the educational success of others in your community to guide you, you decide it is time to take responsibility for yourself. In time there emerges an acknowledgment that you are only letting yourself down by not finishing earlier, and now you will fix that by pursuing your education. You finish your GED and have decided to enroll in college courses and are using this book to guide your success.

Pride in Tribal Community

As with a TCU's presence in the community, a widespread culture of support for getting a higher education ensures the accessibility of education to all who seek it to activate and fulfill dreams that can be achieved without sacrificing tribal identity. Through the cultivation of a sense of ownership in an institution of value and quality, community members are not stuck in a predetermined box; the responsive nature of TCUs allows for the parallel evolutions of individuals and programs that the individuals desire. Many students take great pride in being able to represent a TCU in a positive light through their educational successes, and it behooves mainstream predominantly white postsecondary institutions to take notice.

Because of the prior success of American Indian and Alaska Native college graduates who return home, many Native communities are becoming rich in knowledge on their own volition, independent from outside planners. This self-developed programming creates a value shift in the minds of the community. Imagine yourself among other American Indian and Alaska Native college graduates who respect the core tribal values and in turn place more value on advancing tribal culture. This sense of personal pride is contagious and results in a sense of community and tribal pride, which makes more people seek out education so they, too, can offer more to their community and culture. This snowballs into more associations with more people and social confidence surges, creating a continuous dialogue among community members. People become happy with themselves and each other, creating a populace unified in their commitment to community betterment. Can you imagine the possibility of creating such a rewarding reality?

The development of tribal knowledge along with skills for employment creates an attitude of comfort when it comes to taking leadership roles in the community. The TCU's role allows tribal business and services to know the educational experiences of potential employees and can employ quality people who have community pride embedded in their ethics, along with a community-based concept of professionalism. This reinforces tribal identity among employees, customers, and others who receive tribal services; sovereignty is intentionally enacted on a daily basis through a commitment to the mutual improvement of the community. You might be the student who intends to remain in the tribal workforce and hopes to serve your community as a reflection of what can be gained through educational pursuit. Your individual experience fluently ties together the concepts of culturally specific education to traditional tribal self-determination and individual and community improvement. Ultimately, people like you are influencing others to better themselves.

The stories of student success and pride are numerous and positively overwhelming. Through TCUs, students' skills have been validated, and they are ready to continue the pursuit of their dreams. Due to the educational opportunities in their home communities that support a sense of self-value, students at a TCU learn that everyone is a teacher, a counselor, a learner, and a human capable of everything their hearts and minds envision. Clearly, TCU students present themselves to their families and communities with pride and encouragement, as well as giving joy and respect to the legacies of those of the tribal community who have passed on.

CHAPTER 9

The Circle of Success

Student Voices

- I dared to dream.
- When someone is there who's shown you that your dreams are possible, there's no limit.

It all starts with a dream. Envision yourself five years from now, ten years from now. Where do you want to be? What do you want to be doing? Now hold that vision. Will it require an associate's degree? A bachelor's degree? Or maybe even a graduate degree? Higher education can take you toward that dream—but you have to hold on to that vision of the person you want to become and let it carry you forward.

WHAT IS SUCCESS?

This is a book about the success of American Indian and Alaska Native peoples in higher education. So what does it mean for a Native student to be successful? The way that success is conceptualized is grounded in one's individual and collective identity. For American Indian and Alaska Native students, Native identity will provide the framework through which success is defined. In fact, when American Indian and Alaska Native college students and graduates were asked to describe success in higher education, their responses showed wide variation. This highlighted the fact that each student is an individual with his or her own view of the world. Examples of responses follow.

- Learning to negotiate cultures—your own Native culture and the academic culture.
- Researching and working with the [tribal] culture.
- Benefit my tribal community in some way—know that education is not just for yourself.
- Self-sufficiency—I can support myself, my family, and my extended family.
- Develop and exercise self-determination.
- To develop a voice and be part of decision making.
- Getting a degree and being able to help in ways I couldn't before allows me to dig deeper into my community and be more integral to its success. I particularly look forward to helping Native kids who might fall through the system's cracks succeed.
- Come back, stay in the community they love, and work for the community.
- Use the knowledge I have obtained to help my students—to see progress in the people I help.
- I am a role model in a position to make change in education—it is my responsibility to teach others where I am with my degree.
- You are a role model. Everyone is so proud of you. You've made it.
- You are respected by your colleagues and community members for making an effort to complete your course studies to obtain your degree. You are knowledgeable in your field of study. You understand what people are talking about if they talk about coursework or concerns. You feel a sense of accomplishment and completion.
- Meet my goals and objectives.
- To finish what you have begun. See it through. To be able to pass on that knowledge.
- Ability to learn—a passion for learning—openness to new ideas.
- To grow personally and professionally.
- Demonstrate your potential—skills and knowledge open a door for you.
- It's an accomplishment, a milestone, one of the best things that mainstream culture has to offer me.

These comments from American Indian and Alaska Native students and graduates collectively reveal a clear sense of pride in goals accomplished and new knowledge and skills gained. A foundation for lifelong learning has been established. These students and graduates see themselves as empowered to make changes in their personal lives as well as contributions to their families, communities, and tribes. They see themselves as ready to be role models and decision makers and to implement self-determination. There is an underlying desire to give back to American Indian and Alaska

Native peoples and society in general. Success grows with learning to live into tomorrow. These individuals are experiencing success—and you can, too. Hold on to your dream.

THE JOURNEY OF SUCCESS

Our depiction of the journey of college success takes on a circular form (see Figure 9.1). The circle communicates a continuous cycle where all elements are interconnected and interact with one another. At the core of the circle lies cultural identity. Pathways through college revolve around this foundation of cultural identity. Immediately surrounding the core circle are individual, family, community, and tribe. The close proximity to cultural identity illustrates the strong linkage across all of these dimensions. The outer circle represents, first, what you do to prepare for transitioning into your college pathways. This preparation then leads to your actual experience of higher education. The journey comes full circle with the final linkage representing the possibilities created by a college education for returning to serve your home community, tribe, and the broader world. Each of these elements will be described further.

THE CORE OF THE CIRCLE OF SUCCESS: CULTURAL IDENTITY—IT'S COMPLEX

Identity is a concept grounded in the diversity and complexity of human beings and their social groups. It is important to recognize that identity has

Figure 9.1. The Circle of Success for American Indian and Alaska Native Students in Higher Education

components that make each one of us a unique individual. At the same time we are brought together in groups sharing commonalities in the ways we identify ourselves, the values we hold, and the way we choose to live our lives. As social beings we communicate and interact with each other through shared languages, stories, gestures, and mannerisms. Our languages may be passed down through the oral tradition or may have been recorded in a written form. What is important is that we have the choice to define who we are, decide what is important to us, communicate with each other in the way we choose, and live life guided by principles established by our own social communities.

Native communities and tribes have faced varying challenges in maintaining their collective identities. Some communities have been able to retain their Native languages, whereas others struggle with only a handful of fluent speakers still living. Some have been able to keep their history alive through oral teachings, stories, art, music, and customs, and others are working to revive traditions that have nearly been lost. Connections with Mother Earth and an associated spirituality may still be strong, or these connections may have been disrupted by outside influences. Some tribal members may live on their traditional homelands, while an increasing number are moving to urban locations. What this means is that each student will bring a different frame of reference as to what it means to be a member of a specific tribe, as well as what it means to be collectively identified as American Indian or Alaska Native.

As a college student, it will be important for you to understand who you are. As mentioned in Chapter 5, Huffman suggests that American Indian and Alaska Native students may go through an initial period of alienation during the higher education experience, as they find the process to be unfamiliar and disjointed from life in their home communities. However, with perseverance students can move on to discover that their Native identities are a strength that will carry them through the college experience. This process of transculturation requires that a student be able to walk in two worlds—learning to traverse the world of higher education while being firmly grounded in his or her Native identity.

For students who have grown up away from their tribal communities or Native villages, the college experience is likely to take on a different meaning. Colleges and universities can provide a rich arena in which to explore and become reconnected with your Native identity. Your school may have established partnerships with local tribes to make service learning opportunities or internships available. Through these types of experiences you may be able to immerse yourself in the Native community by living and working there. There may be tribal elders in residence and/or teaching on the campus. As tribal wisdom keepers, elders hold a wealth of knowledge pertaining to traditions and ways of knowing. Look for a Native student center where you can connect with other American Indian and Alaska Native students to bring Native speakers, events, and celebrations to campus. We have known students who have come to campus and discovered archival records that tribal members thought to be lost. These students went on to assume active roles in revitalizing their American Indian and Alaska Native communities. College can provide a key opportunity to better understand your cultural heritage and to explore who you are as a Native person.

CONCENTRIC CIRCLE: INDIVIDUAL, FAMILY, AND COMMUNITY

Student Voices

- I knew I could do it! There was no way I would fail. I made the right choices.
- My own commitment.
- You have to take initiative. No one will do it for you.
- My family said, "Go for it!"
- My family was a natural extension of myself.
- I have strong family values, which are not okay to violate.
- To understand that your need for your family is a given—even if you think you don't need them—keep them within visiting distance.
- When you pursue something unknown, it really matters that your family is behind you.
- I knew I had to get through—my own mindset—to support my family.
- I wanted opportunities for my children—good child care, food, shelter, safety, for them to be healthy.
- Position yourself to benefit your Native community.
- You're leaving a community and coming into a [college] community . . . then come back and work for your community.

Hold on to your family and community. While your individual characteristics, including determination, initiative, and commitment, are important to your success, many American Indian and Alaska Native students from both urban and reservation backgrounds have also found that maintaining close connections to family and community was essential. We see this reflected in the preceding student quotes. American Indian curriculum developers have pointed out that "family and community—to us, it's one and the same."[1] Traditionally, American Indian and Alaska Native education has exemplified the phrase, "It takes a village to raise a child." Family and community members were collectively responsible for the education of their youth with individuals knowledgeable in particular areas (such as healing, storytelling, arts, or hunting) taking responsibility for teaching in those areas. Community members, particularly tribal elders, continue to be the sources for learning traditional knowledge that will keep your community's identity alive.

As you strive to be a successful student in college, it will be important to keep in mind these interconnections between individual, family, and community. You arrive at the door of an institution as an individual, but all that you accomplish will have potential for contributing to the success of your specific tribal or Native community, to other Native communities, and to American Indian and Alaska Native peoples more broadly.

At the same time, maintaining connections to community and family can pose a challenge to staying the course of higher education. Family commitments, such as taking care of relatives during illness, or community commitments, such as attending funerals or major cultural events, may pull you away from your coursework. Your family values may supersede the idea of getting a college degree. Many students have identified a core value of giving back to their Native communities as an indicator of their success. You may feel that by being away from your home community, you are not giving back. How can you deal with this? One student suggests, "Establish rapport with your professors and classmates, explain your situation, always stay in communication with professors and classmates." Let your instructors know that you may feel pulled in different directions. By helping your teachers and peers understand your situation, they may be able to help you figure out a way to juggle all of these various expectations and commitments while staying on the higher education path.

You can figure out ways to incorporate the value of giving back into the projects that you complete for your coursework. For instance, students have created storybook units centered on traditional tribal stories for use in a tribal Head Start program. You may complete a scientific project that involves maintenance of water quality to better ensure the survival of the salmon, trout, and other life of the oceans and rivers. Or you may work on habitat restoration necessary for big game management, such as that impacting the life of bison. You may gain skills to help you become an entrepreneur and start your own business back on your reservation. There are many different ways to give back to your community through your education. It will take creativity to see the connections. It will also likely take a faculty member who is willing to work with you in making your dreams and hopes for the future become reality. Remember—college faculty are there for you, as a student. That is their job—and all it takes is one professor to believe in the possibilities that you see. He or she can work with you to make these possibilities happen. Hold on to your dream.

CONCENTRIC CIRCLE: TRIBAL NATIONS

Tribes hold a unique status in the United States, as sovereign nations with jurisdiction over their lands and tribal members, guaranteed by various treaties with the federal government. The Indian Reorganization Act of 1934 and the Self Determination and Educational Assistance Act of 1975 both recognized the power held by American Indian and Alaska Native peoples to determine directions for their own lives and for their communities. Self-determination for tribal nations represents a political and legal status at the level of tribal government. As such, tribal officials are responsible for decision making about how self-determination is implemented for their tribal nations. Deloria and Wildcat stress the need to simultaneously examine how self-determination is carried out as a part of daily life experience.[2] They highlight the need to ground self-determination in ancestral teachings of place and power through Indigenous ways of thinking and knowing.

Wildcat contends that Indigenous self-determination requires critical reflection—first in understanding who you are and then discovering ways in which your being holistically interconnects with the surrounding world on both physical and spiritual levels. He poses the challenge, "So let us think about self-determination indigenously: about what living with honor means to Peoples still connected to places."[3] Sounds pretty deep, doesn't it? This is the level of thinking that it will take for tribal nations to survive and flourish as distinct entities that continue to carry forward their traditional values and ways of life. College can challenge you to examine issues from various perspectives. To grasp the lived meaning of self-determination will require that you connect with American Indian and Alaska Native scholars and elders who carry the ancestral knowledge that lies at the core of Indigenous self-determination. Stay connected to your tribe.

TRANSITIONING INTO THE OUTER CIRCLE: PREPARING FOR COLLEGE

Transitioning into college may be one of the most rewarding (yet difficult) journeys of your life. The distance you travel may be great—not so much in physical miles but in the distance from your Native cultural values and upbringing to the culture of the college or university that you attend, particularly if you choose to attend a predominantly white institution. Remember, you can hold on to your Native identity while learning to navigate the culture of higher education. Prepare for this by understanding that many different cultures exist. Just because you will be required to learn the culture of the university doesn't mean that you have to give up your Native identity. In fact, a strong sense of Native identity can be a strength that carries you forward to new possibilities that grow out of your college education.

Ask yourself, "What do I want to accomplish with a college education?" Your purpose will be important to consider in selecting a college that fits your needs. If you have the opportunity to participate in precollege programs, they can give you an idea of how you would feel as a student on a particular campus. Many colleges provide opportunities to attend summer camps or participate in weekend experiences during the school year. Know that you can contact the admissions office for a college any time to arrange a visit and a tour of the campus. If you have an idea of the field in which you would like to study, set up a meeting with faculty in that department. Visit the Native American student center and meet some of the current students. As you get a feel for what your experience might be like at a particular college, ask yourself again, "How does this fit into my life plan? Will this college take me toward my vision of where I want to be in five years? Ten years?"

Of course, the coursework you take in high school as well as the habits you establish provide the foundation for learning at the college level.

Many American Indian and Alaska Native students comment that they wish they would have taken more math and science courses to prepare for college. They also stress the importance of good study habits and the need to manage a time schedule that is much more unstructured compared with high school. You will need to take initiative. As expressed by one student, "It is an individual effort. No one else will write your paper or take your exam." Understand and capitalize on your strengths. Self-awareness will lead you to make informed decisions about the directions you choose to go with your education. Be ready to become or continue to be a self-determined learner who can envision a future of success as a student. Your own mindset will be important in carrying you forward on this journey!

A Student's Voice

Give yourself the best building blocks you can. It's important to take high school classes that will push you to be a stronger student, but it's equally important to take classes that foster growth in areas you have interests in (art, theater, etc.). My personal transition to college was extremely difficult—so much, in fact, that I almost didn't go back after my first year. Looking back after so many years of college it seems funny, but then it sure wasn't. It was pretty much hell for me. I had culture shock, missed my family, and was a miserable wreck for months on end. I gained forty pounds in one semester!

As for things that are helpful, I think talking to a guidance counselor is a good idea. If your guidance counselor isn't helping you, find a teacher that likes you and ask them to help. I didn't do any bridge programs myself, but they might be helpful. There's lots of paperwork and deadlines to wade through, and it can all get very confusing. Also, apply to more than one college. For my undergrad I applied for six, which my friends thought was nutty, but then I got to pick from five that accepted me! Applying to more colleges gave me more options, and turned out to be a great idea.

The other thing I would suggest is go visit the colleges. Walk around with and *without* one of the tour guides they give you, and ask people who go there what they *like* about the school and what they *hate* about the school. This is much more informative than any glossy brochure they'll send you. As for general preparation, the more you read, the better off you'll be. It's almost like reading grows brains. If you know what you want to do in college (English, biology, art, etc.), read up on journals from those disciplines. Learning the lingo before you go helps, and gives you an idea of what kinds of things are going on in your school. I looked up all my current professors and reviewed their published research articles before I went to grad school. It gave me an idea of what my department was focusing on at the upper levels, and made me feel more in touch, although at that point I didn't completely understand all the articles themselves.

THE OUTER CIRCLE: THE JOURNEY THROUGH COLLEGE

The importance of connecting with people as you embark on the college journey cannot be overstated. American Indian and Alaska Native students and graduates indicate that a personal relationship with at least one faculty member was key to their success. Wilson identified specific qualities of the faculty-student relationship that students valued—genuineness, accessibility, approachability, and a caring attitude.[4] There will be faculty who take an interest in you. You might not find them immediately, but as you participate in educational activities at your college, they will surface. Be sure to take advantage of office hours. It can be much easier to talk to and get to know a professor on a one-to-one basis. In addition, get to know the staff in the department where you are a student. They understand the system in which you are immersed and can provide guidance in maneuvering your way through paperwork and other requirements. Look for opportunities to connect with other students in your program of study. Students generally find that participating in study groups provides a great boost to their understanding of course material, as well as their sense of belonging in their chosen field.

Maintaining connections with your culture serves as another key factor in ensuring that your higher education journey is successful. Some students who live close to their college prefer to maintain cultural connections by returning home often to participate in cultural events and in learning with their own tribal elders and tradition bearers. For other students, opportunities to connect with your Native culture on campus will be important. This will often be through the Native American student center. This can serve as your home away from home, where you can feel comfortable in being who you are with others of Native background. A Native student advisor is there to answer questions and provide guidance as needed. Look for opportunities to become involved in Native student organizations and campus events centered on American Indian and Alaska Native culture. You can even play a leadership role in making Native culture more visible on your campus and in educating your college community regarding issues of importance to American Indian and Alaska Native communities by assisting with putting on college-wide events.

Finally, adequate financial resources can make or break your college experience. The extensive discussion of financial aid provided for you in Chapter 3 identifies a wealth of options. Getting through the application forms can be a challenge, but stick with it and you can be well rewarded. There are specialists in the college financial aid office who are there to guide you. Be sure to use these resources so you don't feel overwhelmed by all of the forms and procedures. Financial aid or scholarship advisors, as well as a Native American student advisor, may be aware of financial resources that are specifically available to you as a Native student. These resource people are there for you!

A Student's Voice

I built relationships, and I think this is key to success. There is part of academia that promotes a more reserved, formal interaction between faculty and faculty, and faculty and students. I have continually been more successful when I feel respect as well as an element of friendship with faculty. If I think someone cares about how I'm doing, I work harder for them and for myself. Connection and relationship, as well as mentoring and mutual respect, are key, key, key. Find someone you click with, even if it is a professor who is not in your department! Find someone you feel wants *you to succeed* and check in with them from time to time. The other things I did to succeed were: (1) not partying or getting into recreational drugs, (2) maintaining my religion and identity, (3) showing up to class and doing homework regularly, (4) working my butt off, (5) going home on breaks, (6) bravely starting to speak out loud in classroom discussions, and (7) watching two hours of *The Simpsons* every day for my first semester. That might sound funny, but I had never seen *The Simpsons*, because I grew up on a homestead, without cable or TV, and knew nothing of American pop culture. I didn't know what Abercrombie & Fitch was, how to drive on a freeway, or who Britney Spears was. I was forced to do some informal cultural research to discover how to interact with these Midwestern kids I found myself thrown in with. I didn't understand the jokes and references at lunch in the cafeteria until I immersed myself a little more into their world. Which was hard, and weird, and they thought I was weird for a while, but sometimes, "when in Rome do as the Romans do" is good advice. And now I find I love *The Simpsons*.

THE OUTER CIRCLE BECOMES COMPLETE: RETURNING TO SERVE

A Student's Voice

I'm starting to transition into my profession this year. It's a little weird, thinking about working and being a "professional" when I am by nature and culture such a laid-back person. But I also find it very exciting. I have to do some practicum and internships for my program, and I wanted some of that to expand my interest and knowledge of Native peoples and issues. I am going to do an internship with a Native medical center, which I am really looking forward to. I've done observations in village Head Starts and schools with large Native populations, and have chosen research that incorporates Native issues. I have been fortunate to be asked to present at a state and a national conference on issues related to Native student success in higher education. I am in a position now to give mentoring tips and support to other Native students starting out in my program. I love the feeling of giving back! I plan on working for a while in the community I grew up in, and in time broadening my work out to other areas of the state and other issues that impact Alaska Natives and American Indians.

Giving back or reciprocity is a core value of many American Indian and Alaska Native communities. Native students and graduates have indicated that their ability to give back is one of the most significant indicators of their success as a student. Thus, we close the circle of success with the concept of returning to serve. This can occur at several levels. Some graduates go back to their home communities to use their skills and knowledge in providing service for members of their tribes or Native villages. Others choose to serve a Native community in another part of the state or country. Still others serve American Indian and Alaska Native people on a more broad level through involvement in Native organizations and professional associations. Some graduates play a role in educating non-Natives, such as teachers, about the cultural background of the children they teach. As a college graduate, you will serve as a role model of success for American Indian and Alaska Native youth who aspire to go on to receive a college education. We see university graduates as important contributors to the education of current students, as they return to serve as both as role models and as mentors.

Perhaps of most importance is the potential that you will have for assuming a leadership role in making transformational change for American Indian and Alaska Native peoples. Returning to the challenge posed by Wildcat earlier in this chapter, "So let us think about self-determination indigenously: about what living with honor means to Peoples still connected to places."[5] To get at the essence of the lived experience of Indigenous self-determination and to act on its meaning will take well-honed problem-solving and critical-thinking skills. It will require that you be able to examine an issue from multiple angles, as well as be able to anticipate both the potential intended and unintended consequences of your decisions that will come to bear on the lives of your children and the children of seven generations from now. A college education can help develop your potential to make a difference for American Indian and Alaska Native peoples and beyond. This is a critical time for seeing new possibilities to make this a better world as Native and non-Native people together are faced with environmental, social, educational, and health concerns that challenge the way we live on a global level. *Hold on to your dream. You can make a difference!*

FINAL THOUGHT

This chapter has presented the Circle of Success, a model for promoting American Indian and Alaska Native student achievement in higher education. The model is centered on cultural identity as the core of American Indian and Alaska Native student success. Closely linked to cultural identity in a conjoining concentric circle are the interrelated components of individual, family, community, and tribe. The outer circle represents three phases of the journey through college beginning with preparation to transition into college, followed by the actual experience associated with enrollment in college, and then with the final linkage connecting back to American Indian and Alaska Native communities, both locally and more broadly, through a process of returning to serve American Indian and Alaska Native peoples. Following the pattern of life itself, the circle represents the continuity and interconnectedness of all aspects of the educational journey.

More Profiles of Successful College Graduates

We have come full circle—taking you through possibilities for your own success as a student in higher education. As we began the journey through this book, we provided stories of real people—people who had a vision of themselves with a college education, people who pursued their dreams and were making significant contributions to our world. We end the journey with three more stories of successful college graduates who describe their own circles of success that have carried them forward through higher education. Their richly detailed stories vary and illustrate the importance of staying grounded in or learning more about ancestral teachings and cultural identity, while maintaining close connections with family and community throughout the educational process. We challenge you to join with the narrators of these stories in creating your own story as you navigate your way through college. You can serve as a role model for future generations to come. Start by keeping a diary. Synthesize your thoughts into a story that you might share with others. What is important is that *your* story becomes part of the circle of success.

THOMAS PEACOCK is a member of the Fond du Lac Band of Lake Superior Chippewa (Ojibwe); he serves as associate dean and professor in the College of Education and Human Service Professions at the University of Minnesota Duluth.

Tell me about your experience as a student in higher education.

I started school about a million years ago, 1969. Bemidji State University. I remember mailing my application for admission. A friend and I were hitchhiking across the country. We ended up sleeping in a ditch near Watersmeet, Michigan, and I had my application with me. It was just after Neil Armstrong landed on the moon. And I still hadn't sent in my admissions application, yet so I sent it in. Bemidji State at the time was, maybe they still do, taking about anybody that had a heartbeat and could pay their tuition, so that's where I ended up going on the "buddy" plan with one of my high school friends. I had been to Bemidji State as a teenager in an Indian Youth Leadership Program. That was in about ninth or tenth grade, so I was familiar with the campus. And so I was straight out of high school and I didn't want to go in the service. So I decided to go to school. I was good at school. There were only, as I remember, thirteen Native students at Bemidji State at the time. And I remember in my sophomore year, that figure just jumped like to 200. It was that huge wave of Native students coming into higher ed at the time, so I did my undergrad there. That was my first experience in higher ed, and I got in.

Like I say, I was pretty good at school, so that part wasn't too much of an issue when I went to class. I remember barely getting out of Bemidji State with a degree because I spent lots of time in the student union and the usual raising hell like most other students did back then, but I got a teaching degree in social studies and biology as I remember it. And went off to work and doing a little bit of teaching, serving as a JOM coordinator, that kind of thing. Then I pretty much immediately started going to night school here. I was working down in Duluth at the time. And I started into a master's program in ed administration here at the University of Minnesota, Duluth, and did that for a couple years—took night classes and got most of everything done except my paper. And then I didn't finish that paper up for a couple of years. It just sort of sat around. I finished that master's up, and then I went again to summer school immediately pretty much to get my administrative license—my principal's and superintendent's license because by that time I was a school principal. I was on a provisional license, so I finished my administrative license up over at St. Cloud State. I was a principal for about five years and I thought it was time to try something else. I was getting really burned out being a principal. I applied for a Bush Fellowship and then applied for admission to Harvard grad school and got in, and I went off and did that for about three or four years. They throw in another master's degree in the process on the way to the doctorate. So I had my EdD in ed administration and I've pretty much been a school boy. Done a lot of school. So that's my schooling.

How did you choose the higher education institutions you attended?

Bemidji State—I had been in an Indian Youth Leadership Program there as a high school student [as part] of the war on poverty programs. It was an OEO program and it brought Native youth from around Minnesota to something called an Indian Youth Leadership Program, and it was run at the time by Bob Troyer, a wonderful man as I remember, and he was straight out of OEO in Washington. He had moved back to Minnesota. And so like as a ninth or tenth grader I was brought to the Bemidji State campus for that and that really turned me on to Bemidji. And of course I'm from the Duluth area. I'm from Fond du Lac and I wanted to get away a little bit, and I knew that Bemidji State was in the heart of Indian Country. I think that was one of the reasons. The other schools were just schools of convenience. UMD was a school of convenience because I was living in Duluth at the time. It had the degree I wanted. St. Cloud was the same thing. St. Cloud was the only place in the area and I was still living in Bemidji at the time. I had to drive 150 miles to go to school there. Harvard—I wanted to go to Harvard when I was in seventh grade. Some people dream of being astronauts and firemen and all that stuff. I wanted to go there, so I applied for a Bush Fellowship, which gives big scholarships to emergent leaders in Minnesota, Wisconsin, the Dakotas. It's a very generous fellowship and it pretty much paid my ticket to go there. Plus a wonderful stipend—a living stipend. And that was the opportunity. You know, I got one of those and applied for admission at the same time. And so I think without that it would have been more difficult. I probably would have gone anyway and relied on loans and tribal scholarships and that kind of thing. But that really made it easier in terms of not having to worry about money, which is a big part of going to school.

What factors contributed to your success in higher education?

I've always been good at school. When I was a little kid I was good at school. I was in the first reading group. Some people are good at that kind of thing. Reading was easy for me. Math was easy. When I concentrated on school, it was easy all the way through. Of course, I had all kinds of diversions, but you do what you're good at. And I think the other thing is that I enjoy the challenge of writing and that scholarly kind of thinking, particularly in graduate school, particularly when at Harvard. It was about the only place I got the kind of education when I really felt stimulated, scholarly writing. None of the other places I went to school really did that. They were pretty much filling in time and getting credits. But that place was stimulating. When you'd read a book, the instructor would bring in the author of the book to discuss it. It was where Howard Gardner was. And Sarah Lawrence Lightfoot was there. These people that were known nationally and internationally in education—they were all there. The person I took several classes from—Lee Boldman—was "the" person in the leadership and organizational literature. I took classes from him. It was awesome to do that. So that challenge is something that drew me and helped me be successful. It's sort of like doing research nowadays. That presents the same kind of feeling, the same kind of challenge, when I'm writing, it's the same kind of thing.

What challenges did you face as a student in higher education?

I think the kinds of diversions that most people run into. I married early. I was twenty, a sophomore in school and started a family right away. That was difficult—to do that and be a student at the same time. My wife quit school to work so we could make it—those kind of family responsibilities. I was never too much of a hell-raiser. My hell raising didn't get in the way of schooling. I think I was more challenged by social diversions. I was very active at Bemidji State in the Indian club—Council of Indian Students. I was president for a couple of years, and I was very active in that organization. I have to say in hindsight, that place kept me out of class every day. Because that became a way of life—doing club stuff and organizing, because I was the head of it, all of that being part of that community. I skipped a lot classes doing club stuff and hanging out with other Native students in the student union. I think that's what kept my GPA way down as an undergrad, and when I went back to graduate school I decided to not to stay active in the organizations, except when I was at Harvard I was active there because my class schedule was such I could be involved without taking away from school.

How did you adapt to meet these challenges?

Well, when the honeymoon was over, then it was easy to concentrate on school. I mean, I think that it took until I was like a senior in my undergrad before I really decided to settle down and became less active in the club, as I remember it, and concentrated more on school. I was no longer the president of the club. That really did help a lot. I still was active, but by then we had a baby and I just couldn't do a lot of that extracurricular kind of stuff. That sure did settle me down in terms of schooling. When I was at Harvard though . . . I should talk about that, because that was a challenge. I was a single parent by then, I had three kids, and I was raising my kids. So I had gone through the marriage thing. That was very difficult—balancing school. You know, I could handle the school part and the academic part of it, but I also had other responsibilities. So I remember being challenged by school and I loved it. I would tell my kids like every Saturday morning, and Sunday morning, that that was my time to write. I lived about twenty miles south of Boston, so I'd take the trains in every day, and I did most of my reading on the train and at night. What I remember is being exhausted all the time. It's like having two full-time jobs—being a full-time student and then raising three kids and being a full-time parent, more than a full-time parent. I forgot all about that. I sort of block that part out. But I remember just being completely exhausted all the time. And that was my biggest challenge. I never did think of dropping out. You sort of pick and choose what you are going to read. You know instructors would give you fifty articles to read and books and I would have to pick and choose. I'd have to be selective on what I was going to read so I did the best that I could. I did well, so it turned out okay. And until my second semester at Harvard, until I bought my first computer, that was a challenge too because I'd have to send things to a typist and that could only be one draft. And then I finally broke down and bought an old Apple computer. The kids helped me drag it on the subway train home and back—printers and all; it made a huge difference. It's not even comparable in terms of quality of papers and the amount of editing you can do. So that just made a huge difference.

What advice would you give to American Indian individuals interested in obtaining a higher education?

I was thinking back and I've always been very grounded in who I am. You can't tell people to be grounded, but to be grounded in who they are. To be grounded culturally. When I was in college I always was really active in my own community. I helped bring the first social drum back to my reservation. Hadn't been a social drum there in decades, and [there were] pow wows and being active in ceremonies. Making that and family—that kind of grounded. If you have that, you have everything. And then school is just school. I think a lot of people go off to school to find themselves, because you're still young and you can do that. I did that when I was young by becoming very active in the Native organization at school. [I wanted that] kind of community and a sense of community, like a family, like extended family almost. It came from being involved in the Native organization in the college, especially at Bemidji State and at Harvard, where there weren't many Native people in the greater Boston area. Being a part of that circle of people, with the Boston Indian Council. They were like a great fellowship and support for folks like us who were 1,500 miles from our families.

What would your life be like without having gone to college or earning a college degree?

I can't imagine that because like I say, I've always been good at school. I wouldn't have lived my life without college. I can't imagine my life without it because I think we try to do things that we are good at. And I was good at school. I can't imagine doing anything else.

Please describe what you feel are the benefits of going to college and getting your college degree.

I think from a personal perspective, if you buy into Maslow's thing, self-actualization. I'm doing exactly what I always wanted. I think that's helped in my personal life. I knew exactly where I wanted to be. To do research, to write, and to teach. Like now, one of the greatest pleasures that I draw is working with the students, watching them grow. They come in brand new. I work with graduate students primarily now, master's students. Many of them I've known as undergraduate students and I follow them two years later and watch them walk across the stage and hand them their degree. It feels really good that I had something to do with that. I've worked with a lot of Native doctoral students and [I like] to work with them, to help them get that degree, to work with them as their advisor, when they come in the door and they have just a ton of issues—a lot of academic issues—typically writing issues in particular. And then a ton of personal issues come in, lots of responsibilities, way more responsibilities than so many non-Native people have. A lot of family trauma, a lot of difficult situations—to come in and finish and come out with a product that anybody would be proud of—I did this. To hand in their thesis. I'm preparing that next legion of educators to go out there and kick butt and change the world. And to give back.

I think my way of giving back is . . . I decided that that's what I could do. I didn't realize that until I was like fifty years old. So what can I give back? I can write. So then I can give that back. I've been doing a lot of Ojibwe history stuff—one is a history book for little kids. Because I think that is important that Native kids know their history and their culture and their philosophy and their language. So I've been doing that—wrote a couple of other Ojibwe history books. Did a couple education things—book-type things. That's what I can give back. I can use all those skills I learned while in school to try to make a difference in life. So I'm doing exactly what I want. I was telling my wife just the other day I couldn't trade this in. It's hard work, but I wouldn't trade it in a minute. If I had to go do something else, I'd be completely lost.

LeMANUEL "LEE" BITSOI is a proud member of the Navajo Nation. His maternal clan is Kinyaa'áánii (Towering House), and his paternal clan is Hashtl'ishnii (Mud). He is fluent and literate in the Navajo language. He currently lives in Cambridge, Massachusetts, but he travels home often to Naschitti, New Mexico, to spend time with his parents and family. He credits his family for his academic and professional success. As director of minority training in bioinformatics and genomics at Harvard University, he focuses his work on promoting educational opportunities for students of color. Lee is also pursuing his doctorate of education degree in higher education management at the University of Pennsylvania. His story of educational success follows.

I am the youngest of seven in my family. All of us were expected to attend school every day, but sometimes we didn't. All of us graduated from high school, and eventually, all of my brothers and sisters attended college. I was inspired by all of them to pursue higher education; however, it was my adjacent sibling, my sister, Dr. Elvira Bitsoi Largie, who graduated from college first. My mother was also my inspiration. Although she attended school only up to the ninth grade, she was aware of the power of education and how it changed lives. "Get up! Get ready for school!" We heard these phrases every morning before she left for work at the local school where she was the cafeteria manager. My mother, Irene Bitsoi Morris, is an amazing lady who raised my siblings and me as a single parent after my father passed away when I was three months old. (She remarried when I was thirteen.)

My mother has always been my primary role model and teacher. She has provided some of my most profound learning experiences. I remember as a child sitting at the base of her weaving loom and asking her questions about Navajo plants and animals. She never seemed to tire of answering my questions, no matter how trivial they might be. She also shared her wisdom countless times and reinforced the Navajo philosophy of "T'áá hwiih ajit'éégo," which translates to "your success or failure depends upon yourself." Within Navajo philosophy, this ageless tenet of self-sufficiency and self-reliance was communicated to my mother from her parents, grandparents, and great-grandparents. They were her role models and teachers who shared precious knowledge in hopes that she would aspire to live a life in the best manner possible. T'áá hwiih ajit'éégo has been a driving force for me throughout my life. I am grateful for the prayers and the knowledge base of my ancestors that my mother has maintained.

My father left this world when I was an infant, and my mother faced the monumental task of raising my siblings and me as a single parent. I cannot even begin to fathom what she must have endured as she struggled to make ends meet. It was not until later that I realized many of the sacrifices she made while I was growing up, for they had been transparent to me. She relied on T'áá hwiih ajit'éégo. She had a successful career at the local elementary school as a cafeteria manager, despite her limited education. She confided in me once that she would have liked to have had a better education. However, she felt strongly that she was being forced by Catholic nuns to give up her identity (especially her language and culture) for the sake of an education. This form of education was common practice for all schools at that time. (My mother attended four different boarding schools, the last one being Catholic, and she said all of them punished Navajo students for speaking Navajo.) American Indian students at all schools (government, parochial, etc.) could speak English only. Moreover, my mother told me that they had to dress and behave like white people. My mother did not agree with this coercion and chose a different path. At that time, when my mother chose work instead of school, the employment system was somewhat different in that one could work and support a family without a high school diploma. Personally, I believe it was the will of the Creator who made my mother come to realize that higher education would be crucial to the experience of her children.

Today, higher education is imperative to the evolution and development of Native tribal nations. To foster that development, as Native people, we need our young people to become professionals. We need to encourage them to seek out educational opportunities for the betterment of themselves, their families, communities, and nations. Though higher education is very important, we also need to sustain our Native ways of education. We need to encourage our young people to continue to learn our respective languages and cultures by encouraging apprenticeships with artisans, ranchers, weavers, and medicine people.

According to my mother, Navajo philosophy, familial support, along with self-resilience and perseverance, will carry one as far as he or she wishes. The path I chose to venture was based on educational goals and was guided by the sagacious teachings of my mother, specifically T'áá hwiih ajit'éégo. I have relied on my family for support and encouragement as I completed my undergraduate and graduate studies. I learned that I didn't have to replace my identity with higher education but complement it with university credentials. I can only hope to serve as a role model for the next generation and pray that they experience higher education as a complement to their respective identities rather than a risk.

I remember waiting for the summer to end so school could begin. I felt that way all thought my elementary school years. I even looked forward to high school. I attended Tohatchi High School, which is twenty miles from my community of Naschitti. Both of these communities are located in north-western New Mexico of the Navajo Nation. After graduating in the top ten of my high school in 1984, I attended New Mexico State University (NMSU) in Las Cruces. I had applied to NMSU, the University of New Mexico (UNM), and Arizona State University (ASU) and began the application process for Boston University (BU). I chose to apply to the first three schools because I had attended summer programs at each of them and I was familiar with their campuses. I was interested in BU since I had received a catalog and financial aid information from them. It wasn't until later that I found out that I was on their prospective student list based on my demographic information and test score for the ACT. I didn't complete my application because of the expensive application fee. I didn't know that I could have applied for an application fee waiver until much later. (I sometimes wonder where the BU path would have led me.) I received academic scholarships from all three institutions (NMSU, UNM, ASU), but NMSU offered the best financial aid package.

With everything complete, I began my studies at NMSU in Las Cruces in the fall of 1984. I wasn't sure what my major was going to be, but I knew that it was going to be in some sort of engineering discipline. After my first semester, I had the highest GPA within my group of friends. This gave me a boost of confidence and I decided to major in engineering technology (ET). The following year, I continued my studies in ET, but I soon realized that after completion of the program, I would not be an engineer but a technologist. In light of this, as I began my third year, I changed my major to industrial engineering (IE) because I was interested in industry and manufacturing processes and designs. Expertise in IE was (and still is) much needed on the Navajo reservation. Needless to say, since I had changed my major twice, I had a lot of catching up to do with my coursework. By my fourth year at NMSU, I should have been a senior, but I was only in my second year of coursework in IE.

After four years of university life, my circle of friends had expanded. I also began playing volleyball with the NMSU men's collegiate club team. This experience gave me confidence as I began to excel in the sport. I soon became a starter on the team and we began to travel to tournaments throughout the region (New Mexico, Texas, and Arizona). It was a challenge to balance practice time and homework, and I soon found out that one would have to give. I chose volleyball over classes. I didn't regret it, since our club team was able to participate in the national club championships in spring 1988. I dropped two of my classes and concentrated on the remaining three and did well in them. What a thrill it was to play in the national championships! After the spring term, I stayed in Las Cruces for the summer and took classes to make up for the spring term. I had to borrow a student loan to pay for the summer term, since I was determined to pursue IE and finish in two years.

The fall of 1988 was a trying one for me. I missed home since I didn't go home for the summer. In addition, there were a lot of different situations that I encountered at school—some good and some not so good. Since I was a first-generation college student, I really couldn't turn to my mother for guidance or advice. I knew I could rely on her for support, but I wasn't sure she would understand the pressures and temptations that one faces in college. I found college to be fun and became a bit more social with my ever-growing circle of friends. Within this circle, I found that drinking socially was a rite of passage in higher education. I also knew that there were other vices, but I stayed away from them. However, my socialization soon took its toll on my homework. Aside from homework, I was determined to keep my starting spot on the volleyball team, so I concentrated on practice even more. That fall, our team won two preseason tournaments, but I had to withdraw from all of my classes, rather than earn below average grades. I wanted to protect my GPA.

After spending the holiday break at home, I returned in the spring of 1989 with a sense of renewal. I had participated in a couple of ceremonies at home and I was more focused on my studies. When I went to register, I was bit discouraged to find out that my scholarship was not going to be renewed since I had not met the minimum course requirements for the past two semesters. I had no choice but to take out another student loan and work part-time on campus. I registered for the minimum full-time course load, which was twelve credit hours. Practice for the volleyball club began, but I didn't attend for the first couple of weeks. The team captain soon called me and asked me why I wasn't practicing, and I told him that I was planning to concentrate on my studies. He asked me to reconsider and that I would still have a spot on the team should I choose to return by the next week. Again, it was a choice between what I really enjoyed and excelled in versus my studies. I didn't really consider my future career at that time, so I was convinced by my teammates to start playing again. Truthfully, I missed playing, so it didn't take a lot of arm-twisting to convince me to rejoin the club team. I was happy and I didn't mind the extra work I endured to enjoy everything.

By midterm of the spring term, I wasn't able to handle everything. Our team had qualified for the national tournament, which was to be held in California in April, and we began practicing every day, including weekends. I dropped two classes and I felt bad about that, but I had to. I had decided that receiving average grades in two classes was sufficient. My standards were slipping. . . . I was also working a minimum schedule at work, but because I had to finance my own education, I had to work. To make ends meet, I borrowed additional funds to cover the rest of my semester's expenses. Our club team traveled to California for the national tournament, but we finished without making it to the playoffs, so that wasn't a lot of fun. I returned to campus feeling dejected because much of my self-confidence was based on my performance on the court, not in the classroom. I had missed a week of classes and I was behind in homework, so the pressure of finals began to build up. After some deliberation, I decided to withdraw from all of my classes again. I knew that it probably wasn't a good idea, but the alternative was failing my classes. Again, I chose to protect my GPA.

During this troubling time I had a life-transforming conversation with one of my professors. When I went to obtain his signature for my withdrawal card, he asked me why I had fallen behind. He knew that I was on the volleyball club team, but I had missed a few other classes as well. I explained the situation that I was in. Moreover, I explained that I was homesick at times. After listening to me, he asked me why I wanted to become an engineer. I told that I thought that I found it interesting, and I wanted to be rich! He then told me that if I became an engineer, I probably wouldn't be able to return home since there wouldn't be any jobs for me. In addition, he said that I should enjoy what I do for a living. He went on to explain that he became a professor because he liked to teach. He said he wasn't the richest man on campus, but he had a family, a nice home, and a decent car. The last question he asked me was if I liked engineering, and I told him I wasn't sure. In reality, I didn't know why I wanted to become an engineer. I think it was what everyone else wanted me to become and I soon realized that I needed to pursue what I wanted.

I remained in Las Cruces for the summer of 1989. That summer was another important time in my life. Because I had become a very good volleyball player, I began to play outdoor two-man volleyball on grass and sand courts. I became friends with another group of people outside of NMSU, and my social network expanded greatly. A friend of mine (who was already employed as an engineer) had an extra bedroom in his apartment and he offered to let me stay rent-free. All I paid for was half of the utilities. Through another friend, I found a job in a convenience store. I couldn't work on campus because I wasn't registered for classes, and all the summer program jobs had been filled. I was fine with it, since it was the first time I had taken a summer off and just worked and enjoyed myself. I worked during the week and played volleyball after work and on weekends. I also went to weekly parties with my new outdoor volleyball buddies, and this was where I found renewed confidence since people recognized me and had heard of me. It was a fun summer.

The fall semester was around the corner so I registered for classes, but I soon found out that I would have to borrow a lot of money to pay for all of my expenses. There was no alternative. I wasn't sure if my mother could help me, but I asked her anyway. She then questioned what I did over the summer and I told her. I had kept in touch with her during the summer, but I knew she was not pleased with my story. She agreed to send me some money to assist me anyway. I felt good and bad about this. I felt good that she was helping me so I could register, but I felt bad because I knew that she was also struggling to make ends meet. To save on my expenses, I asked my roommate if I could continue to live with him. He agreed and things were looking good. After the first week of classes, I found myself questioning why I was in school. Sitting in my differential equations class, I wondered why I needed to learn math of that sort. Without consulting anyone, I decided to take a semester off and work full-time.

It was tough for the rest of the year. By December, I was tired of being barely able to eke out a living on my paltry income, so I decided to move home to Naschitti. I was really sad to leave my friends and the community that I had built for myself. I had moved on from my high school friends (who had now all graduated) and earned a reputation of being an excellent volleyball player. I commanded respect, but it was at a price—my studies.

In any event, I knew I had to move home and find a job. Rather than wasting time and resources, I decided to take a break, or as Vincent Tinto calls it, "a stop out," which was appropriate for me at that time.

My family was so happy to have me home, but I felt like a failure since I had returned without a degree. At the time though, my family did not care. I was home to make our family whole again. The novelty of my homecoming was short-lived. . . . One morning as my mother was leaving for work, she woke me up and said she needed to talk to me. No one was home at the time, so we had a one-on-one conversation. She took a deep breath and told me that she didn't mind paying for my truck while I was in school. However, now that I was no longer in school, I would need to find a way to pay for it if I wanted to continue to drive it. I knew that must have been hard for her, but I listened. After she left, I felt like I had been given the short end of the stick. How could she be so cruel? Didn't she know the hardships I endured? Of course, I was being selfish. As it turns out, this was the best advice she could give to me at a time when I needed it.

In February 1990, I began work as a census enumerator. I found it very interesting, but I was soon tired of driving to very remote communities and feeling as if I was intruding on people's privacy. In the meantime, I continued to look for another job. I found one as a bookmobile driver for the Navajo Nation Library System (NNLS). After working for a few years, I eventually realized that I needed a bachelor's degree to advance in the job market and become economically independent. This epiphany regarding education came about during my stop out. I also worked in the Research Library of the NNLS, where I encountered many different scholars who used the Native American resources the library held. Often, I found myself engaged in stimulating and intellectual discussions regarding Navajo sovereignty, and they were enlightening. I also met many young Navajo people who were attending higher education institutions all across the country, including Ivy League institutions. I was impressed with them. Many of these scholars and visitors asked me why I had not completed my undergraduate coursework and I soon found myself asking the same question. Other departmental personnel, notably those from the Navajo Nation higher education financial aid office, also asked me. It was my interaction with the scholarship counselors where I found my answer in how I could assist Navajo students like me who were questioning why they were on an educational journey. I came to realize I could be of most assistance through student services as a financial aid counselor or academic advisor.

During my tenure at the NNLS, I took classes at UNM Gallup to complete my requirements for an associate of arts degree from NMSU. I transferred my coursework to NMSU and I received my AA diploma in the summer of 1992. This inspired me to complete my coursework for a bachelor's degree. In addition, my sister Elvira had graduated from UNM and began teaching at our local school in Naschitti. As a full-time mother and wife, she had been able to complete her studies, so I had no excuse! I decided to return to my studies full-time in the spring of 1993.

Instead of returning to NMSU, I transferred to UNM in Albuquerque, which was closer to my home community. I changed my major to education since it was the most attractive field to me for it seemed that through education, I could contribute in more tangible ways to my community and the Navajo Nation. Volleyball was still a part of my life and my reputation had followed me, so I joined the men's collegiate club team at UNM. This time, however, I knew what I was going to face, so I was prepared to balance everything—studies, work, and play. Also noteworthy at UNM was that I was able to take Navajo classes, which was my new interest. In addition to fulfilling my major requirements, I was able to take all of the Navajo courses that were offered at UNM. I am now more fluent and literate in the Navajo language. My instructor, Roseanne Willink, was awesome! I looked to her for advice and guidance and she never failed me. Even when she had to be stern with me about my homework, I enjoyed interacting with her. I came to think of her as an aunt and she played a very important role later on in my academic career. I enjoyed my studies and did very well in my courses. I made the dean's list consistently, and in 1994 I was initiated into Phi Beta Kappa. My mother, my sister Elvira, and her daughter, Seratha, attended my initiation ceremony. They were proud of me.

In 1995, I graduated cum laude, and all of my family attended. It was a very special day! Eleven years after my high school graduation, I had my bachelor's degree. What an awesome feeling! I wasn't an engineer, but I was pleased with what I had studied and my newfound career pathway. I used to wonder where I would have been if I had continued in engineering. However, I no longer looked at my initial university experience with regret. Actually, those years were very fun and happy times. I needed to experience what I did in order to motivate myself. I took a different path, and little did I know where it would lead me.

In the summer of 1995, I returned to the Office of Navajo Nation Scholarship and Financial Assistance (ONNSFA) for a job. Since I had interned there during my summer breaks, I had decided to work there. Unfortunately, all of the counselor positions had been recently filled, so I had to find work elsewhere. In the fall of that year, I was hired as a financial aid advisor at San Juan College (SJC) in Farmington, New Mexico. I enjoyed that job and after a year of working, I decided that I needed a graduate degree to advance in my field. There were a couple of master's programs offered by NMSU, but I had higher aspirations.

During one of my summer internships at ONNSFA, I met Ferlin Clark (current president of Diné College) who is an alumnus of the Harvard Graduate School of Education (HGSE). I was impressed with him, and he inspired me to consider HGSE. After careful consideration, I decided to apply. I was confident that I had the credentials to be admitted, but I needed letters of recommendation—employer, academic, and other. I asked my boss at that time, Roger Evans, the director of financial aid at SJC, for one. Since I had a good relationship with Roseanne Willink at UNM, I asked her for one as well. The third one was a tough choice. I could ask another instructor, but I knew that my application would be strengthened with a letter from a Navajo Nation representative. I decided to ask Roxanne Gorman, my former boss at ONNSFA, for my third letter.

With a prayer and hope, I sent my application in. I waited for several months before I received a bulky envelope in my post office box. I was so nervous, I shook as I opened the package. I knew that if I had received a small envelope, it wouldn't be good news, so I knew it had to be good news. Still, I was shaky as I opened the package. Tears welled up in my eyes as I read the first line. "Dear Mr. Bitsoi: Congratulations! You have been admitted to the Harvard Graduate School of Education." I was so happy, I wanted to shout it out to the world. I sat in the parking lot of the post office and offered a prayer of gratitude to the Creator.

Since I had been admitted one year in advance to the master of education degree program, I waited until the following spring to tell my family. It was very challenging to keep such a secret, but I wanted to wait until I was ready to announce my plans. I told my mother and siblings and they were surprised! After a few moments of silence, they all congratulated me. My mother then commented, in Navajo, that Harvard sounded expensive and that she probably couldn't assist me in paying for my expenses. Her comment made me smile, since I knew that she was offering her support. After a few more moments, she asked me why I had to travel to the other side of the country when there was a university (UNM) located "over the hill." Elvira explained what Harvard was to my mother and she simply nodded. My mother has a way of keeping me grounded.

One of my brothers, Darryl, and his family helped me move to Cambridge in September 1997. The evening we were scheduled to leave, my family gathered at our favorite New Mexican restaurant, Jerry's Café, in Gallup. It was a bittersweet meal. There were tears and smiles. We tried to keep it light, but we all knew this would be a life-changing experience for me. After hugs, tears, and well wishes, we started our drive to the East Coast. My brother started driving first. He drove through the night until we reached Oklahoma City, then I took over. Since I had slept, I drove most of the day, stopping only to refuel and to eat. We made it to Indianapolis by nightfall and spent the night there. We had breakfast early the next morning and began driving again. Our goal was to arrive in New York City by the evening. We were a little behind schedule, but we got there in time for dinner. I'm sure we were a sight, a big GMC pick-up truck with a camper driving through Manhattan. I joked with Darryl and his wife, Lucinda, about how we should have brought our silver and turquoise jewelry and attempt to buy back the island. After dinner in Times Square, we weren't sure what to do. I looked at the map and decided that we could make it to Boston that night. The distance seemed to be shorter than it really was. I also didn't factor in the traffic.

I started driving again and headed north. Since I had never been in New England, I was amazed to find that the coastline was a long corridor of cities. The trip took longer than I anticipated and we arrived around 3 a.m. in Boston. I followed signs to Cambridge and I figured there would be signs pointing to Harvard, but I didn't see any. I had taken one of many routes into Cambridge and I still didn't see any signs for Harvard University. We ended up in Somerville and I stopped to ask for directions at a gas station. The clerk's Cambridge accent was so thick I had to ask him twice for directions to a hotel instead. I still didn't understand him. Since then, I've come to find that there are distinct accents in the Boston metropolitan area.

HGSE was an awesome experience that I will never forget. I will cherish it always! I made some lifelong friends that I still keep in touch with. We provide each other with updates on our lives—doctoral programs, marriages, new jobs, and so on. I was ready for the academic rigor of Harvard, and it was incredible to learn from primary sources! One of my favorite courses was with Derek Bok, former (and current interim) president of Harvard. How wonderful it was to debate higher education issues with him. I had never been taught in the Socratic method, and this was how he taught his course. I was intimidated at first, but after meeting with him in his office, I found him to be harmless. I told him that I was considering dropping his course and he told me that my contributions to the class would be invaluable. I remember feeling good after our meeting. I didn't drop his class and I'm glad I didn't, since I learned so much!

Since my program was only for a year, graduation in June 1997 came too soon. Most of my family drove to Cambridge for my graduation—another special occasion. Some of close friends from college also attended, and it was very emotional. When I moved to Cambridge, I had planned to return to my home community after graduation. However, I decided to remain in New England to work at an Ivy League institution. With support from my family and friends, I was hired at Dartmouth as assistant director of financial aid in 1999. I was then asked to coordinate Native American recruitment. I learned quite a bit in this unprecedented joint appointment. I remained at Dartmouth for two years and returned to Harvard's Native American Program in 2001. Of the many accomplishments at the Native American Program, two stand out in my mind. First, I established working relationships the university admissions offices that remain in place today. Second, I assisted in the process of securing permanent funding for the program. I enjoyed working at the Native American Program, but I aspired to provide a larger impact for all students of color.

In March 2004, I began working in my current position as director of minority training in bioinformatics and genomics. This unique opportunity allows me to work with students of color nationwide. I continue to be involved in the Native American community and am supported wholeheartedly by my faculty supervisor, Professor William Gelbart, Department of Molecular and Cellular Biology. In 2005, I was able to reestablish the Harvard Chapter of the American Indian Science and Engineering Society (AISES) through the resources of my program. I enjoy directing this nationwide program in training more scientists of color in bioinformatics and genomics. I am appreciative for the educational opportunities that this position has made available to me.

Most notably, Gelbart supports my pursuit of the doctorate of education degree in higher education management at the University of Pennsylvania, while I continue working full-time. (My anticipated date of graduation is May 2007.) I believe in advocating for Native American students in higher education; thus, my dissertation is an examination of success factors of Native American males at Harvard College. I chose my research topic to enhance the body of research regarding Native Americans from a positive and encouraging perspective. I hope that my contribution will aid prospective Native American students and their parents. In addition, my research findings could assist high school guidance counselors and university offices—admissions, financial aid, and student support services—to prepare, recruit, and retain Native American students.

On a final note, volleyball continues to be my favorite pastime. After all these years, I still enjoy playing at a competitive level. Of the numerous awards I've received, the most memorable one is winning a silver medal at the 2004 United States Volleyball Association National Championships. What a thrill that was!

DR. GEORGE BLUE SPRUCE JR. comes from the Laguna and Ohkay-Owingeh Pueblo Tribe/s of New Mexico. His claim to fame is that he was the first American Indian dentist in the United States and just celebrated his fifty-year dental class reunion (having graduated in 1956). He attained the title of Assistant Surgeon General in the U.S. Public Health Service and served American Indian people as an administrator of many education and health programs (retiring in 1986 after thirty years of federal government service, mostly with the Indian Health Service). Presently, he is the assistant dean of the newest dental school in the United States (The Arizona School of Dentistry and Oral Health in Phoenix). His other claim to fame is that he is the first and only male tennis player to be inducted into the American Indian Athletic Hall of Fame (1996). Dr. Blue Spruce has a beautiful American Indian wife (Patricia), and they have six children and twelve grandchildren.

Please describe your experience as a student in higher education.

I was told by my high school counselor that Indians did not go to college. That I should think of another marketable skill. That for sure I could not afford to go to dental school. I was the lone American Indian on the college campus. I was put in a fish bowl and everyone watched my every move. I had distractions from non-Indians asking me ignorant questions about my culture. I almost quit school because I was very lonely and was quiet and reserved. My self-esteem was very much damaged. We had no telephone, so I could not call home for support and comfort.

How did you choose the higher education institutions you attended?

My folks sent me to an all-boys Christian Brothers school in Santa Fe, New Mexico, because they heard the brothers would prepare me for college. Which they did. Since I was a good student (valedictorian of my graduating class) the brothers wanted me to go to a Jesuit university. The closest dental school to my home was Creighton University (Omaha, Nebraska).

What factors contributed to your success in higher education?

I had strong family support. I played on the college tennis team and became popular and it boosted my self-esteem. I studied harder than most students because of the strong competition for getting into dental school.

I sacrificed more than most students and worked at many jobs so that I could get into dental school and help pay for my education.

What challenges did you face as a student in higher education?

I had to get very good grades to get into dental school. World War II veterans were returning back to college and the year I was applying to dental school there were over 1,000 applications for the forty-six seats available in the freshman class!

I was very much stereotyped (as an American Indian) and being in that fishbowl the pressures were more for me—because everyone was looking at me to be either successful or I would be another Indian that failed!

How did you adapt to meet those challenges?

I knew I had to study harder than anyone else—so I could meet the criteria for being accepted into dental school. Being captain of the tennis team and being competitive made me stronger in my abilities to meet all challenges. I grew even prouder of my cultural background and wanted to show everyone that this American Indian was going to succeed—and that was the only way it was going to be!

What advice would you give to American Indian and Alaskan Native individuals interested in obtaining a higher education degree?

Make up your mind to accept the challenges that lay ahead. Your goals should be obtainable. Do not bite off more than you can chew. Do not let distractions get in the way, because there will be many. Overcome the obstacles one by one. Take one step at a time.

Know the importance of time—use it wisely and for your intended goals. Remember that time passes rapidly and that one day turns into a week and before you know it you are taking exams and getting grades that can help or hurt you and it is difficult get behind and have to continuously be playing catch-up.

What would your life be like without having gone to college or earning a college degree?

I may not have had a life—since I was drafted into the Korean War (1950) and several of my high school classmates were killed in that conflict. I would not have been able to declare that I am the *first* American Indian dentist in the United States! I would not have been able to become an Assistant Surgeon General and be the director of the many programs that have helped my American Indian people. When people (Indian and non-Indian) hear that I am a doctor—it is like the golden key that opens all doors and gives me the opportunity to be a meaningful leader and decision maker in my programs that benefit all American Indians. It has allowed me to take pride in being a role model and having Indian youngsters want to follow in my footsteps.

Please describe what you feel are the benefits of going to college and getting a college degree.

In this modern age of technology, competition, and decision making, it seems that the college graduate is looked on as the planner, the implementer, the final decision maker for major policies and procedures. The college graduate (with his or her degree) stands at the turnstiles for determining what happens to those that follow. In Indian Country, if American Indian and Alaska Native students do not assume those meaningful leadership roles (decision makers), in my opinion, Indian self-determination will remain a myth!!

APPENDIX A: FACTORS UNDERLYING NATIVE AMERICAN STUDENT SUCCESS—A LITERATURE REVIEW

Citation	Method of Identification	Whose Perspective?	Factors
Patton and Edington (1973)	Survey	135 students from the University of New Mexico (UNM) and 68 from New Mexico State University (NMSU)	NMSU • College GPA • Gender • Indian Club membership • High school rank • Age UNM • College GPA • Public vs. private high school attendance • Having a native roommate • Larger high school graduating class = more persistence • ACT (social science, math) • Major—technology
Wilson (1983)	Opinionnaires, 189 were also interviewed individually and in groups	214 Wisconsin Indian college students and graduates (juniors, seniors, grad students) attending public and private 4-year institutions	• Financial aid • Family support • Having a personal goal • Determination • Intelligence • Composite profile: parent(s) who valued college education, no perception of discrimination before high school, discovery that college was more difficult and less personal than high school, pride in being an Indian, sense of purpose
Falk and Aitken (1984)	Interviews (structured; given list of 20 factors, ranked top 3)	125 students who received financial aid from Minnesota Chippewa Tribe who had attended over 20 different colleges, most of them within Minnesota or bordering states (also 11 college personnel)	• Active family support • Academic preparation • Overt institutional commitment • Financial aid • Personal motivation

(continued)

Appendix A Continued

Citation	Method of Identification	Whose Perspective?	Factors
Schwartz (1995)	Survey	86 randomly selected students attending Northern Arizona University	• More traditional were more successful (based on judgment of researcher, multiple criteria)
Beaty and Chiste (1986)	Program Review (description)	Review of University Preparation Program at University of Lethbridge for Native students in attempt to improve their retention and graduation rates	• Importance of having a "gate keeper" who is a face to face link from student to university (professor, advisor, etc.) • Self-awareness of learning process • Practice in handling gate-keeping encounters • Prepare institutions for students
Huffman, Sill, and Brokenleg (1986)	Survey	38 Native American and 48 white students from University of South Dakota and Black Hills State College	• Cultural identity and retention of Native cultural traditions (vs. high school GPA and parental encouragement for white students)
Kleinfeld, Cooper, and Kyle (1987)	Program review	Authors' review of a postsecondary counseling program located in a K–12 school district in Alaska	• Postsecondary counselor program: an experienced teacher/counselor takes responsibility for seniors and young adults staying at home (stays linked with students across institutions/programs); helps the student get through the forms and financial aid minefield, phones them regularly at school, acts as personal touchstone to the community and an encourager for the student
LaCounte (1987)	Literature review (uses Eastern Montana State College as example)	Author's perspective on Native American college students	• Variables that influence college persistence (financial resources, bilingualism [varies among tribes], and aspiration to occupations visible on or near reservations where they live—want to get degree to go back and help their own people) • Interventions that enhance academic and personal development: orientation, institutional retention efforts, academic and career advising, monitoring academic progress, tutorial support, financial aid, peer counseling, student organizations, cultural events, formal ways to meet professors

Lin, LaCounte, and Eder (1988)	Survey	632 students at a mid-size predominantly white 4-year state college in Montana (87 were Native)	• Suggest that improvement of campus environment (hostility, acceptance, etc.) will lead to improved academic performance
Rindone (1988)	Survey	107 Navajo graduates who had attained at least a 4-year college degree	• Encouragement from parents and family members
Hornett (1989)	Author suggestions	Author's experience	• Student-oriented, caring faculty who are culturally sensitive and open to new ideas • Suggestions for faculty: understand and deal with racism, recognize nontraditional leadership skills, as well as recognize the student's need for a strong support person, long- and short-term goals, self-understanding, and a positive self-image
Wells (1989)	Survey	33 faculty and staff in U.S. colleges and universities serving highest percentage of Native Americans	• Factors derived from lit review: (a) early intervention, (b) summer bridge programs to introduce students to college-level coursework, (c) tailored financial aid programs, (d) academic assessment programs, (e) tutoring and mentoring services, (f) intrusive academic advising, (g) career guidance • Responses: Committee on special education projects, language programs, remedial programs, orientation and attendance programs, tutorials, developmental courses, counseling and faculty advisors and staff, American Indian program, financial aid, student centers and clubs, Native American awareness week, Upward Bound, Cross Cultural Communications Dept., Honors Institute, rural student services

(continued)

Appendix A Continued

Citation	Method of Identification	Whose Perspective?	Factors
Huffman (1990, Spring)	In-depth interviews and questionnaires	30 Native American students who have attended or are attending predominantly non-Indian colleges in South Dakota	• Transculturation—students go through a continuous process of cultural encounters and realignments through which they rediscover their Native identity as a strength and learn to relate to the college culture while retaining their traditional cultural identity
Lin (1990)	Survey	632 students at a mid-size predominantly white college in Montana (includes 87 Native Americans)	• Those from "traditional" families were more task- and achievement-oriented, had higher GPAs and more hours of doing homework ("traditional" defined as authoritarian and parent centered); those from modern families cared more about professors' opinions and skipped more classes
Cibik and Chambers (1991)	Survey	Undergraduate students at a Southwestern state university, 155 Native American, 131 Hispanic, 38 African American, 25 Asian American and 210 Anglo students	• Financial Aid support (vs. contributions from family, friends) • Ability to "go home" often to help family or attend ceremonies and special activities (although this translates into missing classes—could be detrimental) • Native Americans least confident in moving toward degree • Minority students more often give personal betterment as reason for attending college (vs. career, income, social attributes of college life)

Murguia, Padilla, and Pavel (1991)	Interviews	24 junior and senior students of Hispanic and Native American background	• Ethnic enclaves promote social integration • Ethnicity is rooted in biology, family, and friends • Function of ethnicity: self-identity, sense of place in the world, and affective support
Davis (1992)	Interviews	10 American Indian college graduates who were enrolled membersof the Crow, Northern Cheyenne, and Blackfeet tribes	• Family encouragement • Desire to better themselves
Hoover and Jacobs (1992)	Survey (examined perceptions of high school prep, college instruction, personal views of attending college, and study skill abilities)	257 college students who attended the annual American Indian Science and Engineering Society conference	• Slightly positive toward college life and study skills • Less positive toward counseling and career guidance in high school • Slightly more positive toward college instruction and personal feelings toward attending college than toward study skills
Pavel (1992)	Literature review	Author's perspective on American Indians and Alaskan Natives in undergraduate and graduate enrollment as well as the K–12 system	• Intentions in high school • Academic integration • Social integration (prominent but indirect role) • Ethnic enclaves • Advisors who were ethnic matches or were selected by student (served as advocate, provided insider perspective, understood them as people) • Continuity with K–12 (parental involvement, belief in relevance of education, community-based curriculum, appropriate teaching styles, caring teachers and administrators, holistic early intervention)

(continued)

Appendix A Continued

Citation	Method of Identification	Whose Perspective?	Factors
Pavel and Padilla (1993)	Data drawn from the High School and Beyond study (NCES, 1980 to 1986)	Structural equation modeling	• Family background • Postsecondary intentions (both prior to and during college) • Formal and informal academic integration
Benjamin, Chambers, and Reiterman (1993)	Started with quantitative analysis of specified factors (did not predict persistence); then conducted interviews to explore issues listed in factors column	166 new first-time full-time American Indian freshmen enrolling at a medium sized Southwestern state university (quantitative part); 11 from 166 were interviewed	• Early desire to further education • Ability to "go home" often • Ability to assume bicultural patterns, but not assimilate
Steward (1993)	Case studies	2 American Indian seniors enrolled at a predominantly Anglo Midwestern public university	• Stable family system • Academically prepared for college based on high school GPA and ACT scores • Had found comfortable niche on campus • World views similar to Anglo • Expressed a need to be of assistance to others in society • Perceived selves to be socially competent • Well defined vocational goals
Tate and Schwartz (1993)	Survey	84 American Indian undergrad and grad social work students from accredited programs across nation	• Faculty support

			Focus on barriers: individual variability—difficulties associated with cultural differences, being nontraditional students, lack of faculty support
Cross (1993)	Survey	56 American Indian support program administrators at selected 4-year public and private colleges/universities	• American Indian support programs impact enrollment, retention, and graduation • Top 3 important factors specific to programs: institutional support, qualified American Indian staff, community connection • Top 3 student needs: deal with financial difficulties, culture shock and value differences, family issues • Top 3 areas of participation: academic advising, tutoring, financial aid advising
Pipes, Westby, and Inglebret (1993)	Literature review	Authors' perspectives	• Attitudes toward education • Cultural dimensions • Communication variables • Cognitive and learning styles • Attitudes and beliefs regarding health and illness • Strategies for academic achievement (faculty role as cultural broker, oral interaction and teaching strategies, enhancing curricular content)
Barnhardt (1994)	Interviews, student record review, participant observation	50 Alaska Native teacher education graduates from University of Alaska Fairbanks	• Teaching and learning environment responsive to interests and needs of culturally diverse (CD) students • Student support services respectful of interests and needs of CD students • Strong family and community support • Supportive prior school and life experiences • Exceptional individual efforts

(continued)

Appendix A Continued

Citation	Method of Identification	Whose Perspective?	Factors
Dodd, Garcia, Meccage, and Nelson (1995)	Interviews	24 academically successful American Indian students classified as seniors in a state-supported college in Montana	• Family • Student support services • Teachers (caring, concerned) • Coping with prejudice • Maintain identity through special activities and organizations
Burns (1995)	In-depth interviews	5 members of Colville Confederated Tribes attending Spokane Community College (persisted for more than 2 consecutive quarters in same program and achieved at least 2.0 GPA each quarter)	• Precollege preparatory activities • Mobility (physical and emotional) • Alcohol or drugs affected lives profoundly • Biculturalism and dealing with racism • Struggles experienced (emotional pain)—more motivated to prove themselves • Strategies employed to stay (internal: setting attainable educational goals, positive attitude; external: success in extracurricular activities, support from specific people, funding, cultural involvement, taking on identity as role model) • Suggested retention strategies (preplanning for college and initial success, survival strategies, connecting with people who can act as mentors)
Liley (1995)	Survey	75 AI/AN graduates of Utah Graduate School of Social Work (MSW)	• Financial aid • Tutoring support: writing, social work concepts • Special interest of Indian Project staff • Individual consultation with faculty • Study groups with other MSW students • Relevance of curricular components to employment

Monette (1995)	Survey	278 graduates of Turtle Mt. Community College (tribally controlled), earned AA, AAS, or vocational diploma or certificate	• Positive about TMCC academic programs, met student needs, curriculum responsive to tribal education needs, Indian instructors and Indian culture important, met its transfer mission, quality of instruction perceived to be equal to transfer institution
Napier (1995)	Micro-ethnography	9 American Indian with doctoral degrees from Pennsylvania State University's American Indian leadership program	• Motivated to improve education for American Indian children • Family and community ties
Wenzlaff and Brewer (1996)	15 Native participants in a Native American Secondary Teacher Education Program at a predominantly white university	Student perspectives of their success in the program	• Family support • Former tribal college experiences (build self-confidence) • Program peer group • Mentors (faculty, students, administration, project staff) • Professors • Determination to obtain an education and keeping focused on education
HeavyRunner and Morris (1997)	Literature review (resilience)	Authors	• Educators and others working with Indian youth who demand respect for cultural values, beliefs and behaviors foster resilience (10 are identified: spirituality, childrearing/extended family, veneration of age/wisdom/tradition, respect for nature, generosity and sharing, cooperation/group harmony, autonomy/respect for others, composure/patience, relativity of time, nonverbal communication) • Safe families for children • Tribal identity, spirituality, elders, ceremonies, rituals, humor, oral tradition, family, support networking, cultural values, and worldviews (identified by 20 national Native educators/trainers)

(continued)

Appendix A Continued

Citation	Method of Identification	Whose Perspective?	Factors
Boyer (1997)	Survey	1,614 Native American students from 24 different tribal colleges	• Curriculum focus: job training • Curriculum focus: Native culture • Personal attention from faculty and staff (care, understand their needs) • Quality instruction • Affordability • Essential support services (transportation, child care; some indicated a need for more) • Small classes
Brown and Kurpius (1997)	Survey	288 American Indian undergrad students in a large SW university (149 persisters: had obtained BA or were enrolled 5 years later; 139 nonpersisters: had not obtained underground degree (although no data available regarding transfers)	• Academic preparation and aspirations • Academic performance • Interactions with faculty and staff
Buckley (1997)	Ethnography	8 American Indian students in graduate and professional schools at research university (medicine, law, public affairs)	• Construct a surrogate community on campus with those who share their ethnicity (provide community service to those in need "giving back" in city and university and to distant reservations) • Faculty/advisor support
Meyers (1997)	Program review	Author's review of RAIN program at University of North Dakota college of Nursing, WA state teacher certification program on the Tulalip reservation, RAIN program at UCLA, MERITS program at the University of Arizona	• RAIN (ND): Open-door policy, creating a sense of belonging, intrusive monitoring, aggressive advising, mentoring, value clarification, cultural awareness • Tulalip: Courses with strong cross-cultural emphasis, financial assistance, work release time, Native language classes offered, food available in class, students teach

			faculty, instructors learn to use Indian humor and cross-cultural communication skills • RAIN (UCLA): Operated by students, peer counseling, study hall to encourage group study and transportation home, academic, social, and cultural workshops, resources, and talking circles • MERITS: Contract system: regular peer advising, regular grade report sheets, workshops with student dialogue on issues affecting their academic success, tutoring sessions—math, science, writing
Wilson (1997)	Interviews (ethnographic)	60 undergrad students (28 Native American)	• Professor-student relations (accessibility, approachability, and availability; genuineness and caring)
Fore (1997)	Questionnaires (investigated 4 research questions involving direct and mediator relationships among variables in relation to GPA and retention)	59 Native American and 76 Anglo American college students	• Hypothesized mediator relations were not found • Native Americans who endorsed greater perceived support from environment achieved higher GPA 1 year later • Native Americans who endorsed more long-term goals were more likely to graduate or stay in college • For Anglo students, leadership skills and financial aid influenced GPA and retention
Castellanos, Kuh, and Pavel (1998)	Survey (CSEQ data-based Pace's framework, Pascarella's model)	298 American Indian/Alaska Native undergraduate students and 1,698 white students at research-type institutions	• Did not support ethnic differences in level of academic student effort or involvement (white vs. Native) • Social student effort was higher for whites (effect size small) • Perceptions of vocational and practical aspects of environment and perceived gains in science and technology were higher for Natives (effect size small)

(continued)

Appendix A Continued

Citation	Method of Identification	Whose Perspective?	Factors
Taylor (1999)	Interviews	13 Native American undergraduates at predominantly white research institution, who had persisted for more than 1 semester	• Each story is unique • Supportive people (instructors, advisors, parents) • Determination • Challenges: Alienation based on academic struggles, skin color and appearance, covert and overt racial hostility, lack of respect, stereotyping, loneliness, lack of role models, lack of institutional support
Pavel (1999)	Literature review	Various authors	• K–16 partnerships with tribal communities to enhance pre-college academic preparation and postsecondary aspirations • Culturally specific academic and student support services • Mentoring programs • Adequate financial aid • Tribal colleges are exemplars in recruitment, retention, and supportive campus environments
Wiest (1999)	Interviews	15 Native American students	• Family values/influences • Institutional support/programs • Financial support • Culture and community
Jenkins (1999)	Literature review	Author	• Family support • Student support services • Precollege preparation
American Indian Higher Education Consortium and the American Indian College Fund (2000)	Survey	242 Native American graduates from 17 tribal colleges (AA, BA, certificates)	Satisfaction ratings high for: • Major courses • Overall instruction • Small class sizes • Contact with faculty and administrators • Prepared for transfer

Garcia (2000)	Interviews	12 American Indians with a doctoral degree in the state of Montana	• Family support • Ability to function biculturally • Spirituality • Traditional understanding of reciprocity (giving back) • Role models/mentors • Desire to achieve • Pride in cultural heritage
Reyes (2000–2001)	Focus groups	7 Alaska Native students at upper division or graduate levels at the University of Alaska Fairbanks	• Persistence and hard work • Commitment to Native community • Financial support from Native corporations • Family support (both emotional and financial) • Employment • Availability of developmental classes (to develop skills they thought they lacked) • Distance delivery courses • Rural student services • Faculty support
Angspatt (2001)	Interviews	20 American Indian graduates from University of Montana (completed at least BA)	• Academic mentoring • Family support • Goal orientation • Personal motivation
Demmert (2001)	Literature review	ERIC and dissertation abstracts were screened (a more formal evaluation of quality will be reported as part of a larger study)	• Family support • Cultural identity • Personal determination and goal setting • Financial support • Academic skills • Mentoring and supportive faculty • Bicultural curriculum

(continued)

Appendix A Continued

Citation	Method of Identification	Whose Perspective?	Factors
Huffman (2001)	In-depth interviews	69 American Indian (predominantly Lakota), culturally traditional students attending a small Midwestern university	• Transculturation framework • American Indian ethnic identity as emotional anchor • Importance of transculturation threshold leading to self discovery • Ability to engage in two cultural settings • Process of cultural learning
Jackson and Smith (2001)	Interviews	22 Navajo high school graduates, most were involved in college coursework, all were considering college	• Positive factors: Family connections, faculty relation-ships, and connection to homeland and culture (all had conflicting dimensions) • Challenging factors: Discrepancy between high school and college learning environments, vague educational and vocational constructs
Rousey and Longie (2001)	Ethnography of a typical tribal college	Administrator, faculty, and student interviews; parent and staff interviews for community programs; observations; document review for Cankdeska Cikana Community College in North Dakota	• Provision of coordinated social services (especially child care) • Incorporation of cultural-familial values, knowledge, and traditions throughout institution • Location on reservation in context of strong family network available for social support • College changes to meet student needs • Students adjust to academic demands, then as transfer students adjust to social differences in life off reserve (at 4-year institutions would do both at same time) • Staff personally know students and their families

Reed-Inderbitzin (2001)	Program evaluation	54 Building Bridges Conference participants, primarily from SD; 75% Native American	Students evaluated effectiveness of meeting program goals as follows: • Networking opportunities with individuals interested in mental health issues • Role models • Provide info on culturally appropriate research • Provide info relating to bicultural skills
Cole and Denzine (2002)	College Student Experience Questionnaire (CSEQ, Pace, 1998)	544 undergraduate students (74 were American Indian) attending a doctoral program at a public university in the Southwest	• No significant differences between American Indian and white students in their academic engagement
Ness (2002)	Individual interviews and focus groups	13 American Indian students who attended a tribal college (7 had successfully completed their plan of study and 6 had not)	• Strong self-esteem • Sense of resiliency/ability to "bounce back" • Goal completion mentality • Family support system • Financial aid/resources • Arrangements for child care, transportation, etc. • Ability to "walk in two worlds" without losing personal identity • Significant personal connection to faculty/staff member • Access to significant help from support services early in college experience • Participation in cultural activities on and off campus • Avoidance of drug/alcohol abuse

(continued)

Appendix A Continued

Citation	Method of Identification	Whose Perspective?	Factors
Strand and Peacock (2002)	Literature review	Various authors	• Spiritually, mental well-being, emotional well-being, physical well-being • Building self-esteem through belonging, mastery, independence, generosity • Family, fair teachers, close to people at school, get along with people at school, felt that other students were prejudiced • Parents, communities, teachers, school connections; tribal culture; good self-concept, strong sense of direction, tenacity, positive feelings regarding tribal culture (and feeling comfortable living in both worlds); participation in cultural activities; strong positive feelings of belonging to a Native community and family; appreciation of the influence of elders, grandparents, and parents; participation in school curriculum that includes Native history, language, and culture
HeavyRunner and DeCelles (2002)	Literature review	Authors	• Family support for the students • Family rapport with the college staff • Healthy families • Spirituality • Bilingualism • Biculturalism • Kinship • Community
Guillory (2002)	Focus group interviews	30 students (junior, senior, graduate), 2 State Board of Education members, 3 university presidents, and 9 faculty members from Washington State University, University of Idaho, Montana State University	Students • Family support; giving back to tribal community; social supports—other students, faculty, advisor; recruitment/retention programs specific to Native Americans; did not want to return to negative conditions of reservation

			State Board of Education members • Academic preparation; financial resources; role models University presidents • Programs tailored to Native Americans; adequate financial support; nurturing and welcoming environment—culturally, academically, socially; cultural outreach Faculty • Support systems—family, cultural, academic, peer, faculty; financial support; special programs
Jackson, Smith, and Hill (2003)	Interviews	15 successful Native American college students who grew up on reservations (five 4-year colleges in SW); seniors in good standing	• Family support • Structured social support • Faculty/staff warmth • Exposure to college and vocations • Developing independence and assertiveness • Reliance on spiritual resources • Dealing with racism • Nonlinear path • Paradoxical cultural pressure
HeavyRunner and Marshall (2003)	Literature review	Authors	• Understanding inner spirit • Finding sense of direction • Spirituality • Family strength • Elders • Ceremonial strength • Oral traditions • Tribal identity • Support network

(continued)

Appendix A Continued

Citation	Method of Identification	Whose Perspective?	Factors
Ortiz and HeavyRunner (2003)	Literature review	Authors' perspective on Native American students in higher education including 2- and 4-year universities and tribal colleges and universities	• Family support • "Traditional" families • Sufficient academic preparation • Educational aspiration • Attendance at tribal colleges • Academic integration • Support services • Supportive and encouraging faculty • Role models • Assistance with paperwork and forms • Good advising
Aragon (2004a)	3 learning style instruments	Assessment results: convenience sample of 206 AI/AN postsecondary students at community colleges in SW, including 1 tribal college	• "Moderate or average" skills—info processing, self-testing, use of study aids, methodological study, and elaborative processing • Border of "low/moderate"—motivation, ability to select main ideas, fact retention • "Low"—attitude, use of test strategies, concentration, level of anxiety, time management, and deep processing
Aragon (2004b)	3 learning style instruments	Assessment results: convenience sample of 206 postsecondary students at community colleges in SW, including 1 tribal college	• Students are practical, orderly, logical, and earn success by concentration and thoroughness; use both analytical (field-independent) and global (field-dependent) info processing
Waterman (2004)	Individual interviews	12 Haudenosaunee higher education graduates	• Before College Path: Parent expectations, TV was not emphasized, high school guidance played no role, applied to only one college

			• College Path: longer time to finish (2–20 years; stop-outs for 2–15 years) • Support: family, children, siblings, parents, home-going, student group (students go to find their identity; traditional student often did not go), Native faculty/staff, caring faculty (got to know, explained assignments), mentoring (more for men, to leadership and teaching, show informal network of university) • Stress—from family and culture, double curriculum—Native (ex., language) and formal, college is external demand • Maintained their cultural identity • Family support of student • Academically engaged • Community college experience (fixed grades) • Want to "give back"
White Shield (2004–2005)	Literature review	Author	• Opportunities to develop and sustain Indigenous identity and attachment to Native values, behaviors, and realities (requires faculty and staff training, culturally meaningful education specific to Indigenous students, implementation of new recruitment and retention designs, culturally responsive counseling, increased numbers of Indigenous faculty and administrators)
Katz (2005)	Collective case study—interviews, e-mails, observations, and interviews with associates	3 members of Plateau tribes who had graduated from registered nursing programs with at least 2 years of nursing experience	• Family expectations to become educated • Desire to break a cycle of early pregnancy, high school dropout, and alcohol/drug abuse • Desire to serve their communities • Able to deal with pressure/culture shock (support from faculty and staff) • Determination and strength

(continued)

Appendix A Continued

Citation	Method of Identification	Whose Perspective?	Factors
Fox, Lowe, and McClellan (2005)	Literature review	Various authors	• Complex Native identities and experiences • Expectations of higher education: respect for tribal sovereignty and Native cultures, languages, and epistemologies; funding for Native students; coordinated, campus-wide student support (students services and faculty); cooperative relationships between universities and Indian nations • Tribal colleges as exemplars • Native American studies programs • Native staff and faculty • Native voices heard and honored through action
Yang, Byers, and Fenton (2006)	Survey: Basic Human Needs scale and "My Life Then & Now" scale	57 American Indian and Alaska Native students	• Student use of multicultural student support office varied (on average 1–2 times/semester; 4% used daily; 65% do not use at all) • Students feeling adrift and with lower GPAs used office more often • Students feeling self-directed used office less
Villegas and Prieto (2006)	Interviews	45 Alaska Native community leaders, community members, and advocates	• "Successful Alaska Native students are those who can set and achieve goals because they know their own worth and value, understand their responsibility to their community, and are prepared to pursue whatever life path they choose."

APPENDIX B: FINANCIAL AID TERMINOLOGY

Financial aid has its own vocabulary, terms, and abbreviations. To help you speak the "language," the Office of Student Financial Aid at Washington State University has put together an amazing glossary listing some of the most commonly used terms and abbreviations. Please visit www.finaid.wsu.edu/vocab.htm to see this complete list plus helpful links to more information.

Term	Definition
1040 Form, 1040A Form, 1040EZ Form, Tele-Tax Form	FAFSA term—The federal income tax return. Forms used to report income and income tax due/paid to the Internal Revenue Service each year.
1090 Form	FAFSA term—Form used to report interest income or dividend income.
1099 Form	FAFSA term—Form used by business to report income paid to a nonemployee.
401(k)	FAFSA term—A popular type of retirement fund.
AA or AAS	Academic terms—AA—associate of arts degree. Can be earned at most two-year colleges. AAS—associate of applied science degree. Can be earned at some two-year colleges. Also known as associate degree.
Ability to Benefit	FAFSA term—One of the criteria used to establish student eligibility to receive Title IV program assistance is that a student must have earned a high school diploma or its equivalent. Students who are not high school graduates (or who have not earned a GED) can demonstrate that they have the "ability to benefit" from the education or training being offered by passing an approved ability-to-benefit (ATB) test.
Academic Year	Academic term—The period during which school is in session, consisting of 30 weeks of instructional time. The school year runs from the end of August through the middle of May at WSU.
Accrue	Loan term—To accumulate; refers to interest on a loan.
Accrual Date	Loan term—The date on which interest charges on an educational loan begin to accrue. *See also* Unsubsidized Loan.
Academic Advisor	Academic term—The academic person from whom a student receives personal guidance in the processes of choosing a major, picking classes to fulfill graduation and major requirements, as well other academic issues.
AFDC	FAFSA term—AFDC (Aid to Families with Dependent Children) or ADC is a federal program to financially assist families with children.

(continued)

Appendix B Continued

Term	Definition
AGI	FAFSA term—Adjusted gross income (AGI) is a figure taken from the federal income tax form that has been filed in compliance with IRS regulations and guidelines.
Alternative Loans	See Private Loans.
Amortization	Loan term—The process of gradually repaying a loan over an extended period of time through periodic installments of principal and interest.
Appeal	Financial aid term—A written request from a student or their parent(s) asking for consideration to due special or unusual circumstances. For example, if you believe the financial information on your financial aid application does not reflect your family's current ability to pay (e.g., because of death of a parent, unemployment, or other unusual circumstances) you should definitely make an appeal. The financial aid administrator will require documentation of the special circumstances.
Assets	FAFSA term—Assets are elements of the student's and family's financial worth; includes stocks, bonds, checking and savings accounts, trusts, other securities, real estate (this does not include your the family home or family farm), income property, business equipment, and inventory. When calculating the expected family contribution (EFC), all assets are considered.
Asset Equity	FAFSA term—Asset equity is the current market value of an asset minus any debt owed against it. Market value, not the insurance or tax value, is what it could be sold for at the present time. See also Equity.
Assistantship	See Graduate Assistantship.
Associate Degree	Academic term—The degree granted by two-year colleges. See also AA or AAS.
Award Letter	Financial aid term—An official notices from the college's financial aid office to the student applicant providing an analysis of their financial need and the financial aid package awarded. Award letters include the amount, source and type of aid included in the package. The award letter will include the terms and conditions for the financial aid and information about the cost of attendance. Also called Financial Aid Award Notification.
Award Year	The academic year for which financial aid is requested (or received).
B.A. or B.S.	Academic terms—These are undergraduate degrees. Also know as bachelor's degree. B.A. stands for bachelor of arts; B.S. stands for bachelor of science. The type of degree awarded depends on the kinds of courses taken by the student.

Bankruptcy	Legal term—When a person is declared bankrupt, he is found to be legally insolvent and his property is distributed among his creditors or otherwise administered to satisfy the interests of his creditors. Federal student loans, however, cannot normally be discharged through bankruptcy.
Base Year	FAFSA term—For need analysis purposes, the calendar year preceding the award year for which financial aid is requested (i.e., for the 2004–2005 award year, the base year would be the calendar year of 2003).
BIA	Bureau of Indian Affairs, a federal agency responsible for the awarding and disbursement of federal funds to Native Americans.
BIA Grant	A BIA grant program for enrolled members of a tribe (Indian, Eskimo, or Aleut) pursuing an undergraduate or graduate degree at an accredited postsecondary institution. To be eligible for a BIA grant, students must show financial need as determined by the institution they are attending.
Branch Campus	Academic term—A permanent location of a school that is geographically apart from the main campus. Now known as urban campus.
Borrower	Loan term—The person who signed the promissory note and is responsible for repaying the loan.
Budget	See Cost of Attendance.
Cancellation	Loan term—Certain loan programs provide for cancellation (erasing) of the loan under certain circumstances, such as death or permanent disability of the borrower. Some of the federal student loan programs have additional cancellation provisions. For example, if the student becomes a teacher in certain national shortage areas, they may be eligible for cancellation of all or part of the balance of their educational loans. Not all loans have the same provisions.
Capitalized	Loan term—The practice of adding unpaid interest charges to the principal balance of an educational loan, thereby increasing the size of the loan. Interest is then charged on the new balance, including both the unpaid principal and the accrued interest. Capitalizing the interest increases the monthly payment and the amount of money you will eventually have to repay. If you can afford to pay the interest as it accrues, you are better off not capitalizing it. This refers to the Unsubsidized Stafford Loan.
Central Processing System (CPS)	FAFSA term—The federal computer system that receives the FAFSA and calculates the Expected Family Contribution (EFC) and delivers the Student Aid Report (SAR).
Citizen	Federal term—A native or naturalized member of the United States. To receive federal aid you must be a U.S. citizen, a U.S. national, or a permanent resident who has an I-151, I-551, or I-551C.

(continued)

Appendix B Continued

Term	Definition
COA	*See* Cost of Attendance.
Collection Agency	Loan term—A company often hired by the lender or guarantee agency to recover defaulted loans.
Color of Federal Forms	FAFSA term—The FAFSA and SAR change color each year in a four-color rotation: green (2001–2002), blue (2002–2003), yellow (2003–2004), pink (2005–2006). This will help you make sure you're filing the right form for the year.
Commuter Student	Financial aid term—A student who lives at home with his or her parents and commutes to school every day.
Consolidation Loan	Loan term—Consolidation loans allow students to combine different loans, subsidized and unsubsidized, from different lenders or schools to make repayment more manageable. Loans eligible for consolidation include Stafford, PLUS, Perkins, SLS, NDSL, HPSL, and direct loans. Participating lenders pay off the borrower's existing student loans, creating a new loan with a single monthly payment and an extended repayment term of up to 30 years.
Consortium Agreement	Academic term—A written, formal agreement between two institutions eligible to participate in Title IV federal funding programs. The consortium agreement allows a student to enroll in courses at another institution while working toward a degree or certificate.
Cooperative Education	Academic term—A program where the student spends time engaged in employment related to their major in addition to regular classroom study. Also known as "co-op education"
Corrections	FAFSA term—The process of making changes to the original data submitted on the FAFSA. Corrections are made when an error occurred. Changing income information from estimated to actual tax information is one example of an allowable correction. Corrections may be student-made or school-made depending on the type of information being changed.
Co-signer	Loan term—A person who signs the promissory note in addition to the borrower and is responsible for the obligation if the borrower does not pay.
Cost of Attendance (COA)	Financial aid term—The COA is the an estimate of total amount it should cost the student to go to school for the period. The COA must include estimates for tuition and fees, room and board (or rent/food/utilities), allowances for books and supplies, transportation, and personal and incidental expenses. Also known as the budget.
CPS	*See* Central Processing System.
Credit Bureaus	Loan term—Organizations that maintain records on personal financial histories. There are currently three major credit bureaus: TRW, Equifax Credit Information Services, and TransUnion.

Credit Worthy Loan term—An individual with no negative credit history per the criteria established by the lender.

Cumulative Grade Point Average Academic term—The overall average of a student's grades based on a 4.0 scale. Also referred to as "cum gpa."

Custodial Parent FAFSA term—If a student's parents are divorced or separated, the custodial parent is the one with whom the student lived the most during the past 12 months. The student's need analysis is based on financial information supplied by the custodial parent on the FAFSA.

Debt Loan/FAFSA term—An amount of money owed.

Default Loan term—Failure to make scheduled monthly payments according to the agreed-on terms. Default occurs at 180 days when the delinquency date is prior to 10/7/98, and 270 days when the delinquency date is on or after 10/7/98. Defaulting on a government loan will make you ineligible for future federal financial aid, unless a satisfactory repayment schedule is arranged, and can affect your credit rating.

Default Rate Loan term—A school's default rate is the percentage of borrowers who are 120 days or more behind in their loan payments.

Deferment Loan term—A period during which a borrower who meets certain criteria may suspend loan payments. For some loans the federal government pays the interest during a deferment. On others, the interest accrues and is capitalized, and the borrower is responsible for paying it.

Delinquent Loan term—Failure to make monthly loan payments when due. Delinquency begins with the first missed payment. If the borrower misses several payments, the loan goes into default.

Departmental Scholarship Financial aid term—An award of gift assistance that is specifically designated for a recipient in a particular academic department or educational program.

Dependent FAFSA term—For a child or other person to be considered your dependent, they must live with you and you must provide them with more than half of their support. Spouses do not count as dependents in the federal methodology.

Dependent Student Status FAFSA term—Based on the FAFSA definition, a student who is required to include parental income and signatures to file the FAFSA.

Direct Loans Loan term—The William D. Ford Federal Direct Loan Program (aka the Direct Loan Program) is a federal program where the school becomes the lending agency and manages the funds directly, with the federal government providing the loan funds.

(continued)

Appendix B Continued

Term	Definition
Disbursement	School term—Payment; the process by which financial aid funds are made available to students for use in meeting educational and related living expenses. Funds are first applied to the student's tuition and fees account balance.
Discharge	Loan term—To release the borrower from his or her obligation to repay the loan. *See also* Cancellation.
Disclosure Statement	Loan term—Statement explaining specific terms and conditions of student loans, such as interest rate, loan fees charged, gross amount borrowed, and so on. Disclosure statements must accompany each loan disbursement.
Documentation	Financial aid term—A written or printed paper, a supporting reference, or a record that can be used to furnish evidence, proof, or information.
Doctorate	Academic term—Also known as a PhD—A graduate degree beyond a master's degree.
DRN	FAFSA term—The Data Release Number is assigned to a student as a protective measure. For the student to make corrections to or add schools to their SAR, the DRN must be used. It is found only on the paper Student Aid Report.
Due Diligence	Loan term—If a borrower fails to make payments on their loan according to the terms of the promissory note, the federal government requires the lender, holder, or servicer of the loan to make frequent attempts to contact the borrower (via telephone and mail) to encourage him or her to repay the loan and make arrangements to resolve the delinquency.
Early Action/Early Admission/Early Decision	Admission Office terms—An early action program has earlier deadlines and earlier notification dates than the regular admissions process. An early admission program allows exemplary high school juniors to skip their senior year and enroll directly in college. An early decision program has earlier deadlines and earlier notification dates than the regular admissions process, and students who apply to an early decision program commit to attending the school if admitted (which means the student must accept the offer of admission before they see their financial aid package).
EDE	*See* Electronic Data Exchange.
EFT	*See* Electronic Funds Transfer.
Educational Opportunity Grant Program (EOG)	Financial aid term—The Educational Opportunity Grant is a state-funded grant program aimed at the neediest students. The HECB identifies who is eligible and sends to the college a list of the students to be awarded.
Educational Testing Service (ETS)	Admissions term—Company that produces and administers the SAT and other educational achievement tests.

EFC | *See* Expected Family Contribution.

Electronic Data Exchange (EDE) | FAFSA term—Program used by schools to electronically receive FAFSA results from the federal processor and to submit corrections to the federal processor.

Electronic Funds Transfer (EFT) | Loan term—Schools and their preferred lenders wire funds for Stafford and PLUS loans directly to participating schools without requiring an intermediate check for the student to endorse. The money is transferred electronically instead of using paper, and hence is available to the student sooner.

Eligible Noncitizen | Federal term—Someone who is not a U.S. citizen but is nevertheless eligible for federal student aid. You are an eligible noncitizen, generally, if you are a U.S. permanent resident with an Alien Registration Receipt Card (I-551), a conditional permanent resident (I-551C), or any other eligible noncitizen with an Arrival-Departure Record (I-94) from the U.S. Immigration and Naturalization Service showing any of the following: "Refugee," "Asylum Granted," "Indefinite Parole," "Humanitarian Parole," or "Cuban-Haitian Entrant." Noncitizens who hold student visas or exchange visitor visas are not eligible for federal student aid.

Eligible Program | Federal term—A course of study that leads to a degree or certificate and meets the U.S. Department of Education's requirements for an eligible program. To get federal financial aid, you must be enrolled in an eligible program, with two exceptions: If a school has told you that you must take certain coursework to qualify for admission into one of its eligible programs, you can get a FFEL for up to 12 consecutive months while you're completing that coursework. You must be enrolled at least half-time, and you must meet the usual student aid eligibility requirements. If you're enrolled at least half-time in a program to obtain a professional credential or certification required by a state for employment as an elementary or secondary school teacher, you can apply for a Federal Perkins Loan, Federal Work-Study, a FFEL Stafford loan (or your parents can get a Parent PLUS Loan) while you're enrolled in that program.

Emancipated | Legal term—To release a child from the control of a parent or guardian. Declaring a child to be legally emancipated is not sufficient to release the parents or legal guardians from being responsible for providing for the child's education. The criteria to be found independent are much stricter.

Endowment | Scholarship term—Funds owned by an institution and invested to produce income to support the operation of the institution. Many educational institutions use a portion of their endowment income for financial aid. A school with a larger ratio of endowment per student is more likely to give larger financial aid packages.

(continued)

Appendix B Continued

Term	Definition
Enrolled	Academic term—A student must register for class and complete and submit at least one lesson to be considered enrolled.
Enrollment Status	Academic term—An indication of whether you are a full-time or a part-time student. Generally you must be enrolled at least half-time (and in some cases full-time) to qualify for financial aid.
Entitlement	Entitlement programs award funds to all qualified applicants. The Pell Grant is an example of such a program.
Entrance Counseling	Loan term—Counseling provided to a student loan borrower about debt and accumulated indebtedness. Counseling is required before the student receives the first disbursement of the student's first loan. Also referred to as entrance interview.
EOG	See Educational Opportunity Grant Program.
Equity	FAFSA term—The net dollar value of ownership in a piece of property.
Exceptional Need	Financial aid term—An eligibility criterion in the Federal SEOG and Federal Perkins Loan programs. Exceptional need for SEOG is defined in statute as the lowest expected family contributions at an institution. The law does not define the term for the Federal Perkins Loan Program.
Exit Counseling	Loan term—Counseling provided to a student loan borrower about debt and accumulated indebtedness. Counseling is required before the student leaves school either due to competition of a program (graduation) or ceasing of enrollment (withdrawal or transfer). Also referred to as exit interview.
Expected Family Contribution (EFC)	Federal term—The amount of money that the family is expected to be able to contribute to the student's education, as determined by the federal methodology need analysis formula approved by Congress. The EFC includes a parent contribution (if the student is dependent) and a student contribution (student and spouse if married and independent). It also looks at family size, number of family members in college, taxable and untaxed income, and asset equity. The EFC is used to determine financial need which is the difference between the COA and the EFC.
FAFSA	See Free Application for Federal Student Aid.
FAFSA on the Web	Federal term—The federal Web site where a student may complete and file the Free Application for Federal Aid application online.
Family Size	FAFSA term—For dependent students—the number of people (including parents and the student applicant) that the parents support. For independent students—the number of people (including the student and spouse if married) that the student will support.

Federal Direct Student Loan Program (FDSLP)	Loan term—The collective name for Direct Subsidized, Direct Unsubsidized, and Direct PLUS Loan programs. The FDSLP is similar to the FFELP, except that funding comes directly from the U.S. Treasury rather than from private lending institutions.
Federal Family Education Loan Program (FFEL)	Loan term—The collective name for Federal Stafford (both subsidized and unsubsidized) and Federal Parent PLUS Loan programs. Funds for these three programs are provided by commercial lenders and the loans are guaranteed by the federal government.
Federal Methodology (FM)	FAFSA term—Formula used to determine an expected family contribution (EFC) for Pell Grants, campus-based programs, and FFEL programs. The federal methodology takes family size, the number of family members in college, taxable and nontaxable income, and asset equity (excluding family homes and family farms) into account.
Federal Processor	FAFSA term—The organization that processes the information submitted on the Free Application for Federal Student Aid (FAFSA) and uses it to compute eligibility for federal student aid.
Federal Stafford Subsidized and Unsubsidized Loan Programs	See Stafford Loans.
Federal Parent PLUS Loan	See Parent PLUS Loan.
Federal Work-Study (FWS)	Financial aid term—Program providing undergraduate and graduate students with part-time employment during the school year. The federal government pays a portion of the student's salary, making it cheaper for departments and businesses to hire the student. For this reason, work-study students often find it easier to get a part-time job. Eligibility for FWS is based on need. Money earned from a FWS job is not counted as income for the subsequent year's need analysis process.
Fellowship	School term—A form of aid given to graduate students to help support their education. Some fellowships include a tuition waiver or a payment to the university in lieu of tuition. Most fellowships include a stipend to cover reasonable living expenses (e.g., just above the poverty line).
FFELP	Financial aid term—Federal Family Education Loan Program.
File	Financial aid term—The student's file is comprised of all paper and electronic documentation submitted to the Financial Aid Office for the student.
File Review	Financial aid term—The process of comparing documentation submitted by the student and/or parents against the information presented on the FAFSA to check for accuracy before making or finalizing awards.

(continued)

Appendix B Continued

Term	Definition
Financial Aid	Financial aid term—Collectively, the term for all funds awarded to the student and the family to help them pay for the student's education. Major forms of financial aid include gift aid (grants and scholarships) and self-help aid (loans and work). Funds may be from federal, state, university, or private sources.
Financial Aid Award Notification	Financial aid term—See Award Letter.
Financial Aid Counselor	Financial aid term—Financial Aid Office personnel who are available to student and parents to answer questions about financial aid and to assist in the process of applying and receiving financial aid funds. Also called financial aid coordinators.
Financial Aid Office (FAO)	Financial aid term—The college office that is responsible for the determination of financial need and the awarding of financial aid. Also known as Office of Student Financial Aid.
Financial Aid Package	Financial aid term—The complete collection of grants, scholarships, loans, and work study employment from all sources (federal, state, institutional, and private) offered to a student to enable them to attend the college or university. Note that unsubsidized Stafford loans and PLUS loans could be considered financing options that are available to the family to help them meet the EFC.
Financial Aid PROFILE	Scholarship term—The CSS/Financial Aid PROFILE application is used by many colleges to gather information to help them award private, nonfederal student aid funds.
Financial Aid Transcript (FAT)	Financial aid term—A record of all federal aid received by students at each school attended. The record is usually obtained electronically from the NSLDS (National Student Loan Data System). The record is used to assess the amount of federal financial aid the student has received and to prevent the award of federal funds for which the student or the parent of a dependent student is not eligible.
Financial Need	Financial aid term—The difference between the COA and the EFC is the student's financial need—the gap between the cost of attending the school and the student's resources. The financial aid package is based on the amount of financial need. The process of determining a student's need is known as need analysis.
First-Time Borrower	Loan term—A first-year undergraduate student who has no unpaid loan balances outstanding on the date he or she signs a promissory note for an educational loan.
Fixed Interest	Loan term—In a fixed interest loan, the interest rate stays the same for the life of the loan. The Perkins Loan has a fixed interest rate. See also Variable Interest.

Forbearance — Loan term—Temporary cessation of regularly scheduled payments or temporarily permitting smaller payments than were originally scheduled.

Free Application for Federal Student Aid (FAFSA) — FAFSA term—Form used to apply for Pell Grants and all other need-based aid. As the name suggests, no fee is charged to file a FAFSA.

Full-time — Academic term—At schools measuring progress in semesters full-time enrollment is at least 12 semester hours per term for undergraduates and 9 semester hours per term for graduate or professional degree students. Most financial aid programs require that the student be enrolled at least half-time to be eligible for aid. Some programs require the student to be enrolled full-time.

Gapping — Financial aid term—When the student's full demonstrated need cannot be met. *See also* Unmet Need.

Garnishment — Loan term—The practice of withholding a portion of a defaulted borrower's wages to repay his or her loan, without their consent.

Gift Aid — Financial aid term—A type of aid, such as grants and scholarships, which does not need to be repaid.

GPA — *See* Grade Point Average.

Grace Period — Loan term—The period that begins the day after a educational loan borrower ceases to be enrolled at least half-time at an eligible school, ends the day before the repayment period begins, and during which payments of principal are not required. (There is no grace period for the PLUS Loan or private/alternative loans.)

Grade Level — Loan term—A student's academic class level, as provided by a school official on the student's application and promissory note. Determines the annual borrowing limit allowed for Stafford Loans.

Grade Point Average (GPA) — Academic term—An average of a student's grades for the term: usually a grade is converted based on a 4.0 scale (4.0 is an A, 3.0 is a B, and 2.0 is a C, etc.) multiplied by the number of credits for which the grade was awarded. *See also* Cumulative Grade Point Average.

Graduate Assistantship — Academic term—There are two types of graduate assistantships: teaching assistantships (TA) and research assistantships (RA). TAs and RAs receive a full or partial tuition waiver and a small living stipend. TAs are required to perform teaching duties. RAs are required to perform research duties, not necessarily related to the student's thesis research.

Graduate Student — Academic term—A student in a postsecondary institution who is enrolled in a master's or higher level degree program.

(continued)

Appendix B Continued

Term	Definition
Graduated Repayment	Loan term—A schedule where the monthly loan payments are smaller at the start of the repayment period and gradually become larger.
Grant	Financial aid term—A type of financial aid based on financial need that the student does not have to repay.
Gross Income	Financial aid term—Income before taxes, deductions, and allowances have been subtracted.
Guarantee Agency or Guarantor	Loan term—State agency or private nonprofit institution that insures student loans for lenders and helps administer the FFELP. Guarantee agencies also oversee the student loan process and enforce federal and state rules regarding student loans.
Guarantee Fee	Loan term—A small percentage of the loan that is paid to the guarantee agency to insure the loan against default. The insurance fee is usually 1% of the loan amount (and by law cannot exceed 3% of the loan amount).
Guaranteed Student Loan (GSL)	Loan term—Former name for the Stafford Loans.
Half-Time	Academic term—At schools measuring progress in semesters, half-time enrollment is at least 6 semester hours per term for undergraduates or at least 6 semester hours per term for graduate or professional degree students. Most financial aid programs require that the student be enrolled at least half-time to be eligible for aid. Some programs require the student to be enrolled full-time.
Health Education Assistance Loan (HEAL)	Financial aid term—A low-interest loan administered by the U.S. Department of Health and Human Services. It is available to medical school students pursuing medicine, osteopathy, dentistry, veterinary medicine, optometry, podiatry, clinical psychology, health administration, and public health. Undergraduate pharmacology students are also eligible.
Health Professions Loan (HPL)	Financial aid term—A low-interest loan administered by the U.S. Department of Health and Human Services. It is now known as the Primary Care Loan (PCL).
Holder	Loan term—The lender, institution, or agency that holds legal title to a loan. The holder may be the bank that issued the loan, a secondary market that purchased the loan from the bank, or a guarantee agency if the borrower defaulted on the loan.

Income — FAFSA term—The amount of money received from employment (salary, wages, tips), profit from financial instruments (interest, dividends, capital gains), or other sources (welfare, disability, child support, Social Security, and pensions).

Income Contingent Repayment — Loan term—Under an income contingent repayment schedule, the size of the monthly payments depends on the income earned by the borrower. As the borrower's income increases, so do the payments. The income contingent repayment plan is not available for PLUS Loans.

Independent Student Status — FAFSA term—An independent student is one who is not required to provide parental information and signature when completing the FAFSA form. *See also* Dependent Student Status.

Individual Retirement Account (IRA) — FAFSA term—One of several popular types of retirement funds. It is not legal to borrow money from your IRA to help pay for your children's education.

INS — Federal term—Immigration and Naturalization Service, the former name of the federal agency responsible for administering immigration procedures and assigning citizenship status. Now known as USCIS, United States Citizen and Immigration Services.

In-State Student — Academic term—A student who has met the legal residency requirements for the state and is eligible for reduced in-state student tuition at public colleges and universities in the state. (Also referred to as resident.)

Insurance Fee — Loan term—Fee passed on by the lender to the federal government as insurance against default. Insurance fees are charged as the loan is disbursed, and typically run to 1% of the amount disbursed. *See also* Guarantee Fee.

Interest — Loan term—Amount charged to the borrower for the privilege of using the lender's money. Interest is usually calculated as a percentage of the principal balance of the loan. The percentage rate may be fixed for the life of the loan, or it may be variable, depending on the terms of the loan. All federal loans issued since October 1992 use variable interest rates that are pegged to the cost of U.S. Treasury Bills.

Internal Revenue Service (IRS) — Federal term—Federal agency responsible for enforcing U.S. tax laws and collecting taxes.

Internship — Academic term—Part-time job during the academic year or the summer months in which a student receives supervised practical training in their field. Internships are often very closely related to the student's academic and career goals and may serve as a precursor to professional employment. Some internships provide very close supervision by a mentor in an apprenticeship-like relationship. Some internships provide the student with a stipend, some don't.

(continued)

Appendix B Continued

Term	Definition
Lender	Loan term—A bank, credit union, savings and loan association, or other financial institution that provides funds to the student or parent for an educational loan. Note: Some schools now participate in the Federal Direct Loan program and no longer use a private lender, since loan funds are provided by the U.S. government.
Loan	Loan term—A type of financial aid that must be repaid, with interest. The federal student loan programs (FFELP and FDSLP) are a good method of financing the costs of your college education. These loans are better than most consumer loans because they have lower interest rates and do not require a credit check or collateral. The Stafford Loans and Perkins Loans also provide a variety of deferment options and extended repayment terms.
Loan Consolidation	*See* Consolidation Loan.
Loan Debt Counseling	Loan term—Counseling provided to a student about debt and accumulated indebtedness. Counseling is required both before the student receives the first disbursement of the first loan and again whenever the student withdraws from the university, drops below half-time enrollment, or is scheduled to complete an academic program. These are commonly referred to as entrance or exit counseling; also know as entrance and exit interviews.
Loan Guarantee Agency	*See* Guarantee Agency.
Loan Forgiveness	Loan term—The federal government cancels all or part of an educational loan because the borrower meets certain criteria (e.g., is performing military or volunteer service).
Married	FAFSA term—For establishing independency a student who is married at the time the FAFSA is filed for the first time for the year that aid is being requested.
Master's Degree	Academic term—One of several degrees granted by graduate schools.
Master Promissory Note (MPN)	Loan term—The Master Promissory Note takes the place of the annual loan applications for Stafford funds. After completing the initial application, students just need to complete the confirmation letter to receive funds. MPNs are valid for 10 years or until the student changes school or lender and/or has a break in their education.
Maturity Date	Loan term—The date when a loan comes due and must be repaid in full.
Merit-based	Scholarship aid term—Financial aid that is merit-based depends on your academic, artistic or athletic merit, or some other criteria, and does not depend on the existence of financial need. Merit-based awards use your grades, test scores, hobbies, and special talents to determine your eligibility for scholarships.

Mortgage	Legal term—A loan of funds for purchasing a piece of property that uses that property as security for the loan. The lender has a lien on the property and will receive the property if the borrower fails to repay the loan.
MPN	*See* Master Promissory Note.
National Service Trust	Federal term—President Clinton's national community service program. If you participate in this program before attending school, the funds may be used to pay your educational expenses. If you participate after graduating, the funds may be used to repay your federal student loans. Eligible types of community service include education, human services, the environment, and public safety.
Need	Financial aid term—The difference between the COA and the EFC is the student's financial need—the gap between the cost of attending the school and the student's resources. The financial aid package is based on the amount of financial need. The process of determining a student's need is known as need analysis.
Need Analysis	Financial aid term—The process of determining a student's financial need by analyzing the financial information provided by the student and his or her parents (and spouse, if any) on a financial aid form. The student must submit a need analysis form to apply for need-based aid. The need analysis form is the FAFSA.
Need-Based	Financial aid term—Financial aid that is need-based depends on your financial situation as reported on the FAFSA. Most government sources of financial aid are need-based.
Need-Blind	Admission term—Under need-blind admissions, the school decides whether to make an offer of admission to a student without considering the student's financial situation. Most schools use a need-blind admissions process. A few schools will use financial need to decide whether to include marginal students in the wait list.
Net Income	FAFSA term—This is income after taxes, deductions, and allowances have been subtracted.
New Borrower	*See* First-Time Borrower.
Nonfiler's Statement	Financial aid term—A statement from a student, parent or spouse indicating that they did not file a federal tax return during the year in question and stating their total income for that same period.
Nonresident Student	Academic term—A student who has not met the legal residency requirements for the state for fee-paying purposes. These students are charged a higher tuition rate than state residents. (Also known as out-of-state.)
Nontransferable Funding	Financial aid term—This is college funding that cannot be transferred to another college or university.
NSLDS	Federal term—National Student Loan Database System. This automated system maintained by the Department of Education and schools will replace all paper financial aid transcripts except for mid-year transfer students. Students may access their total borrowing history via the NSLDS Web site.

(continued)

Appendix B Continued

Term	Definition
Number in College	FAFSA term—The number of eligible students in the household that will be attending college at least half-time between July 1 of the current year to June 30 of the future year in a program that leads to a degree or certificate.
Nursing Student Loan (NSL)	Loan term—A low interest loan program administered by the U.S. Department of Health and Human Services and available to students enrolled in nursing programs. This is a federal aid program.
Origination	Loan term—The process whereby the lender, or a servicing agent on behalf of the lender, handles the initial application processing and disbursement of loan proceeds.
Origination Fee	Loan term—Fee payable by the borrower and deducted from the principal of a loan prior to disbursement to the borrower. For federally backed loans, the origination fee is paid to the federal government to offset the cost of the interest subsidy to borrowers. For private loan programs, the origination fee is generally paid to the originator to cover the cost of administering and insuring the program.
Orphan	Financial aid term—For independence, a student whose parents are both deceased or the supporting parent is deceased.
Outside Resource	Financial aid term—A type of aid or benefits from outside the university but available to the student because of enrollment in college. Outside resources are counted after need is determined. Outside scholarships, prepaid tuition plans, and VA educational benefits are examples of outside resources.
Outside Scholarship	Financial aid term—A scholarship that comes from sources other than the university or federal or state governments.
Out-of-State Student	Academic term—A student who has not met the legal residency requirements for the state for fee-paying purposes. These students are charged a higher tuition rate than state residents. (Also known as nonresident.)
Overaward	Financial aid term—A student who receives federal financial aid may not receive awards totaling more than his or her financial need.
Packaging	Financial aid term—The process of assembling a financial aid package.
Parent Contribution (PC)	FAFSA term—A part of the EFC for dependent students. An estimate of the portion of your educational expenses that the federal government believes your parents can afford based on the FAFSA information.

Parent PLUS Loan	Loan term—Federal Parent PLUS Loan (also known as Parent Loan for Undergraduate Students). Parents may borrow to help pay for their children's education. This loan is made to the parent by a lender such as a bank, credit union, or savings and loan association. Interest rates are linked to the 52-week Treasury Bill rates but may not exceed 9%. PLUS loans may be used to replace EFCs. Also known as a FFEL Loan program.
PARS	Financial aid term—Packaging Aid Resource System. A computer program that is used to automatically package awards for students who have complete financial aid files and for whom all required tracking items are complete.
Pell Grant	Financial aid term—A federal grant based on the student's financial need and designed to go to the neediest students first.
Perkins Loan	Financial aid term—Formerly the National Direct Student Loan Program, the Federal Perkins Loan allows students with exceptional financial need to borrow up to $3,000/year for undergraduate school and up to $5,000/year for graduate school.
PhD or Doctorate	Academic term—One of several degrees granted by graduate schools.
PIN	Federal term—The Personal Identification Number from the U.S. Department of Education that serves as an electronic signature on the FAFSA on the Web and to sign certain other legal documents.
Postsecondary	Academic term—This term means "after high school" and refers to all programs for high school graduates, including programs at two- and four-year colleges, and vocational and technical schools.
Prepaid Tuition Plans	A college savings plan that is guaranteed to rise in value at the same rate as college tuition. For example, if a family purchases shares that are worth half a year's tuition at a state college, they will always be worth half a year's tuition, even 10 years later when tuition rates will have doubled.
Prepayment	Loan term—Paying off all or part of a loan before it is due.
Preregistration	Academic term—The same processes as registration, however, done in advance of a term, often several months ahead. For example, Fall 2002 preregistration started in March 2002. Preregistration is the same as reserving a seat in a particular classes in advance.
Prime Rate	Loan term—The fluctuating interest rate that banks charge to their best business customers. Private/alternative loans have interest rates that fluctuate based on the prime rate.
Principal	Loan term—The amount of money borrowed or remaining unpaid on a loan. Interest is charged as a percentage of the principal. Insurance and origination fees will be deducted from this amount before disbursement.

(continued)

Appendix B Continued

Term	Definition
Private Loans	Loan term—Educational loan programs established by private lenders to supplement the student and parent education loan programs available from federal and state governments.
Professional Judgment (PJ)	Financial aid term—For need-based federal aid programs, the financial aid administrator may adjust the EFC, adjust the COA, or change the dependency status (with documentation) when extenuating circumstances exist. For example, if a parent becomes unemployed, disabled, or deceased, the FAA can, on written appeal, decide to use estimated income information for the award year instead of the actual income figures from the base year. This delegation of authority from the federal government to the financial aid administrator is called Professional Judgment (PJ).
PROFILE	Scholarship term—The CSS/Financial Aid PROFILE application is used by many colleges to gather information to help them award private, nonfederal student aid funds.
Promissory Note	Loan term—The binding legal document that must be signed by the borrower before loan funds are disbursed by the lender. The promissory note states the terms and conditions of the loan, including repayment schedule, interest rate, deferment policy, and cancellations. The borrower should keep this document until the loan has been repaid.
Quality Assurance (QA)	Federal term—Quality assurance is a federal program under the authority of the Department of Education. At a Quality Assurance participant school, students are exempt from the Federal Verification Program. Students who are instructed on the Student Aid Report to submit tax returns and verification worksheets should first check with the financial aid office to determine if they are required under Quality Assurance.
RA Room Waiver	Scholarship term—Resident (Hall) Advisor. As a condition of their employment in the residence halls, RAs receive a waiver of the cost of their room bill provided by the Housing Office. This value is counted as a resource in determining total financial aid.
Reciprocity	Scholarship term—An agreement between two or more states agreeing to discount the cost of tuition to eligible residents of the agreeing states.
Register for Classes	Academic term—The processing by which a student chooses a class schedule for a particular term. The schedule include picking classes by day, time, and instructor. *See also* Preregistration.
Regular Student	A regular student is one who is enrolled or accepted for enrollment at an institution for the purpose of obtaining a degree, certificate, or other recognized educational credential offered by that institution. Generally, to receive

	federal student financial aid from the programs discussed in this guide, you must be a regular student. There are exceptions to this requirement for some programs.
Renewable Scholarships	Scholarship term—A scholarship that is awarded for more than one year. Usually the student is required to maintain certain academic standards to be eligible for subsequent years of the award. Some renewable scholarships are automatically renewed, which means there is no need to resubmit paperwork. Others require the resubmission of paperwork.
Repayment Schedule	Loan term—The repayment schedule discloses the monthly payment, interest rate, total repayment obligation, payment due dates, and the term of the loan.
Repayment Period or Term	Loan term—The Repayment Period of a loan is the period during which the borrower is required to make payments on his or her loans. When the payments are made monthly, the term is usually given as a number of payments or years.
Resident	Academic term—A student who is considered a legal resident for tuition and fee paying purposes. These students are then charged the in-state student tuition. See also In-State Student.
ROTC Scholarship	Scholarship term—Reserve Officer Training Corps (ROTC) scholarships available for army, navy, and air force at many colleges and universities throughout the United States. These scholarships cover tuition and fees, books and supplies, and include a subsistence allowance.
Sallie Mae	Loan term—(Formerly known as SLMA or the Student Loan Marketing Association) The nation's largest secondary market and holds approximately one third of all educational loans.
SAP	Federal and academic term—Satisfactory Academic Progress. A student must meet these minimum standards in order to continue receiving federal aid. If a student fails to maintain an academic standing consistent with the school's SAP policy, they are unlikely to meet the school's graduation requirements.
SAR	See Student Aid Report.
SAT	Admissions term—Scholastic Assessment Test. One of the two national standardized college entrance examinations used in the United States. The other is the ACT. The SAT (previously known as the Scholastic Aptitude Test) is administered by the Educational Testing Service (ETS). Most universities require either the ACT or the SAT as part of an application for admission.
Scholarship	Scholarship term—Scholarships are a form of financial aid given to students to help pay for their education. Some scholarships may be used only to pay tuition expenses or to offset the costs of room or board expenses. Scholarships are a form of gift aid and do not have to be repaid. Many scholarships are available only to students in specific courses of study or are based on specific academic, athletic, or artistic talent.

(continued)

Appendix B Continued

Term	Definition
Scholarship Search Services	Scholarship term—Search services that assist student in finding possible scholarships. There are now many free search programs available, therefore students should never pay a fee for the same services.
Secondary Market	Loan term—A secondary market is an organization that buys loans from lenders, thereby providing the lender with the capital to issue new loans. Selling loans is a common practice among lenders, so the lender you make your payments to may change during the life of the loan.
Secured Loan	Loan term—A loan backed by collateral. If you fail to repay the loan, the lender may seize the collateral and sell it to repay the loan. Auto loans and home mortgages are examples of secured loans. Educational loans are generally not secured.
Selective Service Registration	FAFSA term—Registration for the military draft. Male students who are U.S. citizens and have reached the age of 18 and were born after December 31, 1959, must be registered with Selective Service to be eligible for federal financial aid.
Self-Help Aid	Financial aid term—Financial aid in the form of loans and student employment.
Separation Date	Registrar term—The date the student ceases to be enrolled on at least a half-time basis at an eligible school. Separation starts either the grace or repayment period.
Semester	Academic term—In a semester based school, one of two terms that comprise an academic year.
SEOG	*See* Supplemental Educational Opportunity Grant.
SEP	*See* Statement of Educational Purpose.
Service Academy	Federal term—The U.S. Air Force Academy, U.S. Coast Guard Academy, U.S. Merchant Marine Academy, U.S. Military Academy, and U.S. Naval Academy are service academies. Admissions is highly selective, as students must be nominated by their congressional representative to apply.
Servicer	Loan term—The servicer collects payments on a loan and performs other administrative tasks associated with maintaining a loan portfolio. Loan servicers disburse loans funds, monitor loans while the borrowers are in school, collect payments, process deferments and forbearances, respond to borrower inquiries and ensure that the loans are administered in compliance with federal regulations and guarantee agency requirements.

Simple Interest

Loan term—Interest that is paid only on the principal balance of the loan and not on any accrued interest. Most federal student loan programs charge simple interest. Note, however, that capitalizing instead of paying the interest on an unsubsidized Stafford loan is a form of compounded interest.

Simplified Needs Test

FAFSA term—If the parents have an adjusted gross income of less than $50,000 and every family member was eligible to file an IRS Form 1040A or 1040EZ (or wasn't required to file a federal income tax return), the federal methodology ignores assets when computing the EFC.

Stafford Loans

Loan term—Stafford Loan Program—Low-interest loans that are made to students attending school at least half-time. Loans are made by a lender such as a bank, credit union, or savings and loan association. These loans are insured by the guaranty agency in each state and reinsured by the federal government. Interest rates are linked to the 52-week Treasury Bill rates but may not exceed 8.25%. Stafford Loans that come in two forms, subsidized and unsubsidized. Subsidized loans are based on need; unsubsidized loans aren't. The interest on the subsidized Stafford Loan is paid by the federal government while the student is in school and during the 6-month grace period. The Subsidized Stafford Loan was formerly known as the Guaranteed Student Loan (GSL). The Unsubsidized Stafford Loan was formerly known as the Supplemental Loan for Students (SLS) Loan. Unsubsidized Stafford Loans may be used to replace the EFC. These are federal aid programs.

State Student Incentive Grants (SSIG)

Financial aid term—A state-run financial aid program for state residents. The states receive matching funds from the federal government to help them fund the grant program.

Statement of Educational Purpose

Financial aid term—The SEP, Statement of Educational Purpose, is required from any student who is awarded a State Need Grant. The absence of this document from a student's file will prevent the grant funds from releasing.

Student Aid Report (SAR)

FAFSA term—Student Aid Report. Produced by the federal government via the Central Processor in response to a student filling out the Free Application for Federal Student Aid (FAFSA). This information is sent to the student as a paper form that may be used to submit corrections. The report contains all the information supplied on the FAFSA and is provided to the student by the federal processor. The SAR will also indicate Pell Grant eligibility, if any, and the EFC. SARs may also be used to make manual corrections to the FAFSA data. The Financial Aid Office receives the same information electronically.

Student Contribution

FAFSA term—The amount of money the federal government expects the student to contribute to his or her education based on the FAFSA information and is included as part of the EFC.

(continued)

Appendix B Continued

Term	Definition
Subsidized Loan	Loan term—With a subsidized loan, such as the Perkins Loan or the Subsidized Stafford Loan, the government pays the interest on the loan while the student is in school, during the 6-month grace period and during any deferment periods. Subsidized loans are awarded based on financial need and may not be used to finance the family contribution. *See* Stafford Loans for information about subsidized Stafford Loans. *See also* Unsubsidized Loan.
Supplemental Education Opportunity Grant (SEOG)	Financial aid term—Federal grant program for undergraduate students with exceptional need. SEOG grants are awarded by the school's financial aid office, and provide up to $4,000 per year. To qualify, a student must also be a recipient of a Pell Grant. This is a federal aid program.
Teaching Assistantship (TA)	Academic term—A form of financial aid awarded to graduate students to help support their education. Teaching assistantships usually provide the graduate student with a waiver of all or part of tuition, plus a small stipend for living expenses. As the name implies, a TA is required to perform teaching-related duties.
Term	Registrar term—A educational period. Also referred to as semesters.
Title IV Loans	Federal term—Title IV of the Higher Education Act of 1965 created several education loan programs which are collectively referred to as the Federal Family Education Loan Program (FFELP). These loans, also called Title IV Loans, are the Federal Stafford Loans (Subsidized and Unsubsidized), Federal PLUS Loans, and Federal Consolidation Loans.
Title IV School Code	FAFSA term—When you fill out the FAFSA you need to supply the Title IV Code for each school to which you are applying.
Transcript	Admissions term—A list of all the courses that a student has taken at a particular high school or college with the grades that the student earned in each course. Also referred to as an academic transcript.
Tuition	Admissions term—The cost of instruction; the amount charged by a school for the classes in which a student enrolls. May also be referred to as tuition and fees.
Undergraduate Student	Registrar's term—Any student who is enrolled in a bachelor's degree program.
Unearned Income	FAFSA term—Income not from wages, salaries, or tips, i.e., interest income, dividend income, and capital gains.
Unmet Need	Financial aid term—In an ideal world, the Financial Aid Office would be able to provide each student with the full difference between their ability to pay and the cost of education. Due to budget constraints the FAO may provide the student with less than the student's need (as determined by the FAO). This gap is known as the unmet need.

Unsecured Loan	Loan term—A loan not backed by collateral, representing a greater risk to the lender. The lender may require a co-signer on the loan to reduce their risk. If you default on the loan, the co-signer will be held responsible for repayment. Most educational loans are unsecured loans. In the case of federal student loans, the federal government guarantees repayment of the loans. Other examples of unsecured loans include credit card charges and personal lines of credit.
Unsubsidized Loan	Financial aid term—A loan for which the government does not pay the interest. The borrower is responsible for the interest on an unsubsidized loan from the date the loan is disbursed, even while the student is still in school. Students may avoid paying the interest while they are in school by capitalizing the interest, which increases the loan amount. Unsubsidized loans are not based on financial need and may be used to finance the family contribution. The Stafford Unsubsidized Loan and the Parent Loan for Undergraduate Students are both unsubsidized loans. *See also* Stafford Loans for information about unsubsidized Stafford Loans.
Untaxed Income	FAFSA term—All income received that's not reported to the IRS or is reported but that is not subject to taxation. May include Social Security benefits, Earned Income Credit, welfare payments, untaxed capital gains, interest on tax-free bonds, clergy and military allowances, and others.
Urban Campus	Academic term—A permanent location of a school that is geographically apart from the main campus. Formerly known as branch campuses.
USCIS: United States Citizenship and Immigration Services	Federal term—USCIS—United States Citizenship and Immigration Services—The new name of the federal agency responsible for administering immigration procedures and assigning citizenship status. Formerly known as Immigration and Naturalization Service (INS).
U.S. Department of Education (ED or USED)	Federal term—Government agency that administers several federal student financial aid programs, including the Federal Pell Grant, the Federal Work-Study Program, the Federal Perkins Loans, the Federal Stafford Loans, and the Federal PLUS Loans.
U.S. Dept. of Health and Human Services (HHS)	Federal term—Government agency that administers several federal health education loan programs, including the HEAL, HPSL, and NSL loan programs.
VA	Federal term—Veterans Administration, which administers benefits for a variety of veteran's programs, including educational benefits.
Variable Interest	Loan term—In a variable interest loan, the interest rate changes periodically. For example, the interest rate might be pegged to the cost of U.S. Treasury Bills (e.g., T-Bill rate plus 3.1%) and be updated monthly, quarterly, semi-annually, or annually. All Stafford Loans and PLUS loans have variable annual rates.

(continued)

Appendix B Continued

Term	Definition
Verification	FAFSA term—Verification is a process of checking the accuracy of data supplied by on the FAFSA to ensure accurate reporting and resolve inaccuracies. Students may receive an indication on their SAR that they have been selected for a process called verification.
Veteran	FAFSA term—For federal financial aid purposes such as determining dependency status, a veteran is a former member of the U.S. Armed Forces (Army, Navy, Air Force, Marines, or Coast Guard) who served on active duty and was discharged other than dishonorably (i.e., received an honorable or medical discharge).
Veteran's Benefits	Financial aid term—Assistance provided by the federal government to eligible veterans and service persons for the purpose of financing education or training programs. Must be counted as an outside resource when packaging financial aid. Also referred to as VA Benefits.
W2 Form	FAFSA term—The form listing an employee's wages and tax withheld. Employers are required by the IRS to issue a W2 form for each employee, usually by the end of January, each year.
Ward of the Court	FAFSA term—Independence criteria.
Withdrawal Date	Registrar's term—The date the student withdraws from enrollment, as determined by the school.
Work Study (WS)	Financial aid term—Work study is a financial aid award that gives a student the opportunity to work part time. There are both federal and state work study programs.

NOTES

Notes to Chapter 2

1. National Indian Education Association, *Preliminary Report on No Child Left Behind in Indian Country* (Washington, DC: National Indian Education Association, 2005).

2. M. Villegas and R. Prieto, *Alaska Native Student Vitality: Community Perspectives on Supporting Student Success* (Anchorage, AK: Alaska Native Policy Center at First Alaskans Institute and Institute for Social and Economic Research, University of Alaska Anchorage, 2006).

3. Marjane Ambler, "Tribal Colleges Redefining Success," *Tribal College Journal* 16, no. 3 (Spring 2005).

4. College Board, *Education Pays Update* (New York: College Board, 2005).

5. Jeffrey Dransfeldt, "College Choice Has Many Factors," *Ventura College Press*, May 9, 2005. Available at www.venturacollegepress.com.

6. Jay Mathews, "Six Ways to Be Happy with Your College Choice," *Washington Post*, October 5, 2004. Available at www.washingtonpost.com.

7. Barry Schwartz, *The Paradox of Choice: Why More Is Less* (New York: Harper-Collins, 2004).

8. Peter Senge, *The Fifth Discipline: The Art and Practice of the Learning Organization* (New York: Doubleday, 1990); Peter Senge, Art Kleiner, Charlotte Roberts, Richard B. Ross, and Bryan J. Smith, *The Fifth Discipline Fieldbook: Strategies and Tools for Building a Learning Community* (New York: Doubleday/Currency, 1994); Peter Senge, Art Kleiner, Charlotte Roberts, Rick Ross, George Roth, and Bryan Smith, *The Dance of Change: The Challenge of Sustaining Momentum in Learning Organizations* (New York: Doubleday/Currency, 1999); Peter Senge, Nelda Cambron-McCabe, Timothy Lucas, Bryan Smith, Janis Dutton, and Art Kleiner, *Schools That Learn: A Fifth Discipline Fieldbook for Educators, Parents, and Everyone Who Cares about Education* (New York: Doubleday/Currency, 2000).

9. Senge et al., *The Fifth Discipline Fieldbook*, 194.

Notes to Chapter 3

1. College Board, *Trends in College Pricing* (New York: College Board, 2005); College Board, *Trends in Student Aid* (New York: College Board, 2005).

2. College Board, *Trends in College Pricing*, 18.

3. College Board, *Trends in Student Aid*, 2.

4. U.S. Department of Education, Federal Student Aid, *Funding Education Beyond High School: The Guide to Federal Student Aid* (Jessup, MD: ED Pubs, Education Publication Center, 2006).

5. Ibid., 2.

6. Ibid., 3–4.

7. Ibid., 5.

8. Jacqueline E. King, "Working Their Way through College: Student Employment and Its Impact on the College Experience." (ACE Center for Policy Analysis, American Council on Education, 2006). Available online at www.acenet.edu.

9. Nellie Mae's Web site is www.nelliemae.com.

10. Use Nellie Mae's online budget calculator at www.nelliemae.com/calculators for assistance.

11. Cheryl D. Blanco, *Early Commitment Financial Aid Programs: Promises, Practices, and Policies* (Jointly sponsored by the Pathways to College Network, the College Board, and the Western Interstate Commission for Higher Education, 2005), 7.

12. Indian Resource Development, *Sources of Financial Aid Available to American Indian Students* (Las Cruces, NM: Indian Resource Development, 2006). Free copies of the book can be obtained from the Indian Resource Development, PO Box 30001, MSC 3IRD, Las Cruces, New Mexico 88003-8001; phone (505) 646-1347; fax (505) 646-7740; email ird@nmsu.edu.

13. To access the online guides, visit the American Indian College Fund Web site at www.collegefund.org/scholarships/guides.html. The handbooks take students step-by-step through the process of deciding to go to college, learning about financial aid, and money management. The series uniquely promotes success in college by featuring stories of personal struggle and of how educational and cultural success are intertwined.

Notes to Chapter 4

1. Iris HeavyRunner and Richard DeCelles, "Family Education Model: Meeting the Student Retention Challenge," *Journal of American Indian Education* 41, no. 2 (2002).

2. R. Hingson et al., "Magnitude of Alcohol-Related Mortality and Morbidity among U.S. College Students Ages 18–24: Changes from 1998 to 2001," *Annual Review of Public Health* 26 (2005): 259–79.

3. Ibid.

4. Ibid.

5. Ibid.

6. R. W. Hingson, T. Heeren, R. C. Zakocs, A. Kopstein, and H. Wechsler, "Magnitude of Alcohol-Related Mortality and Morbidity among U.S. College Students Ages 18–24," *Journal of Studies on Alcohol* 63, no. 2 (2002): 136–44.

7. R. C. Engs, B. A. Diebold, and D. J. Hansen, "The Drinking Patterns and Problems of a National Sample of College Students, 1994," *Journal of Alcohol and Drug Education* 41, no. 3 (1996): 13–33; C. A. Presley, P. W. Meilman, J. R. Cashin, and R. Lyerla,

Alcohol and Drugs on American College Campuses: Use, Consequences, and Perceptions of the Campus Environment, vol. 3: 1991–1993 (Carbondale, IL: Core Institute, Southern Illinois University, 1996); C. A. Presley, P. W. Meilman, and J. R. Cashin, *Alcohol and Drugs on American College Campuses: Use, Consequences, and Perceptions of the Campus Environment, vol. 4: 1992–1994* (Carbondale, IL: Core Institute, Southern Illinois University, 1996); H. Wechsler, J. E. Lee, M. Kuo, M. Seibring, T. F. Nelson, and H. P. Lee, "Trends in College Binge Drinking during a Period of Increased Prevention Efforts: Findings from Four Harvard School of Public Health Study Surveys, 1993–2001," *Journal of American College Health* 50, no. 5 (2002): 203–17.

8. Hingson et al., "Magnitude of Alcohol-Related Mortality," 2002.

9. Presley et al., *Alcohol and Drugs on American College Campuses*, 1996.

10. Hingson et al., "Magnitude of Alcohol-Related Mortality," 2002.

11. Wechsler et al., "Trends in College Binge Drinking," 2002.

12. H. Wechsler, B. Moeykens, A. Davenport, S. Castillo, and J. Hansen, "The Adverse Impact of Heavy Episodic Drinkers on Other College Students," *Journal of Studies on Alcohol* 56, no. 6 (1995): 628–34.

13. Wechsler et al., "Trends in College Binge Drinking," 2002.

14. Hingson et al., "Magnitude of Alcohol-Related Mortality," 2002.

15. J. R. Knight, H. Wechsler, M. Kuo, M. Seibring, E. R. Weitzman, and M. Schuckit, "Alcohol Abuse and Dependence among U.S. College Students," *Journal of Studies on Alcohol* (May 2002).

16. Virginia Smith Harvey, "Resiliency: Strategies for Parents and Educators," in Andrea S. Canter, Leslie Z. Paige, Mark D. Roth, Ivonne Romero, and Servio A. Carroll (eds.), *Helping Children at Home and School II: Handouts for Families and Educators* (Bethesda, MD: National Association of School Psychologists Publications, 2004), S5-79–S5-82.

17. Ibid., S5-80.

18. J. M. Gottman, J. Declaire, and D. P. Goleman, *Raising an Emotionally Intelligent Child* (New York: Fireside Press, 1998).

19. Harvey, "Resiliency," S5-80.

20. Edward C. Anderson and Scott McDowell, *Towards a Theology of Strengths* (Paper presented at the National Conference on Identifying and Developing Students' Strengths, Eastern University, St. Davids, PA, October 26, 2001).

21. Deborah Spaide, *In Helping Ourselves by Helping Others*, n.d., available at www.soulrise.com/common/helping.htm.

22. Allan Luks and Peggy Payne, *The Healing Power of Doing Good: The Health and Spiritual Benefits of Helping Others* (Lincoln, NE: iUniverse, 2001).

23. Source material for this section is available online at www.tcpnow.com/holidaykit/part2/hd2.6a.html; the Legacy Project can be found online at www.legacyproject.org.

24. Harvey, "Resiliency," S5-81.

Notes to Chapter 5

1. Alberto F. Cabrera, Personal communication (February 7, 2007).

2. Maria Elena Reyes, "Tortured Victory or Joyful Accomplishment? Successful Eskimo and Latina College Students," *Race, Gender and Class* 8, no. 1 (2001).

3. See for example, Brian F. French and William Oakes, "Reliability and Validity Evidence for the Institutional Integration Scale," *Educational and Psychological Measurement* 64, no. 1 (February 2004): 88–98; and Laura I. Rendón, Romero E. Jalomo,

and Amaury Nora, "Theoretical Considerations in the Study of Minority Student Retention in Higher Education," in John M. Braxton (ed.), *Reworking the Student Departure Puzzle* (Nashville, TN: Vanderbilt University Press, 2000).

4. Clifford Adelman, *The Toolbox Revisited: Paths to Degree Completion from High School through College* (Washington, DC: U.S. Department of Education, 2006).

5. ACT, *Courses Count: Preparing Students for Postsecondary Success* (Iowa City, IA: ACT, 2005).

6. Aaron P. Jackson, Steven A. Smith, and Curtis L. Hill, "Academic Persistence among Native American College Students," *Journal of College Student Development* 44, no. 4 (July/August 2003): 548–65.

7. Maria Elena Reyes, "What Does It Take? Successful Alaska Native Students at the University of Alaska Fairbanks," *Journal of College Student Retention* 2, no. 2 (2000): 141–59.

8. Florence McGeshick Garcia, "Warriors in Education: Persistence among American Indian Doctoral Recipients," *Tribal College Journal* 9, no. 3 (May 2000): 46–48.

9. Terry Huffman, "Resistance Theory and the Transculturation Hypothesis as Explanations of College Attrition and Persistence among Culturally Traditional American Indian Students," *Journal of American Indian Education* 40, no. 3 (2001): 1–23.

Notes to Chapter 6

1. U.S. Department of Education, National Center for Education Statistics, *The NPEC Sourcebook on Assessment, Volume 1: Definitions and Assessment Methods for Critical Thinking, Problem Solving, and Writing*, NCES 2000–172, prepared by T. Dary Erwin for the Council of the National Postsecondary Education Cooperative Student Outcomes Pilot Working Group: Cognitive and Intellectual Development (Washington, DC: U.S. Government Printing Office, 2000).

2. Ibid.

Notes to Chapter 7

1. Marjane Ambler, "Tribal Colleges Redefining Success," *Tribal College Journal* 16, no. 3 (Spring 2005): 8–10.

2. Ibid., 10.

3. AnnMaria Rousey and Erich Longie, "The Tribal College as Family Support System," *American Behavioral Scientist* 44, no. 9 (2001): 1492–504.

Notes to Chapter 8

1. *Annual College Guide for American Indians* (Boulder, CO: *Winds of Change* Magazine in association with the American Indian Science and Engineering Society, 2005).

2. American Indian Higher Education Consortium and the Institute of Higher Education Policy, *Building Strong Communities: Tribal Colleges* (ERIC Document no. ED451818, 2001), 6.

3. National Center for Education Statistics, *Status and Trends in the Education of American Indians and Alaska Natives* (NCES 2005-108) (Washington, DC: U.S. Government Printing Office, 2005).

4. Marjane Ambler, "Of the Community, by the Community, and for the Community," *Tribal College Journal* 12, no. 4 (2001): 8–9.

Notes to Chapter 9

1. E. Inglebret, *Conceptual Framework for Developing Culturally Responsive Teacher Education Curriculum for Northwest Indian College: A Grounded Theory.* Unpublished doctoral dissertation, Washington State University, Pullman, Washington, 2001, 101.

2. V. Deloria, "Higher Education and Self-Determination," in V. Deloria Jr. and D. R. Wildcat , *Power and Place: Indian Education in America* (Golden, CO: Fulcrum Resources, 2001), 123–33; D. R. Wildcat, "The Question of Self-Determination," in V. Deloria Jr. and D. R. Wildcat , *Power and Place: Indian Education in America* (Golden, CO: Fulcrum Resources, 2001), 135–50.

3. Wildcat, "The Question of Self-Determination," 150.

4. P. Wilson, "Key Factors in the Performance and Achievement of Minority Students at the University of Alaska, Fairbanks," *American Indian Quarterly* 21, no. 3 (1997): 535–44.

5. Wildcat, "The Question of Self-Determination," 150.

REFERENCES AND BIBLIOGRAPHY

ACT. (2005). *Courses Count: Preparing Students for Postsecondary Success.* Iowa City, IA: ACT.

Adelman, C. (2006). *The Toolbox Revisited: Paths to Degree Completion from High School through College.* Washington, DC: U.S. Department of Education.

Ambler, M. (2001). "Of the Community, by the Community, and for the Community." *Tribal College Journal* 12(4): 8–9.

Ambler, M. (2005). "Tribal Colleges Redefining Success." *Tribal College Journal* 16(3): 8.

American Indian Higher Education Consortium and the American Indian College Fund. (2000). *Creating Role Models for Change: A Survey of Tribal College Graduates.* Alexandria, VA: American Indian Higher Education Consortium and the American Indian College Fund.

American Indian Higher Education Consortium and The Institute for Higher Education Policy. (2001). *Building Strong Communities: Tribal Colleges as Engaged Institutions.* ERIC Document Reproduction Service No. ED451818.

American Indian Science and Engineering Society. (2005). *Winds of Change Annual College Guide for American Indians.* Boulder, CO: American Indian Science and Engineering Society Publishing.

Anderson, E. C., and McDowell, S. (2001, October). *Towards a Theology of Strengths.* Paper presented at the National Conference on Identifying and Developing Students' Strengths, Eastern College.

Angspatt, J. (2001). *Barriers and Contributions to American Indian Academic Success at the University of Montana: A Qualitative Study.* Unpublished doctoral dissertation, University of Montana.

Aragon, S. R. (2004a). "Learning and Study Practices of Postsecondary American Indian/Alaskan Native Students." *Journal of American Indian Education* 43(2): 1–18.

Aragon, S. R. (2004b). "Information Processing Patterns of Postsecondary American Indian/Alaska Native Students." *Journal of American Indian Education* 43(3): 1–20.

Barnhardt, C. (1994). *Life on the Other Side: Alaska Native Teacher Education Students at the University of Alaska-Fairbanks.* Unpublished doctoral dissertation, University of British Columbia. ERIC Document Reproduction Service No. ED382415.

Beaty, J., and Chiste, K. B. (1986). "University Preparation for Native American Students: Theory and Application." *Journal of American Indian Education* 26(1): 6–13.

Benjamin, D. P., Chambers, S., and Reiterman, G. (1993). "A Focus on American Indian College Persistence." *Journal of American Indian Education* 32: 24–39.

Blanco, C. D. (August, 2005). *Early Commitment Financial Aid Programs: Promises, Practices, and Policies.* Boulder, CO: Western Interstate Commission for Higher Education.

Boyer, P. (1997). "First Survey of Tribal College Students Reveals Attitudes." *Tribal College Journal* 9(2): 36–41.

Brown, L. L., and Kurpius, S. E. R. (1997). "Psychosocial Factors Influencing Academic Persistence of American Indian College Students." *Journal of College Student Development* 38(1): 3–12.

Buckley, A. (1997). *Threads of Nations: American Graduate and Professional Students.* ERIC Document Reproduction Service No. ED444771.

Burns, S. L. W. (1995). *A Qualitative Study of the Retention of Colville Confederated Tribe American Indian Students in Spokane Community College.* Unpublished doctoral dissertation, Gonzaga University, Spokane, WA.

Cabrera, A. F., and La Nasa, S. M. (Eds.). (2000). *Understanding the College Choice of Disadvantaged Students: New Directions for Institutional Research.* San Francisco: Jossey-Bass.

Cabrera, A. F., La Nasa, S. M., and Burkum, K. R. (2001). *On the Right Path: The Higher Education Study of One Generation.* University Park, PA: Center for the Study of Higher Education, The Pennsylvania State University.

Castellanos, J., Kuh, G., and Pavel, D. M. (1998, November). *American Indian and Alaska Native Students and the Student Involvement Model.* Paper presented at the Annual Convention of the Association for the Study of Higher Education, Miami, FL.

Cibik, M., and Chambers, S. (1991). "Similarities and Differences among Native Americans, Hispanics, Blacks, and Anglos." *NASPA Journal* 28(2): 129–39.

Cole, J. S., and Denzine, G. M. (2002). "Comparing the Academic Engagement of American Indian and White College Students." *Journal of American Indian Education* 41(1): 19–34.

College Board. (2005a). *Education Pays Update.* New York: College Board.

College Board. (2005b). *Trends in College Pricing.* New York: College Board.

College Board. (2005c). *Trends in Student Aid.* New York: College Board.

Cross, S. L. (1993). *A Cross-Sectional Study of Selected Four-Year Public and Private Colleges and Universities in the United States with American Indian (Native American) Student Support Programs.* Unpublished doctoral dissertation, Michigan State University.

Davis, J. (1992). "Factors Contributing to Post-Secondary Achievement of American Indians." *Tribal College Journal* 4(2): 24–30.

Deloria, V. (2001). "Higher Education and Self-Determination." In V. Deloria Jr. and D. R. Wildcat, *Power and Place: Indian Education in America* (pp. 123–33). Golden, CO: Fulcrum Resources.

Demmert, W. G. (2001). *Improving Academic Performance among Native American Students: A Review of the Research Literature.* Charleston, WV: ERIC Clearinghouse on Rural Education and Small Schools.

Dodd, J., Garcia, F., Meccage, C., and Nelson, J. R. (1995). "American Indian Student Retention." *NASPA Journal* 33(1): 72–78.

Dransfeldt, J. (May 9, 2005). "College Choice Has Many Factors." *Ventura College Press*. Available online at www.venturacollegepress.com.

Engs, R. C., Diebold, B. A., and Hansen, D. J. (1996). "The Drinking Patterns and Problems of a National Sample of College Students, 1994." *Journal of Alcohol and Drug Education* 41(3): 13–33.

Falk, D., and Aitken, L. (1984). "Promoting Retention among American Indian College Students." *Journal of American Indian Education* 23(2): 24–31.

Fore, C. L. (1997). *Factors Influencing Academic Achievement among Native American College Students*. Unpublished doctoral dissertation, Oklahoma State University.

Fox, M. J. T., Lowe, S. C., and McClellan, G. S. (2005). *Serving Native American Students*. New Directions for Student Services, No. 109. San Francisco: Jossey-Bass.

French, B. F., and Oakes, W. (February 2004). "Reliability and Validity Evidence for the Institutional Integration Scale." *Educational and Psychological Measurement* 64(1): 88–98.

Garcia, F. M. (2000). "Warriors in Education: Persistence among American Indian Doctoral Recipients." *Tribal College Journal* 11(3): 46–48, 50.

Gottman, J. M., Declaire, J., and Goleman, D. P. (1998). *Raising an Emotionally Intelligent Child*. New York: Fireside Press.

Guillory, R. (2002). *Factors Related to Native American Students' Persistence in Higher Education: A Comparative Analysis of Student and State and University Officials' Perceptions*. Unpublished doctoral dissertation, Washington State University, Pullman.

Harvey, V. S. (2004). "Resiliency: Strategies for Parents and Educators." In A. S. Canter, L. Z. Paige, M. D. Roth, I. Romero, and S. A. Carroll (Eds.), *Helping Children at Home and School II: Handouts for Families and Educators* (pp. S5-79–S5-82). Bethesda, MD: NASP Publications.

HeavyRunner, I., and DeCelles, R. (2002). "Family Education Model: Meeting the Student Retention Challenge." *Journal of American Indian Education* 41(2): 29–37.

HeavyRunner, I., and Marshall, K. (2003). "'Miracle Survivors': Promoting Resilience in Indian Students." *Tribal College Journal* 14(4): 14–18.

HeavyRunner, I., and Morris, J. S. (1997). "Traditional Native Culture and Resilience." *Research/Practice* 5(1): 1–6.

Hingson, R. et al. (2005). "Magnitude of Alcohol-Related Mortality and Morbidity among U.S. College Students Ages 18–24: Changes from 1998 to 2001." *Annual Review of Public Health* 26: 259–79.

Hingson, R. W., Heeren, T., Zakocs, R. C., Kopstein, A., and Wechsler, H. (2002). "Magnitude of Alcohol-Related Mortality and Morbidity among U.S. College Students Ages 18–24." *Journal of Studies on Alcohol* 63(2): 136–44.

Hoover, J., and Jacobs, C. (1992). "A Survey of American Indian College Students: Perceptions toward Their Study Skills/College Life." *Journal of American Indian Education* 32: 21–29.

Hornett, D. (1989). "The Role of Faculty in Cultural Awareness and Retention of American Indian College Students." *Journal of American Indian Education* 29(1): 12–18.

Huffman, T. (1990, Spring). "The Transculturation of Native American College Students." *Proteus: A Journal of Ideas* 7: 8–14.

Huffman, T. (2001). "Resistance Theory and the Transculturation Hypothesis as Explanations of College Attrition and Persistence among Culturally Traditional American Indian Students." *Journal of American Indian Education* 40(3): 1–23.

Huffman, T., Sill, M., and Brokenleg, M. (1986). "College Achievement among Sioux and White South Dakota Students." *Journal of American Indian Education* 25(2): 32–38.

Inglebret, E. (2001). *Conceptual Framework for Developing Culturally Responsive Teacher Education Curriculum for Northwest Indian College: A Grounded Theory.* Unpublished doctoral dissertation, Washington State University, Pullman.

Jackson, A. P., and Smith, S. A. (2001). "Postsecondary Transitions among Navajo Indians." *Journal of American Indian Education* 40(2): 28–47.

Jackson, A. P., Smith, S. A., and Hill, C. L. (2003). "Academic Persistence among Native American College Students." *Journal of College Student Development* 44(4): 548–65.

Jenkins, M. (1999). "Factors which Influence the Success or Failure of American Indian/Native American College Students." *Research and Teaching in Developmental Education* 15(20): 49–52.

Katz, J. (2005). "'If I Could Do It, They Could Do It': A Collective Case Study of Plateau Nurses." *Journal of American Indian Education* 44(2): 36–51.

King, J. E. (2006, May). "Working Their Way through College: Student Employment and its Impact on the College Experience." ACE Center for Policy Analysis, American Council on Education. Available at www.acenet.edu.

Kleinfeld, J., Cooper, J., and Kyle, N. (1987). "Post-Secondary Counselors: A Model for Increasing Native Americans' College Success." *Journal of American Indian Education* 27(1): 9–16.

Knight, J. R., Wechsler, H., Kuo, M., Seibring, M., Weitzman, E. R., and Schuckit, M. (2002, May). "Alcohol Abuse and Dependence among U.S. College Students." *Journal of Studies on Alcohol* 63: 263–70.

LaCounte, D. (1987). "American Indian Students in College." In D. J. Wright (Ed.), *Responding to the Needs of Today's Minority Students* (pp. 65–79). New Directions for Student Services, No. 38. San Francisco: Jossey-Bass.

Liley, D. G. (1995). *Twenty Years of Diversity: An Examination of American Indian Alaska Natives Master of Social Work Graduates from the University of Utah Graduate School of Social Work: Implications for Recruitment, Support, and Curriculum.* Unpublished doctoral dissertation, University of Utah.

Lin, R. L. (1990). "Perceptions of Family Background and Personal Characteristics among Indian College Students." *Journal of American Indian Education* 29(3): 8–15.

Lin, R. L., LaCounte, D., and Eder, J. (1988). "A Study of Native American Students at a Predominantly White College." *Journal of American Indian Education* 27: 8–15.

Luks, A., and Payne, P. (2001). *The Healing Power of Doing Good: The Health and Spiritual Benefits of Helping Others.* iUniverse.com.

Mathews, J. (2004). "Six Ways to be Happy with Your College Choice." *Washington Post*, October 5. Available online at www.washingtonpost.com.

Meyers, G. B. (1997). "Keeping Students in College—What's Working?" *Winds of Change* 12(1): 58–59.

Monette, G. C. (1995). *Follow-up Study of the Graduates of an American Indian Tribally-Controlled Community College.* Unpublished doctoral dissertation, University of North Dakota, Grand Forks.

Murguia, E., Padilla, R. V., and Pavel, M. (1991). "Ethnicity and the Concept of Social Integration in Tinto's Model of Institutional Departure." *Journal of College Student Development* 32: 433–39.

Napier, L. A. (1995). "Educational Profiles of Nine Gifted American Indian Women and Their Own Stories about Wanting to Lead." *Roeper Review* 18(1): 38–44.

National Center for Education Statistics. (2005). *Status and Trends in the Education of American Indians and Alaska Natives* (NCES 2005-108). U.S. Department of Education, National Center for Education Statistics. Washington, DC: U.S. Government Printing Office.

National Indian Education Association. (2005). *Preliminary Report on No Child Left Behind in Indian Country*. Washington, DC: National Indian Education Association.

Ness, J. E. (2002). "Crossing the Finish Line: American Indian Completers and Non-Completers in a Tribal College." *Tribal College Journal* 13(4): 36–40.

Nora, A., and Cabrera, A. F. (1992). *Measuring Program Outcomes: What Impacts Are Important to Assess and What Impacts Are Possible to Measure for the Talent Search Program*. Washington, DC: U.S. Department of Education, Office of Policy and Planning.

Ortiz, A., and HeavyRunner, I. (2003). "Student Access, Retention, and Success: Models of Inclusion and Support." In M. K. P. Benham and W. J. Stein (Eds.), *The Renaissance of American Indian Higher Education* (pp. 215–40). Mahwah, NJ: Lawrence Erlbaum Associates.

Patton, W., and Edington, E. D. (1973). "Factors Related to Persistence of Indian Students at the College Level." *Journal of American Indian Education* 12: 19–23.

Pavel, D. M. (1992). *American Indians and Alaska Natives in Higher Education: Research on Participation and Graduation*. ERIC Digest EDO-RC-92-2.

Pavel, D. M. (1999). "American Indians and Alaska Natives in Higher Education: Promoting Access and Achievement." In K. G. Swisher and J. W. Tippeconnic (Eds.), *Next Steps: Research and Practice to Advance Indian Education* (pp. 239–58). Charleston, WV: ERIC Clearinghouse on Rural and Small Schools.

Pavel, D. M., and Padilla, R. V. (1993). "American Indian and Alaska Native Post-secondary Departure: An Example of Assessing a Mainstream Model Using National Longitudinal Data." *Journal of American Indian Education* 32(2): 1–23.

Pipes, M. A., Westby, C. E., and Inglebret, E. (1993). "Profile of Native American Students." In L. W. Clark and D. E. Waltzman (Eds.), *Faculty and Student Challenges in Facing Cultural and Linguistic Diversity* (pp. 137–72). Springfield, IL: Charles C. Thomas.

Presley, C. A., Meilman, P. W., Cashin, J. R., and Lyerla, R. (1996a). *Alcohol and Drugs on American College Campuses: Use, Consequences, and Perceptions of the Campus Environment*, Vol. III: 1991–1993. Carbondale, IL: Core Institute, Southern Illinois University.

Presley, C. A., Meilman, P. W., and Cashin, J. R. (1996b). *Alcohol and Drugs on American College Campuses: Use, Consequences, and Perceptions of the Campus Environment*, Vol. IV: 1992–1994. Carbondale, IL: Core Institute, Southern Illinois University.

Reed-Inderbitzin, D. L. (2001). *Building Bridges of Success and Bi-Cultural Competence with Native American Students: A Goal-Oriented Program Evaluation*. Unpublished doctoral dissertation, University of South Dakota.

Rendón, L. I., Jalomo, R. E., and Nora, A. (2000). "Theoretical Considerations in the Study of Minority Student Retention in Higher Education." In John M. Braxton (Ed.), *Reworking the Student Departure Puzzle*. Nashville, TN: Vanderbilt University Press.

Reyes, M. E. (2000). "What Does it Take? Successful Alaska Native Students at the University of Alaska Fairbanks." *Journal of College Student Retention* 2(2): 141–59.

Reyes, M. E. (2001). "Tortured Victory or Joyful Accomplishment? Successful Eskimo and Latina College Students." *Race, Gender and Class* 8(1): 82–98.

Rindone, P. (1988). "Achievement Motivation and Academic Achievement of Native American Students." *Journal of American Indian Education* 28(1): 1–8.

Rousey, A., and Longie, E. (2001). "The Tribal College as Family Support System." *American Behavioral Scientist* 44(9): 1492–504.

Schwartz, B. (2004). *The Paradox of Choice: Why More Is Less*. New York: Harper-Collins.

Schwartz, J. L. (1995). *Native Americans in a Southwestern University: A Study of the Impact of Traditionality on Success in Higher Education.* Unpublished doctoral dissertation, Northern Arizona University, Flagstaff.

Senge, P. (1990). *The Fifth Discipline: The Art and Practice of the Learning Organization.* New York: Doubleday.

Senge, P., Cambron-McCabe, N., Lucas, T., Smith, B., Dutton, J., and Kleiner, A. (2000). *Schools That Learn: A Fifth Discipline Fieldbook for Educators, Parents, and Everyone Who Cares about Education.* New York: Doubleday/Currency.

Senge, P., Kleiner, A., Roberts, C., Ross, R. B., and Smith, B. J. (1994). *The Fifth Discipline Fieldbook: Strategies and Tools for Building a Learning Community.* New York: Doubleday/Currency.

Senge, P., Kleiner, A., Roberts, R., Ross, R., Roth, G., and Smith, B. (1999). *The Dance of Change: The Challenge of Sustaining Momentum in Learning Organizations.* New York: Doubleday/Currency, 1999.

Spaide, D. (n.d.). *In Helping Ourselves by Helping Others.* Online document available at www.soulrise.com/common/helping.htm.

Steward, R. (1993). "Two Faces of Academic Success: Case Studies of American Indians on a Predominantly Anglo University Campus." *Journal of College Student Development* 34(3): 191–96.

Strand, J., and Peacock, T. (2002). *Nurturing Resilience and School Success in American Indian and Alaska Native Students.* ERIC Digest ED471488.

Tate, D., and Schwartz, C. (1993). "Increasing the Retention of American Indian Students in Professional Programs in Higher Education." *Journal of American Indian Education* 33(1): 21–31.

Taylor, J. S. (1999, November). *America's First People: Factors which Affect Their Persistence in Higher Education.* Paper presented at the Annual Meeting of the Association for the Study of Higher Education, San Antonio, TX. ERIC Document Reproduction Service No. ED437874.

Terenzini, P. T., Cabrera, A. F., and Bernal, E. M. (2001). *Swimming Against the Tide: The Poor in American Education.* New York: College Entrance Examination Board.

U.S. Department of Education, Federal Student Aid. (2006). *Funding Education beyond High School: The Guide to Federal Student Aid.* Jessup, MD: ED Pubs, Education Publication Center.

U.S. Department of Education, National Center for Education Statistics. (2000). *The NPEC Sourcebook on Assessment, Volume 1: Definitions and Assessment Methods for Critical Thinking, Problem Solving, and Writing.* NCES 2000-172, prepared by T. Dary Erwin for the Council of the National Postsecondary Education Cooperative Student Outcomes Pilot Working Group: Cognitive and Intellectual Development. Washington, DC: U.S. Government Printing Office.

Villegas, M., and Prieto, R. (2006). *Alaska Native Student Vitality: Community Perspectives on Supporting Student Success.* Anchorage: Alaska Native Policy Center at First Alaskans Institute (www.firstalaskans.org).

Waterman, S. J. (2004). *The Haudenosaunee College Experience: A Complex Path to Degree Completion.* Unpublished doctoral dissertation, Syracuse University.

Wechsler, H., Lee, J. E., Kuo, M., Seibring, M., Nelson, T. F., and Lee, H. P. (2002). "Trends in College Binge Drinking during a Period of Increased Prevention Efforts: Findings from Four Harvard School of Public Health Study Surveys, 1993–2001." *Journal of American College Health* 50(5): 203–17.

Wechsler, H., Moeykens, B., Davenport, A., Castillo, S., and Hansen, J. (1995). "The Adverse Impact of Heavy Episodic Drinkers on Other College Students." *Journal of Studies on Alcohol* 56(6): 628–34.

Wells, R. (1989). *A Survey of American Indian Students*. Canton, NY: St. Lawrence University. ERIC Document Reproduction Service No. ED 311778.

Wenzlaff, T. L., and Brewer, A. (1996). "Native American Students Define Factors for Success." *Tribal College Journal* 7(4): 40–43.

White Shield, R. (2004–2005). "The Retention of Indigenous Students in Higher Education: Historical Issues, Federal Policy, and Indigenous Resilience." *Journal of College Student Retention* 6(1): 111–27.

Wiest, P. E. (1999). *Stories of Academic Achievement: Case Studies of Successful Native American Students*. Unpublished doctoral dissertation, Arizona State University, Tempe.

Wildcat, D. R. (2001). "The Question of Self-Determination." In V. Deloria Jr. and D. R. Wildcat, *Power and Place: Indian Education in America* (pp. 135–50). Golden, CO: Fulcrum Resources.

Wilson, J. G. (1983). *Wisconsin Indian Opinion of Factors which Contribute to the Completion of College Degrees*. Report from the Postdoctoral Fellowship Program. ERIC Document Reproduction Service No. ED237274.

Wilson, P. (1997). "Key Factors in the Performance and Achievement of Minority Students at the University of Alaska, Fairbanks." *American Indian Quarterly* 21(3): 535–44.

Yang, R. K., Byers, S. R., and Fenton, B. (2006). "American Indian/Alaska Native Students' Use of a University Student Support Office." *Journal of American Indian Education* 45(1): 35–48.

INDEX

ABOUT THE AUTHORS

D. MICHAEL PAVEL (CHiXapkaid, ancestral name; Skokomish, tribal affiliation), Associate Professor of Higher Education at Washington State University, is a nationally renowned researcher on issues dealing with American Indian and Alaska Native students' access to and achievement in higher education. He is an enrolled member of the Skokomish Nation and active traditional bearer. A frequent speakers at events across the country, Dr. Pavel is married to Susan Pavel and has two sons, Kaid'dub and Akea.

ELLA INGLEBRET is an Assistant Professor in the Department of Speech and Hearing Sciences at Washington State University. She has administered a highly successful program designed to recruit and graduate American Indian and Alaska Native students in the field of speech-language pathology for the past eighteen years. Her current research focuses on identifying factors associated with Native student success in higher education.